T0301585

Christian Theology and Market Economics

Christian Theology and Market Economics

Edited by

Ian R. Harper

Sidney Myer Chair and Executive Director, Centre for Business and Public Policy, Melbourne Business School, University of Melbourne, Australia

Samuel Gregg

Director of Research, Acton Institute, USA

Edward Elgar
Cheltenham, UK • Northampton, MA, USA

Published by
Edward Elgar Publishing Limited
The Lypiatts
15 Lansdown Road
Cheltenham
Glos GL50 2JA
UK

Edward Elgar Publishing, Inc.
William Pratt House
9 Dewey Court
Northampton
Massachusetts 01060
USA

A catalogue record for this book
is available from the British Library

Library of Congress Control Number: 2008932869

ISBN 978 1 84720 377 9

Printed and bound in Great Britain by MPG Books Ltd, Bodmin, Cornwall

Contents

Contributors

Philip Booth is Editorial and Programme Director at the Institute of Economic Affairs and Professor of Insurance and Risk Management at the Cass Business School, City University, London.

Geoffrey Brennan is Professor of Economics in the Research School of Social Sciences at the Australian National University and holds a regular Visiting Professorship jointly in Political Science at Duke University, Durham, North Carolina, and Philosophy at the University of North Carolina, Chapel Hill.

Ricardo F. Crespo is Profesor del Área Economía and Secretario Académico at the IAE Management and Business School, Universidad Austral in Buenos Aires.

Stephen J. Grabill is Research Scholar in Theology at the Acton Institute in Grand Rapids, Michigan and Executive Editor of the *Journal of Markets & Morality*.

Samuel Gregg is Director of Research at the Acton Institute in Grand Rapids, Michigan and Adjunct Professor at the Pontifical Lateran University in Rome.

Ian R. Harper is Sidney Myer Professor of Commerce and Business Administration and Executive Director of the Centre for Business and Public Policy, at the Melbourne Business School, University of Melbourne.

Peter S. Heslam is Director of Transforming Business at the University of Cambridge. He is a Fellow of the Faculty of Divinity, a Senior Member of Trinity College and a Fellow of the Royal Society of Arts in London.

Eric L. Jones is Professorial Fellow at the Melbourne Business School, University of Melbourne, Emeritus Professor of La Trobe University, Melbourne and Visiting Professor at Exeter University.

Gordon Menzies is Senior Lecturer in Economics in the School of Finance and Economics at the University of Technology, Sydney.

Michael J. Miller is Director of Programs and Education at the Acton Institute, Grand Rapids, Michigan.

Paul Oslington is Professor of Economics and Finance at the University of Notre Dame, Australia, and Visiting Fellow, St Marks National Theological Centre and Australian Centre for Christianity and Culture, Canberra.

Anthony M.C. Waterman is Emeritus Professor of Economics, University of Manitoba and Fellow of St John's College, Winnipeg.

Acknowledgement

The editors gratefully acknowledge the willingness of our contributors to meet tight deadlines and to accommodate our various editorial requests. We also acknowledge with thanks the editorial assistance of David Rozenbes who checked references and standardized style across the range of contributions to this volume.

Introduction
Ian R. Harper and Samuel Gregg

The subject of God and Mammon is fraught with considerable confusion, strong disagreement and widespread misunderstanding. While Christianity has always insisted that, ultimately, the Kingdom of God is not of this world, Christians hold sharply divergent views on what this means for their relationship with the things of this world. For centuries, many Christian men and women have taken the radical option of literally separating themselves from the world, and renouncing the private ownership of material goods. In more recent times, we have observed the emergence of the so-called 'Prosperity Gospel', which seems to hold that material success and the ownership of considerable wealth are signs of God's favour.

The vast majority of practising Christians – Orthodox, Protestant and Roman Catholic alike – have taken a more nuanced position. It involves a delicate balance between what Christian faith has taught as the necessity for humans to use worldly things in a creative, joyful, free and responsible manner, and the imperative of maintaining a certain detachment so that the possession and use of material goods, however large or small, remains understood as a means to an end, rather than an end in itself.

Perhaps the delicacy of this balance, and the failures of Christians throughout the centuries to maintain it, has contributed to the ambiguity so often found in patristic, medieval, early-modern and contemporary Christian thought on subjects such as the purpose and nature of economics and the moral status of private business. It may also have resulted in the tendency of theologians and economists to talk past each other when it comes to sustained conversation about the relationship, if any, between theological reflection and what might be called 'the economic way of thinking'.

Part of the problem flows from the fragmented approach to the acquisition of knowledge that is characteristic of many contemporary universities. It is entirely possible for a theology student never to receive even a cursory introduction to economics. Nor is it common for economics or business students to receive any formal (or even informal) instruction in the rudiments of Christian theology. Even many economists who also happen to be convinced and active Christians essentially dissociate their religious beliefs and convictions from anything related to their economic research. On one

1

level, this is understandable. All academic disciplines should enjoy a high degree of autonomy as they seek to expand and deepen knowledge of the area according to the norms and rules that make, for example, physics different from philosophy. Yet it is also true that classic Christianity does not and has never understood itself to be grounded upon irrationality or unreason. The Christian God is a reasonable God – He is the *Logos*, as the original Greek of the first chapter of St John's Gospel makes clear. To the extent that academic disciplines such as economics, management or business purport to be grounded on reason, they surely have something in common with Christianity.

The purpose of this book is not to resolve in a definitive manner all the usual questions that arise at the multiple intersections between Christian theology and morality, economics and business. Rather, the essays seek to demonstrate that a meaningful conversation between the disciplines is both possible and rewarding. The irony, of course, is that 250 years ago, few scholars would have imagined a need to restart such a conversation, precisely because so many of these areas were thoroughly integrated in European universities from about the 11th century until the middle of the 19th century.

Creating such a conversation necessitates voices that can claim genuine expertise in a range of intellectual disciplines. Hence this volume consists of contributions from economists, business theorists, philosophers, historians of ideas and a number of people with formal training in theology. They also belong to different Christian confessions, and thus bring to their analyses a range of similar and dissimilar theological predispositions. Readers will, however, be struck by the remarkable convergence of views and conclusions. One reason for this, of course, is that Christianity, economics and business have had a great deal to do with each other for centuries, both on the practical and theoretical levels. As John T. Noonan notes in his definitive text on the vexed and much misunderstood subject of usury, 'Most obviously, the scholastic theory of usury is an embryonic form of economics. Indeed it is the first attempt at a science of economics known to the West' (1957, p. 2).

History, it has been said, is the great teacher of wisdom, and it is for this reason that the first half of this book focuses upon tracing the long and complex history of Christian reflection upon and contributions to economics as a distinct branch of inquiry and knowledge. Indeed, the first chapter, 'Aristotle's science of economics', by Ricardo Crespo outlines the essence of economic theory as it existed in the pre-Christian West. Economics was not even recognized as a distinct intellectual discipline at the time of Aristotle and he only devoted a small proportion of his writings to this topic. Crespo introduces Aristotle's notion of *oikonomike*, the use of things necessary to the life of virtues. In Greek, *oikonomike* translates to 'the economic'. For Aristotle, *oikonomike* is essentially moral as it can only be aimed at the good (virtuous).

Crespo asks whether economics is a science for Aristotle and what kind of science it is. He suggests that, for Aristotle, economics was a practical science, distinguishable from a theoretical or technical science. Practical science must deal with facts to better predict outcomes, even though these are not always universal and are better understood as generalizations. Practical science originates in human decision and choice, and Crespo explains why Aristotle defines practical science as an 'immanent action'. Aristotle considered that practical science is not an exact science, since humans will find themselves in varying situations and may act differently each time. A discussion on how practical science is a science follows, and Crespo explains its three characteristics. In the latter part of the chapter, Crespo discusses the consequences of 'the economic' and why Aristotle believes institutions are important in the economic domain. According to Aristotle, institutions can foster habits that lead to established actions. These actions lead to virtues built through things like education and law. Accurate science can be facilitated through institutions, which can in turn precipitate better predictions.

Chapter 2, authored by Stephen Grabill, focuses upon Christianity's pre-Enlightenment contribution to economic thought. Grabill shows how the scholastic method applied by medieval and early-modern Christian moral theologians to economic problems led to new discoveries and insights in economics over the course of centuries. He notes that the historical background of economics was deeply Christian in both theory and practice. Grabill discusses the significance of scholastic economics and the economic historians who promoted its importance in the study of price, money and value.

Noting that scholastic economics has its critics, Grabill argues that it is very difficult to understand why economists and historians seem anxious to deny its importance to modern economics. In this connection, Grabill attempts to shed light on the issue of usury – according to him, the least understood idea in the history of economics. He notes that discussions on any topic within scholastic economics must acknowledge the intellectual shift of the 14th and 15th centuries pioneered by Catholic moral theologians. He also devotes considerable attention to the 'late-scholastic' Spanish theologians (more popularly known as the 'School of Salamanca') of the 16th and 17th centuries, who Grabill describes as the group closest to having been the 'founders' of scientific economics.

Shifting the discussion to the Enlightenment period, Samuel Gregg, in Chapter 3, concentrates on some of the major thinkers during the period of the Scottish Enlightenment, a time when Scotland transitioned, at times almost violently, from a semi-feudal mercantilist set of economic arrangements towards the conditions of a more market-orientated, commercial society – a transition that involved intense argument between those who supported free trade and those who believed in mercantilism. Gregg's main focus is on two scholars, Gershom Carmichael and Francis Hutcheson, both widely regarded as fathers of the Scottish Enlightenment, his aim being to illustrate that the Scottish Enlightenment's distinctly market-orientated contributions to economic theory did not involve a radical break with Christian thought.

Noting the influence exerted upon Carmichael of the writings of the Lutheran natural-law scholar, Samuel von Pufendorf, Gregg illustrates that Carmichael was a supporter of free trade precisely because he accepted many of the premises and economic ideas that are to be found in the thought of Christian natural-law theorists such as Pufendorf, who in turn drew upon late-scholastic Catholic thinkers. Carmichael's reflection on the nature of business, contracts and property was, Gregg illustrates, very much consistent with the established wisdom of 16th- and 17th- century Christian intellectuals on economic issues.

Francis Hutcheson, Gregg reminds us, was a student of Carmichael and, like his teacher, very influenced by natural law. As a lecturer, Hutcheson further refined Carmichael's economic ideas, with one of his students being Adam Smith. Much of Hutcheson's early writings focused on the importance of the division of labour for economic development and the emergence of money-exchange economies – themes much echoed by Smith in his *The Wealth of Nations* ([1776] 1904). While not discounting the decidedly non-Christian influences exerted upon Smith, most notably by the sceptical philosopher, David Hume, Gregg suggests that it is a mistake to discount the influence of 'Christian-Enlightenment' thinkers such as Carmichael and Hutcheson upon Smith, a conviction underlined by the generally positive view adopted by convinced Christians such as William Robertson and Hugh Blair of the commercial society emerging in 18th-century Scotland.

Taking us from the 18th century to the present, Paul Oslington's chapter (Chapter 4) considers the relationship between Christian theology and economics in the post-Enlightenment period. Oslington notes that most of the interest in the connection has come from theologians and scholars of religion but has been limited by their modest level of economic knowledge. He analyses the research of Jacob Viner and Anthony Waterman to assist in understanding the contribution of Christian theology to economic thought since the Enlightenment. Both Viner and Waterman (the latter having formal qualifications in both economics and theology) saw the 18th and 19th centuries as an important period in the relationship between theology and economics. The chapter also acknowledges other economists who have made large contributions to this topic, such as William Paley and T.R. Malthus. Oslington focuses much of his attention on the relationship between theology and economics in Britain and America. The 19th century in Britain saw a complete separation between theology and all sciences due to specialization and professionalization. Keynes saw the 1860s as the moment when Christianity moved away from the philosophical world of England. In America the clerical teachers and textbook writers regarded the dissemination of Adam Smith's economics as a religious task. By the late 19th century, however, a gradual process of secularization was taking place. But this did not stop the discussion of economics in churches in both countries. By contrast, the exclusion of theological faculties from Australian universities created a legacy of non-engagement between theologians and economists that continues to the present day.

Looking at recent developments, Oslington notes that papers on the intersection of theological and economic thought often encounter difficulty in being published in mainstream economics journals. This discourages, he argues, many economists and theologians from engaging in the discussion, and weakens the incentives for economists to acquire training in theology and so to develop the relationship. He also identifies a lack of incentives for theologians to inform themselves about economics. The end result, Oslington argues, is a poorly-informed discussion on both sides between theologians and economists. Despite this, Oslington contends that from the mid-1970s onwards there has been a revival of discussion of the relationship between theology and economics as a result of the labours of a small number of writers.

Taking the discussion to a more theoretical level, Geoffrey Brennan and Anthony Waterman examine the relationship between economic theory and Christian theology in Chapter 5. They begin by providing definitions of each belief – what is considered economics and what theology. In comparing the two disciplines, Brennan and Waterman organize the relationship between theology and economics into four broad categories: independence (the view that one has no effect upon the other); dependence (the idea that one emanates from the other); convergence (the two ideas intersect); and clash (there are conflicts between the two). Potential clashes are also evident in the different styles adopted by theologians and economists. Scripture is seen as the fundamental text for theology whereas, observe Waterman and Brennan, there is no equivalent ultimate source for economics.

The final section of their chapter focuses on two concepts that lie at the heart of economics and that prove troublesome to theologians – rationality and scarcity. Economists proceed on the methodological assumption that people choose rationally; in other words, that their choices reflect their best efforts to maximize their own welfare given their beliefs about the connection between the two. This view of human nature seems to fly in the face of every theologian's conception of human sinfulness and frailty. The notion that people are the best judges of their own best interests when left to their own devices is fundamentally at odds with the biblical witness and Christian teaching down the ages. This difference in the 'angle of vision' is likely to remain a source of dissention in discussion between economists and theologians.

A further stumbling-block is the economist's idea of scarcity, which follows from the assumption of rationality. Rational choice implies the preexistence of scarcity. We have to choose between A and B because we cannot have both. Scarcity is thus the relation of *resources* to *wants*, and because of the latter is inescapably subjective. Many theologians are uneasy with the economists' conception of scarcity for at least three reasons:

1. Scarcity is a nasty example of the 'problem of evil'. Why did God create a world in which many, perhaps most, of his creatures are doomed to a Darwinian 'struggle for existence'?
2. An assumption of scarcity can come across as a bland acceptance of inequality, which offends the sensibilities of many present-day theologians, for whom inevitable poverty and a permanently stratified society is inconsistent with the Christian Gospel.
3. Most seriously, ineluctable scarcity in human affairs is an affront to a central Christian conviction: that the new life in Christ transcends all the limitations of time and space in which we now exist. When Christ fed the multitude with a few loaves and fishes, he taught thereby that God has liberated us from scarcity, or at any rate will do so very soon. This world *ought not* to be a place in which we are constrained by physical limits.

Brennan and Waterman conclude that, on these points at least, there will always be an unavoidable clash between economics and Christian theology.

Discussion of these more theoretical aspects of the intersection between theology and economics is continued by Gordon Menzies in Chapter 6, 'Economics as identity'. The chapter takes the form of a Platonic dialogue between two types of identity. Menzies examines the notion that economic theory can influence personal identity in as powerful a way as a person's theological commitments. Menzies presents these forms of identity via the device of two representative agents: 'economic man', invented by John Stuart Mill, and 'theological man', represented by the Apostle Paul's reference to each person being 'in Adam'. Menzies attempts to arrive at a better understanding of 'economic man' by contrasting him with 'theological man'.

In the first act, both representative agents introduce themselves and try to gain an understanding of each other. The representative agents agree on a name for each other; 'economic man' is named John, and 'theological man' is named Mary. John introduces a number of economists who have shaped his ideas while Mary cites biblical texts to identify herself. Each representative agent becomes a critical observer of the other, which forces them to further explain, and therefore understand, their respective forms of identity. John, for instance, is interested in whether Mary can live in the modern world and whether theology and science – especially economic science – can coexist in modern times, and Mary provides a sound explanation of her position. John, however, is put under the microscope as Mary questions whether a social science is really 'social' and if some forms of economics might not actually discourage social cooperation.

The final four chapters of the book move towards more immediate and practical discussions of economic life with which Christians, especially those living in market-oriented commercial orders, are invariably concerned. Michael Miller (Chapter 7) notes that business is often viewed by Christians and non-Christians alike in a negative manner, even as an essentially dishonest profession where scandals and corruption are rife. Miller seeks to dispel this perception, contending that business benefits the whole of society and has moral value. He suggests that dishonesty in business is not rewarded in the long term. Miller also observes that business creates economic value, technological innovation and improves everyone's standard of living. Business, according to Miller, is also an opportunity for collaboration, for interactions with different people and for developing skills that might not otherwise have been acquired.

Performing diligent and hard work, Miller comments, has been a constant message of Scripture, and the Christian tradition promotes a spirituality of work matched by no other religion, with the exception of Judaism. Jesus warns against corruption and attachment to riches, and not work or business itself. At the same time, Miller warns that business – like any other legitimate enterprise – needs to be grounded in basic moral goods. Markets and free enterprise highlight the importance of choice. But, Miller comments, from the standpoint of Christian theology (and human reason), choice is but one aspect of human freedom, and must be guided by the acquisition of theological and moral virtues, especially the virtue of prudence (a virtue, Miller stresses, that is essential to success in business). Miller finishes his chapter with a brief critique of corporate social responsibility theory and practice, and the manner in which it actually damages a sound understanding of the moral life in business and market economies.

Philip Booth's chapter (Chapter 8) also examines the relationship between Christian ethics and the theory and practice of modern business in a globalized world. Using Catholic social teaching as a prototype for developed – and developing – Christian reflection on the modern social order, Booth notes a qualified but clear acceptance of the market economy, not only because of the market's ability to produce utilitarian economic benefits but also because Catholic social ethics appreciate the opportunities for integral human flourishing that exist in modern business economies.

Booth observes, however, that this general acceptance does not imply the absence of tensions between particular features of modern business life and the demands of Christian ethics. In this regard, four different aspects of inequality feature significantly: the very high wages earned by some senior executives; the very low wages received by others; the low level of product prices received by primary producers; and the high levels that firms can charge for goods based on intellectual property. Booth discusses the responsibilities of managers, shareholders and directors and their relation to the claims of moral law. He also discusses the trade-offs between the levels of wages and employment faced by business. Booth's treatment of these matters underlines the indispensable role played by a properly formed Christian conscience in addressing these issues, as well as important economic and moral reasons why looking to the state to resolve them is not always the optimal approach – morally or economically.

Ian Harper and Eric Jones in Chapter 9 focus attention upon the increasing level of affluence in modern commercial societies and whether this has turned into a disease – 'affluenza'. By this they mean a tendency for people to measure and compare themselves exclusively according to their material wealth. Harper and Jones look at the moral challenges that our society faces in a more affluent world. They underline the positive and negative effects of affluence upon society, and the different attitudes that emerge as a consequence of increased wealth. Ironically, they state, economic analysis illustrates the ways in which affluence can damage economic productivity, inasmuch as it undermines a willingness to work, not to mention ethics in the workplace. Such complacency, Harper and Jones comment, seems to be evident in younger sections of the workforce who are yet to experience more testing economic times.

In affluent societies, Harper and Jones note, people are inclined to spend their disposable income on improving their status in society. At the same time, greater affluence brings with it a sensation of liberation as people's incomes increase and they are exposed to things beyond the boundaries of what they were used to. Harper and Jones also observe that, despite all the particular opportunities to engage in immoral acts, there are people who reject such seductions and instead spend much of their time, energy and monetary income on the pursuit of non-material goods. Only a few decades ago, some of these same non-material goods would have been unobtainable by people too poor and time-constrained to engage in such activities. The ambiguity of affluence for Christians, according to Harper and Jones, is further underlined by their awareness that affluence has the capacity to distract people from the purpose and meaning of life, which Christians believe is found when we love God and our neighbours as we love ourselves. But, Harper and Jones argue, Christians can also find positive results from affluence, such as the greater resources that people can commit to helping those less fortunate. They also note that developed, affluent countries have a much better record in upholding human rights and solving environmental problems than poorer, underdeveloped nations.

Taking the discussion to a global level, Peter Heslam, in Chapter 10, contends that theology and the Christian Church should engage with business in order to help alleviate poverty. Heslam draws on Richard Niebuhr's 'typology' to identify different Christian attitudes towards business, and explains how much of the Church's teachings can be made relevant to modern business. Heslam compares two theological paradigms – *transformation* and *liberation* – to show how theology can embrace and promote business's capacity to improve the material welfare of the poor substantially and permanently in the developing world. He states that business has become the chief agent of social transformation in today's world, and that Christian business people have an opportunity to bring transformation to the world's poor. They realize that globalization can serve the common good. The Church constantly highlights the plight of the poor, but Heslam insists that Christians must rethink their approach to poverty alleviation because government aid and assistance have not provided adequate solutions. Business and private enterprise are able to provide longer-term solutions, especially through improved technology and innovation.

Our intention in compiling this volume was to reach out to those of our professional colleagues who know little if anything of the Christian faith, let alone Christian theology, and at the same time to those of our Christian brothers and sisters who evince deep suspicion or at least puzzlement over our involvement with 'the economic'. Our hope is that the quality of the contributions gathered here will attract a readership within both groups and make connections that have long been abandoned or never yet made in people's minds.

We are not so ambitious as to seek a complete reconciliation of economics and theology. At some level, this is probably impossible given the respective 'worldly' and 'other worldly' foci of the two disciplines. On the other hand, if the papers collected here help to break down interdisciplinary misunderstandings and promote a deeper curiosity on the part of economists and theologians to know more of what lies beyond the bounds of their respective disciplines, our efforts will be amply rewarded.

PART I

Christianity and the history of economic thought

1. Aristotle's science of economics

Ricardo F. Crespo

INTRODUCTION

This chapter explores the Aristotelian conception of economic science. First, the notion of *oikonomike* is introduced and the question addressed whether economics was a science for Aristotle. We then ask what kind of science, within Aristotle's classification, is economics. The characteristics of practical sciences are then examined and, finally, the consequences of economics being a practical science for Aristotle are deduced. The present study relies both on Aristotle's textual analysis and interpretation of his thought to translate his teachings into today's language and apply them to today's economics.

WHAT IS ARISTOTLE'S *OIKONOMIKE?*

First of all, we should note that the economy of Aristotle's time was unlike any developed economy in the modern world. Economics as a discipline had not been established and Aristotle devoted only a few pages to the discussion of economic issues. However, his ideas about *oikonomike* may serve as a useful starting point for an Aristotelian analysis of economic science.

Aristotle considers *oikonomike* as the use of the things necessary to the Good Life – that is, the life of virtues. Aristotle's *oikonomike* is more than 'household management', a common enough understanding of the term among historians of economic thought. He pointed out that *oikonomike* deals with the house but also with the civil community, the *polis* (cf. Aristotle, 1958, *Politics* I, 8, 1256b 12–14; I, 10, 1258a 19–21; I, 11, 1259a 33–6). It is subordinate to politics because the things used by *oikonomike* are a necessary condition for the very existence of the *polis* (cf. ibid., III, 9, 1280b 31–2).

For Aristotle, *oikonomike* can only be aimed at the good – it is essentially moral. He distinguishes another related concept, *chrematistics*, which is a technique subordinate to *oikonomike* dealing with the acquisition of those things used by it.[1] This technique, by contrast, is not essentially oriented towards the good. Therefore, while for Aristotle, a harmful *oikonomike* is unthinkable, two kinds of chrematistics are possible: a subordinated, limited and natural one; and a wicked, unnatural, unlimited one. Thus *oikonomike* is an act, the right act of using things in order to achieve the good (that is, virtuous) life. Accordingly, virtue is needed as a habit to facilitate the performance of the act. Moreover, *oikonomike* was embedded in its political environment.

WAS ECONOMICS A SCIENCE FOR ARISTOTLE?

At the very beginning of the *Nicomachean Ethics* (1962), Aristotle states (I, 2, 1094b 4–6) that politics:

> ordains which of the sciences should be studied in a state . . . and we see even the most highly esteemed of capacities fall under this, e.g., strategy, economics, rhetoric; now since politics uses the rest of the sciences, and since, again, it legislates as to what we are to do and what we are to abstain from, the end of this science must include those of the others, so that this end must be the good for man.

Taking into account the whole context of the treatment of *oikonomike* in *Politics*, Aristotelian scholars have usually interpreted this passage in support of economics being, for Aristotle, a practical science (see, for example Newman, 1951, p. 133; Natali, 1980, p. 117; Berti, 1992, p. 89; Miller, 1995, pp. 6–11; Reeve, 2006, p. 206). Politics is the 'most architectonical' (*Nicomachean Ethics* I, 2, 1094a 27) Aristotelian practical science. Ethics and *oikonomike* are also practical sciences for Aristotle.

There is even a terminological similarity between politics (*politike*) and *oikonomike* that is worth pointing out. In his commentary on Aristotle's *Politics*, Ernest Barker (1959, pp. 354–5) remarks:

> 'Politics' in the Greek is an adjectival form – as if we should say 'the political'. What is the noun which it implies? Strictly, it is the noun 'science' (*episteme*). But sciences may be, in Aristotle's view, practical as well as theoretical, and since the science of politics is largely practical, we may say that 'the political' implies the noun 'art' or 'capacity' (*techne* or *dynamis*) no less than it implies the noun 'science'. In a word, it implies both. 'Politics' is the scientific study of the *polis*, and of all things political, *with a view to political action* or the proper exercise of the political 'art'.

Oikonomike is also a Greek adjective: it translates as 'the economic'. Crespo (2006) offers a similar analysis of the ontology of 'the economic' for Aristotle, suggesting a fourfold meaning of the term. Aristotle uses the adjective to refer to all that relates to the use of wealth in order to achieve the Good Life. He does not use it with corresponding nouns. Thus, it is in fact a substantivated adjective.

Crespo (2006) argues that the expression 'the economic' is an analogical term. Analogical terms have different but related meanings, one of which is the 'focal' or primary meaning to which the other, derivative, meanings refer and are connected. The four different meanings advanced in that paper are as follows:

1. *A human action* The focal meaning of *oikonomike* is its definition, namely, the action of using the things that are necessary for life (live at all) and for the Good Life (live well). When Aristotle speaks about 'life at all', he is referring to what is achieved at home (*oikos*). When he talks about the Good Life, he is referring to what is attainable in the *polis*, and which is the end of civil community. According to him, the latter concept of life has a precise moral meaning; it is a life of virtues by which human beings achieve happiness.

2. *A capacity* Aristotle also considers *oikonomike* as a capacity, that is, an ability or power. In this case, it is a power to perform economic actions. *Oikonomike* as capacity is a derived sense of *oikonomike*, because the capacity of using exists for the sake of the action of using. Given that capacities are defined by their ends or functions (Aristotle, *De Anima* II, 4, 415a 16–21), these ends are ontologically prior to the very capacities and correspond to the focal meaning in a case of an analogical term such as *oikonomike*.

3. *A habit* According to Aristotle, the repetition of actions engenders and consolidates habits that facilitate the very action. In effect, Aristotle speaks about household management as a kind of prudence (*Nicomachean Ethics* VI, 8; cf. also Aristotle, *Eudemian Ethics* I, 8, 1218b 13). *Oikonomike* as a kind of habit is another derived sense of *oikonomike*. It is the habit that helps the performance of *oikonomike* as the action of using necessary things for living well.

4. *'The economic' science* Finally, *oikonomike* is also, as stated above, 'the economic' science. Newman (1950, I, p. 138) states that: 'Political economy almost originated with him'. For Peter Koslowski (1985, p. 2): 'Economic science is an integral part of the hierarchically ordered sciences of human action and societal interaction'.

These various related meanings of *oikonomike* help us to confirm, as asserted above, that 'the economic' is, for Aristotle, a practical science. But what is a practical science? And why is 'the economic' a practical science?

WHAT KIND OF SCIENCE IS 'THE ECONOMIC'?

We begin by considering the meaning of practical science. Aristotle distinguishes between theoretical, practical and poietical (or technical) sciences. The distinction corresponds to their different subjects (Aristotle, *Metaphysics* VI, 1, 1025b 20–21 and cf. 1025b 19ff. and XI, 7, 1063b 36–1064a):

1. Theoretical science deals with those things that are not feasible or modifiable but that can only be contemplated. Theoretical sciences according to Aristotle include metaphysics, physics and mathematics. Theoretical science is the strictest notion of science for Aristotle.
2. Practical science deals with those subjects that originated in human decision or choice. They have a practical aim (*Metaphysics* II, 1, 993b 21–2; see also *Nicomachean Ethics* I, 2, 1095a 6 and II, 2, 1103b 27–8).
3. Technical science deals with artifacts and the rules for their production.

   Both practical and technical sciences deal with human actions. How do we then differentiate practical from technical sciences? In *Metaphysics*, Aristotle distinguishes between two kinds of human actions: first, immanent actions, that is, actions whose end is the action itself, such as seeing, thinking or living – the results of immanent actions remain in the agent; second, transitive actions, where the 'result is something apart from the exercise (and thus) the actuality is in the thing that is being made' (*Metaphysics* IX, 8, 1050a 30–31). Transitive actions are actions the results of which transcend the agent and are something different from the agent as, for example, a product. Aristotle calls immanent action *prâxis* and transitive action *poíesis* (*Nicomachean Ethics* VI, 4, 1140a 1).

   All human actions are both immanent and transitive, except in the case of a fully immanent action (to think or to love). For example, when somebody works, there are two results: an 'objective' result, such as the product or service (transitive aspect), and a 'subjective' result, such as an increase in ability or self-fulfilment of the agent, as well as the moral good of the act (immanent aspect). For Aristotle, this latter – the immanent aspect – is the more relevant. It is the one sought for its own sake, not for any further reason. Aristotle affirms that, 'we call that which is in itself worthy of pursuit more complete than that which is worthy of pursuit for the sake of something else' (ibid. I, 7, 1097a 30–31). In other words, Aristotle attributes more relevance to the intrinsic or immanent aspect of action – that which is in itself worthy of pursuit – because it is this aspect whose end is the very fulfilment or perfection of the agent. For him, the external aspect of action is merely instrumental.

Given this explanation, we have to add that for Aristotle, the subject of practical sciences is the immanent aspect of human actions and the subject of technical (or poietical) sciences is the transitive aspect of those human actions. What kind of action is 'the economic'? We have seen that *oikonomike* is an action of using, in Greek, *chresasthai*. What kind of action, immanent or transitive, is *chresasthai*? 'To use' is a transitive action insofar as the thing used is consumed or wasted when used. However, the complete action of *oikonomike* is to use what is necessary to satisfy the agent's requirements to live well: this is the immanent consideration of use, for it is using for the sake of the proper perfection. The action of *chrematistike*, on the other hand, is clearly transitive.

IN WHAT SENSE IS PRACTICAL SCIENCE – AND THUS ECONOMICS A SCIENCE?

Aristotle established the characteristics of science in his logical treatise called *Posterior Analytics*. The object of science must be necessary and not perishable (Aristotle, *Posterior Analytics* I, 4, 73a 23–4; I, 6, 74b 14; I, 8, 75b 24). It is not knowledge on something particular, but universal (ibid., I, 4, 73b 26 and I, 31, 87b 28–35; *De Anima* II, 5, 417b 23). Finally, it has a deductive or syllogistic demonstrative form.

It is difficult to align practical science with this concept of science. In effect, human action is neither necessary, nor imperishable nor universal, and practical arguments are often inductive, dialectical, metaphorical or topical. However, Aristotle addresses the issue in the quoted passages of the *Metaphysics*. Following the suggestion of Gauthier and Jolif (1970, pp. 23–5 and 453–5), we might interpret 'science' like 'the economic', as an analogical term. Thus, there is a strict as well as a looser meaning of science. The strict meaning corresponds to theoretical science, the science described in the *Posterior Analytics*. Aristotle refers to practical science as a science by similarity: *kat' homoiótesin* (cf. *Nicomachean Ethics* VI, 3, 1139b 20). This is a middle ground between strict science (theoretical), and prudence and action. This analogical meaning of science is not the clearest and most central. However, practical science owns the characteristic common to all kinds of sciences, namely, being a 'state of capacity to demonstrate (*héxis apodeiktiké*)' (ibid., VI, 3, 1139b 32) within the limitations inherent to its subject matter, human choice and human action (contingent, variable, free, singular).

Aristotle recognizes this 'weaker' character. He asserts in *Nicomachean Ethics* that:

> Our treatment discussion will be adequate if it has as much clearness as the subject-matter admits of; for precision is not to be sought for alike in all discussions, any more than in all the products of the crafts. Now fine and just actions, which political science investigates, exhibit much variety and fluctuation . . . We must be content, then, in speaking of such subjects and with such premises to indicate the truth roughly and in outline. (Ibid., I, 3, 1094b 11–27)

Aristotle identifies two reasons for this 'inexactness' of practical sciences: 'variety' and 'fluctuation' of actions. That is, there are lots of possible different situations and the human being may change his or her decisions. This is why, for Aristotle, human action is always singular. He says:

> We must, however, not only make this *general statement*, but also apply it to the individual facts. For among statements about conduct those which are general apply more widely, but those *which are particular are more true*, since conduct has to do with *individual* cases, and our statements must harmonize with the facts in these cases. (Ibid., II, 7, 1107a 31–3, emphasis added)

And also:

> [A]ctions are in the class of *particulars*, and the particular acts here are voluntary. What sort of things are to be chosen, and in return for what, it is not easy to state; for there are many differences in the *particular* cases. (Ibid., III, 1, 1110b 6–8, emphasis added)

Properties of actions are variable. An action may be just or unjust according to the situation; and the concrete determination or content of a just situation is also variable (cf. ibid., V, 10, 1137b 28–30 on equity: 'about some things it is impossible to lay down a law . . . For when the thing is indefinite the rule is also indefinite'). Aristotle also affirms this with regard to wealth, beauty and courage, among others. This is why he says, for example, that 'a young man is not a proper hearer of lectures on political science; for he is inexperienced in the actions that occur in life, but its discussions start from these and are about these' (ibid., I, 3, 1095a 2–4). He often compares politics with medicine in this respect, as in the next quotation. In sum:

> [M]atters concerned with conduct and questions about what is good for us have no fixity, any more than matters of health. The general account being of this nature, the account of particular cases is yet more lacking in exactness; for they do not fall under any art or set of precept, but the agents themselves must in each case consider what is appropriate to the occasion, as happens also in the art of medicine or of navigation. (Ibid., II, 2, 1104a 4–9)

We must remember that practical science, as conceived by Aristotle, ends in action. However, the more 'practical' practical sciences are, the less general they become. By leaving generality behind to move towards con-crete reality, science limits its scope. This ought to be kept in mind as we should look for a balanced position: if we try to include all relevant factors in a concrete situation, we lose generality and, thus, explanatory power for different situations in the conclusions we reach. But as we try to gain gen-erality, we lose contact with reality as it actually is, and thus explanatory, predictive and normative 'efficiency'. Moreover, could we speak about pre-diction in the above described conditions? What is the solution to this choice between accuracy and generality? It may help to analyse what happens in other sciences.

This problem occurs not only in practical science but also in physics. What are the essentials of its subject matter? If physics reduced its scope to that which is strictly necessary, it would not have much to do. It also has to deal with what is probable. But in this case the results are not often univer-sals (which express essences), but generalizations that express general, though not always necessary, properties. Consequently, generalizations may fail. However, though not completely certain, prediction is sufficiently accurate, thus allowing for science.

As already stated, *Posterior Analytics* is the book in which Aristotle char-acterizes science. It belongs to the set of logical books Aristotle called *Organon* (i.e., 'instruments' of thinking). J.M. Le Blond, in his classic *Logique et Méthode chez Aristote*, maintains that 'the books composing the *Organon* are more concerned with *expositing* science in a rigorous way than with *doing* science. His scientific books, on the other hand, focus on research and they are the ones that reveal the method' (1939, p. 191). In other words, the *Organon* contains a theory of science, while the scientific books are actual science that does not always follow the precepts of the theory.[2] As Hankinson states, 'one can trawl the whole of Aristotle's con-siderable scientific *oeuvre* without netting a single instance of a fully worked-out syllogism' (1995, p. 113). General theory must be adequate to the empirical data (ibid., p. 137).

In fact, in his studies – especially biological (*On the Part of Animals*, *The History of Animals*), physical (*Meteorology*), and practical (*Ethics and Politics*) – Aristotle gives plenty of room for experience and does this in order to discover and also verify scientific principles. He says in *Generation of Animals* (concerning his observations about the generation of bees) that 'credit must be given rather to observation than to theories, and to theories only if what they affirm agrees with the observed facts' (III, 10, 760b 31; cf. also *De Anima*, I, 1, 639b 3ff. and 640a 14ff.). That is, some principles in some sciences are based on empirical data leading to generalizations, not to universals. Universals are grasped by a sort of intellectual intuition – called abstraction – which presupposes experience but is not based on a complete enumeration of cases. Moreover, in some cases, one or a few instances suffice to abstract the universal. Generalizations, however, are based on enumeration of empirical or experimental cases. Le Blond shows how Aristotle uses experience in detailed observation as well as in experiment: 'flux and reflux of the research going from facts to theories and from theories to facts' (1939, p. 242). This clearly explains why Aristotle states in *Nicomachean Ethics* (VI, 8) that 'a boy may become a mathematician but not a philosopher or a natural scientist'. The reason, he adds, is that the philosopher and the natural scientist need experience. As he states in *On Generation and Corruption*:

> [L]ack of experience diminishes our power of taking a comprehensive view of admitted fact. Hence those who dwell in intimate association with nature and its phenomena are more able to lay down principles such as to admit of a wide and coherent development. (I, 2, 316a 5–8)

Summing up, generalizations from the point of view of Aristotle's strict science are not scientific, for science deals with universals. However, the contingency of the subject matter justifies the use of generalizations instead of universals in science. Even in *Posterior Analytics*, Aristotle considers as objects of science occurrences that are only general connections, premises or rules (I, 30, 87b 19ff.; II, 12, 96a 8–9). If this is applicable to physics, there are more reasons for applying it to human action as subject matter, for freedom adds an extra quota of contingency. This is the stuff of practical science.

There are two sources that allow generalization in practical sciences: first, an anthropological natural basis; and second (and compatible with the former), the recurrence of habits. This is because in the realm of human action 'in most respects the future will be like the past has been' (Aristotle, *Rhetoric* II, 20, 1394a 7–8). Hence, generalizations in practical science are actual dispositions or habits (see Wieland 1999). This is why close contact with facts is necessary in practical science. The more stable the habits and tendencies, the more predictable the outcomes. In any case general tendencies may change: they are not firmly established universals. Aristotle develops a theory about the stability of habits (*Nicomachean Ethics*, VII, 9, 1151b 25–7 and VII, 10, 1152a, 26–7). When habits are sufficiently stable as to constitute social institutions, practical science is firmly based. Therefore, institutions are very important for they consolidate tendencies and habits and facilitate accurate science. Thus, according to this meaning of 'the economic', we can predict better when social institutions are solidly established; yet, even so, nothing is definitive. We return to this point in the conclusion.

The meaning of *oikonomike* as practical science is analogical in respect to 'economic' human action. Although being a practical science, science for Aristotle is different from action and from practical wisdom (prudence): 'practical wisdom [*phrónesis*] cannot be science [*epistéme*]' (ibid., VI, 5, 1140b 2).

We have spoken of practical science as a middle ground between prudence (a habit) and theoretical science. In effect, while prudence deals with the particular, practical science tries to formulate generalizations. Although these generalizations cannot be exact but only probable, this should be the task of practical science and cannot be considered as a weakness of it but as the appropriate way to tackle its subject. As Kraut asserts, Aristotle 'is asking us to have different expectations of different fields: not *higher* standards for some fields and *lower* for others, but *different* standards' (2006, p. 87). No matter how different, the task of practical science is still to try to generalize. Politics, Aristotle states, 'legislates as to what we are to do and what we are to abstain from' (*Nicomachean Ethics* I, 2, 1094b 4–6). Ideally, Reeve comments, 'the scope of deliberation should be minimal; that of universal law maximal' (2006, p. 211). However, the tension remains: inasmuch as it tends to universality, it moves further away from reality.

WHAT ARE THE CHARACTERISTICS OF PRACTICAL SCIENCE?

As already noted, practical science is not exact science – the truth of the practical is not fixed. Other characteristics of practical science include the following:

First, practical science must be closely linked to the concrete case. 'Now no doubt', Aristotle says, 'it is proper to start from the known. But "the known" has two meanings: "what is known to us" which is one thing; and "what is knowable in itself" which is another. Perhaps, then, for us at all events, it is proper to start from what is known to us' (*Nicomachean Ethics* I, 4, 1095b 2–4). That is, we must start from the manifest surface facts to discover the causes.

Second, another distinctive feature of practical sciences is their pragmatic end. Aristotle states that 'the end of this kind of study [politics] is not knowledge but action' (ibid., I, 3, 1095a 6) and that 'we are not conducting this inquiry in order to know what virtue is, but in order to become good' (ibid., II, 2, 1103b 27–8). He adds in his *Metaphysics* that 'the end of theoretical knowledge is truth, while that of practical knowledge is action' (II, 1, 993b 21–2). Nowadays, social sciences are theoretical studies of practical subjects. Then one can ask: what is their epistemological condition?

Aquinas completes Aristotle on this point: he distinguishes three principles to decide whether a science is theoretical or practical: the subject matter, the end and the method. This threefold classification leaves room for 'mixed' cases, as those theoretical studies of practical subjects just mentioned above. Aquinas asserts in *De Veritate* (Aquinas, 1949)

> Knowledge is said to be practical by its order to act. This can happen in two ways. Sometimes *in actu*, i.e., when it is actually ordered to perform something . . . Other times, when knowledge can be ordered to act but it is not now ordered to act . . . in this way knowledge is virtually practical, but not *in actu*. (q. 3, a. 3)

This is an important point because current social sciences – including economics – although they may try to be only theoretical, are virtually ordered towards action. Thus, although a particular science may be theoretical *secundum finem*, or may have both theoretical and practical aspects, its implicit orientation towards action determines its epistemological framework.

The third characteristic of practical sciences is normativeness. Inexactness, closeness to reality and pragmatic aim are features of the practical sciences stemming from the singularity of human action, as conceived by Aristotle. The normative character of practical sciences has to do with their pragmatic aim. The statement that 'it is rational to act in a concrete way' is both a positive and a normative statement. Practical sciences have an ethical engagement arising from the immanent aspect of human action. In transitive human actions, a triple rationality may be distinguished: practical or moral, technical and logical. Practical immanent rationality permeates the whole action to the extent that, as already explained, the existence of a purely technical transitive action cannot be sustained. Whatever may be the action, it is always essentially ethical. Since human action is ethical, and since economic action is human action, therefore, political economy has an ethical commitment. Concerning our field of study, Gilles-Gaston Granger (1992, p. 80) states that, within the economic arena, braiding the different perspectives of rationality seems to be necessary in order to attain an effective definition of concepts.

Finally, reference should be made to the methodological devices characteristic of practical sciences. The abundant bibliography on this topic could be summarized as a proposal of methodological plurality. In *Politics* and *Nicomachean Ethics*, Aristotle admirably combines axiomatic deduction, inductive inference, dialectic arguments, rhetoric, imagination, examples and topics. Some authors, beginning with Burnet (1900), have stated that there was a predominance of dialectics and topics in such a way that practical science would lack scientific character (see, for example, Hennis, 1963).

The reaction from the Aristotelian scholars led to a deep study of the method of practical science. The result of this study is: 1) in *Politics* and *Nicomachean Ethics*, there are typical scientific demonstrative arguments (see, for example, Barnes, 1980, pp. 494–5 and Barnes, 1993, p. 29): they are 'a state of capacity to demonstrate' (*Nicomachean Ethics* VI, 3, 1139b 31). 2) This science provides what all sciences provide, *pisteue* – that is, certainty (ibid., VI, 3, 1139b 34). 3) It is transmissible, as all sciences are: this is why Aristotle writes *Politics* and *Nicomachean Ethics*. 4) It has a hierarchical order: all practical sciences are subordinated to politics (ibid., I, 2, passim and *Politics* III, 12, 1282b 14) and they are (implicitly) subordinated to metaphysics, 'the most authoritative of the sciences' (*Metaphysics* I, 2, 982b 5).

CONCLUSION

From an Aristotelian point of view, the science of 'the economic' is practical science. The subject matter of practical sciences, among them economics, entails a kind of 'living science' where the principles are few and most of the conclusions are variable according to the cases.

Generalizations in these sciences are possible, thanks to the tendencies of some kind of actions to be repeated. As Alasdair MacIntyre explains, predictability in the social sciences is only imperfectly possible. However, it is often achievable thanks to knowledge of: 1) statistical regularities; 2) the way people carry out their need to schedule and coordinate their social actions; and 3) the awareness of the causal regularities of both nature and social life (see MacIntyre, 1984, pp. 102–3 and Wieland, 1996).

Given these conclusions, there are several reasons why institutions matter greatly in the economic realm. Institutions both embody and reinforce steady habits. That is, there are two directions of analysis: on the one hand, how habits shape institutions; and on the other, how institutions encourage habits. Concerning the first direction, habits, especially good habits, make actions more predictable and thus facilitate the consolidation of institutions. According to Aristotle, the incontinent man is unpredictable; by contrast, the virtuous man, who is continent, is more predictable because he/she perseveres. 'A morally weak person', he says, 'does not abide by the dictates of reason' (*Nicomachean Ethics*, VII, 9, 1151b 25–7). 'A morally strong person remains more steadfast and a morally weak person less steadfast than the capacity of most men permits' (ibid., VII, 10, 1152 a, 26–7). In this way virtues facilitate the predictability of acts and help constitute institutions, which are embodiments of regular behavior patterns towards a defined end.

In the opposite direction, institutions foster habits, for they reinforce the realization of determined acts through rewards and punishments. According to Aristotle, the main means to foster these actions are education and law. First, education, in the broad Greek sense of *paideia*, is the shaping of personal character. This is why, 'it makes no small difference, then, whether we form habits of one kind or of another from our very youth' (ibid., II, 1, 1103b 24). Second, law bears a pedagogical objective (cf. ibid., X, 9, 1179b 31–1180a 4). Aristotle understands that a set of concrete virtues leads humans to their natural excellence. This process begins with the teaching of those virtues, conveniently consolidated by laws.

Hence, there are two reasons why the presence of institutions is relevant. First, they are relevant for the very possibility of economic science. As explained, practical sciences (economics among them) may make generalizations and predictions thanks to the repetition of acts. Institutions help in the consolidation of habits. Second, predictability and institutions facilitate economic coordination. Coordination is possible when acts are foreseeable. Thus, we can conclude, in an Aristotelian-minded spirit, that economic coordination is more easily achievable and economic science can more accurately postulate generalizations within a virtuous environment.

This condition does not diminish freedom but, on the contrary, it presupposes and fosters it. Aristotle considers virtue as a state of character concerned with choice, lying in a mean (that is, the mean relative to us), and this being determined by a rational principle, that principle by which a person of practical wisdom (prudence) would determine it. The word 'choice' means that the main act of moral virtue is the right decision; the decision of doing here and now what is needed for good behaviour. This right decision presupposes a good discernment on means and ways of acting. This is the role of practical wisdom. 'Choice' also indicates that the good action is wanted and elected in itself: intention matters. Hence, virtues facilitate good acts without annulling freedom; on the contrary, they suppose a constant free behaviour. Consequently, an implication of Aristotle's conception of economic science is that, if the society in which an economy functions is free and virtuous, economics will be more precise in its predictions.

2. Christianity's pre-Enlightenment contribution to economic thought[1]
Stephen J. Grabill

INTRODUCTION

The complicated relationship between Christianity and economics before
the 18th century is a story that has largely remained untold for at least five
interrelated reasons. First, there are very few storytellers who are capable
of constructing a narrative from the myriad of medieval documents, texts,
penitential handbooks, theological manuals, papal bulls and consilia in
which the elements of the story are embedded. These source documents are
always written either in a classical language or an old dialect of a vernacu-
lar language, so linguistic proficiency in Greek, Latin and often Hebrew, in
addition to Italian, Spanish, French, German and Dutch, is necessary to
handle the sources. Second, the scope of the story is so immense that it is
difficult to know where to begin. Third, there is relatively little interest in
the story being told at all. Fourth, the narrow specialization and disciplinary compartmentalization of the modern university discourages scholars
in religion, economics and intellectual history from 'crossing the border'
into adjoining disciplines. Finally, and perhaps most important of all,
Western intellectuals (since the 18th century) have downplayed the
Christian roots of modern academic disciplines such as astronomy, physics,
biology, politics, philosophy and economics. Among the mainstream
writers of economic history, secularization has shown itself either in the
glib dismissal or snide rejection of the economic ideas of the scholastics as
'sterile', 'analytically unsophisticated', 'specious theological dogmatism'
and/or 'casuistic'.

To assess Christianity's pre-Enlightenment contribution to economic
thought accurately, it is important to respond to the aforementioned criticisms of scholastic economics. In so doing, two basic starting points will
inform our approach. Jeffrey T. Young and Barry Gordon capture the
essence of the first starting point. They write: 'Modern historical scholarship has shown that the Scholastic doctors of the thirteenth century
addressed economic moral issues in the context of European regional

25

economies that had experienced substantial economic growth over the pre-
ceding two centuries' (Young and Gordon, 1992, p. 3). Lying just beneath
the surface of this seemingly banal observation lurks an implication with
far-reaching significance: to develop a full understanding of how learned
people at the time grasped the significance of population growth, urban-
ization, long-distance trade, innovations in production techniques and the
rising commercial middle class, an analyst must appreciate how they developed arguments pro and con, reasoned from premises to conclusions and
tested their assumptions about the causes of various economic phenomena in relation to their religious and theological starting points. In other
words, it is imperative to grasp the basics of scholastic method, what it is
and what it is not; and if this is done, an honest investigator will reach conclusions about scholasticism that are quite the opposite of the descriptors
above. Second, the predominantly positivist philosophical and methodological assumptions of a sizeable number of economic historians has led
to a severing of economic ideas from their original historical, philosophical, theological and institutional contexts in the debate over the prehistory
of economics. This implies that to tell the complicated story of the relationship between Christianity and economics before the 18th century, it
is also necessary to enter the contemporary debate over the prehistory of
economics.

The aim of this chapter is to show that the application of scholastic
method by Christian moral theologians to economic problems resulted in
revolutionary insights and new-found discoveries in economic thought over
the course of centuries. These insights and discoveries were eventually
refined into ideas that have profoundly shaped the world of modern economics. If this thesis can be sufficiently established here, then it seems
reasonable to expect the burden of proof to fall back upon the critics to show
that scholastic economics has made no analytically sophisticated contribution to modern economics. The most significant insight to emerge from this
study is that economics as a discipline cannot be detached from a historical background that was profoundly Christian in both theory and practice.
To guide this investigation, then, we first examine the historiographical
arguments against giving scholastic economics a more significant place in
economic history textbooks; next we enter the contemporary debate over
the prehistory of economics; and finally we conclude by pointing out how
the recent interest in the 16th- and 17th-century Spanish jurist-theologians
in and around Salamanca serves as a tipping point in the revision of economic history.

THE CONTESTED PLACE OF SCHOLASTIC ECONOMICS IN ECONOMIC HISTORIOGRAPHY

For many intellectuals nowadays moral theology has come to signify a passé form of religious thinking that embraces irrationality and dogmatism, and economic historians have likewise espoused this line of thought. In fact, generally speaking, the identification of scholastic economics (or the 'canonical concept of market behaviour', as it is sometimes called) with Aristotelian metaphysics and ecclesiastical authority has made modern economic historians reticent or, at the very least, unreceptive to acknowledging any sophisticated analytical contribution to the discipline by the 'schoolmen' or the 'doctors' – their 16th- and 17th-century heirs.

Among 20th-century economic historians, Jacob Viner (1978), Raymond de Roover (1948, 1949, 1963, 1967, 1969, 1971, 1974), Marjorie Grice-Hutchinson (1952, 1978, 1990, 1993) and Joseph Schumpeter (1954) were the first to shed new light on the analytical significance of the scholastic contribution to price, money and value. But they laboured alone and their research was often assailed by positivist critics within the neoclassical mainstream. Undeterred, however, they persevered and their work has come to inspire a new generation of revisionist economists (Alvey, 1999, 2004; Black, 2006; Oslington, 2003, 2005; Yuengert, 2004), economic historians (Abellán, 1979; Backhouse, 2002; Camacho, 1985, 1990, 1998a, 1998b; Chafuen, 2003; de Soto, 1996; Gordon, 1975; Langholm, 1979, 1983, 1984, 1987, 1992, 1998, 2003; Lowry, 1969, 1987a, 1987b; Lowry and Gordon, 1998; Noonan, 1957; Nuccio, 1974, 1984–91; Pribram, 1983; Rothbard, 1995; Young and Gordon, 1992), political economists (Gregg, 2007; Hutchinson, 1988; Nuccio, 1965; Piedra, 2004; Young, 1997), philosophers (Mochrie, 2006; Widow, 1997), and moral theologians (Grabill, 2007; Muñoz, 1998, 2001; Sirico, 1998) who now write economic history from a broader, history-of-ideas perspective in contrast to the conventional positivist historiography of the neoclassical mainstream.

Mark Blaug, a prolific British economist, is typical of most mainstream historians with regard to his method and philosophical assumptions. For example, despite acknowledging that the scholastic tradition has been frequently misinterpreted concerning its utility-cum-scarcity understanding of value and the role of common estimation in determining a just price, Blaug repeats the standard criticism of the tradition on usury, namely, that 'money capital is sterile' (Blaug, 1997, p. 30). For, as modern commentators commonly suppose, the scholastic understanding of *cambium*, which closely parallels Aristotle's treatment in *Politics*[2] (1958) and *Nicomachean Ethics*[3] (1962), led ecclesiastical officials to prohibit interest from being taken on any loan – commercial or otherwise – since all interest was regarded as 'a breed of barren metal'.[4] But, as the medievalist, Odd Langholm, assesses the ecclesiastical debate over usury, a somewhat different evaluation emerges:

> It is not that usury is wrong because money *cannot* breed; it is rather that money *should not* be made to breed, because this is an unnatural use of money, such as in money-changing, usury, and debasement . . . The only natural use of money is to serve as a medium of exchange. This is money's true end. But the end for which a thing is invented is subordinated to man's end, reinterpreted by the Scholastics in Christian terms. Making money breed is wrong because it is inspired by cupidity, said Albert the Great. (Langholm, 1987, pp. 128–9).

Cupidity, however, is neither a necessary nor a sufficient motivation of currency exchange; other less malicious, more pragmatic motivations are certainly possible, if not likely, as the schoolmen and the doctors themselves acknowledged. Some schoolmen (such as Henry of Ghent [ca. 1217–93] and Guido Terrena [?–1342]), in fact, came to acknowledge the usefulness of money-changers, just as Albert the Great (ca. 1206–80) and Thomas Aquinas (1225–74) had acknowledged the need for professional merchants. In his *Genovese Sermon* (1243), Albertanus of Brescia (ca. 1190–?), a little-known medieval jurist and representative of the emerging *podesta* (magistracy) literature,[5] taught that wealth creation and the intelligent use of one's acquisitions were virtuous activities:

> Now we must consider the third exercise of virtue, as Cicero says. The third is the moderate and intelligent use of our acquisitions. Here we should note that we ought always to win over to ourselves those who come for our advice and assistance and profit from them and make use of their friendship and riches with moderation and intelligence in keeping with the peculiar nature of virtue. For, as the same Cicero said, 'It is characteristic of virtue both to reconcile the spirits of men and to unite them for their usefulness, that is, their benefit'. We ought to derive, then, benefit, wealth, and advantages from them. (Albertanus of Brescia, 1243, pp. 632–3)

The intelligent use of profit, derived from money (e.g., capital) risked in an entrepreneurial venture, is a formal aspect of the thought of the 15th-century casuists, Saint Bernardine of Siena (1380–1444), a Franciscan, and Saint Antonine of Florence (1389–1459), a Dominican. According to Bernardine, when a business person lends from balances held for commercial purposes, he 'gives not money in its simple character, but he also gives his capital' (as quoted by Gordon, 1975, p. 197). Elsewhere, he writes:

> [W]hat, in the firm purpose of its owner, is ordained to some probable profit, has not only the character of mere money or a mere thing, but also beyond this, a certain seminal character of something profitable, which we commonly call

capital. Therefore, not only must its simple value be returned, but a super-added value as well. (As quoted by Gordon, 1975, p. 198)

In describing how any loan may result in profit forgone (*lucrum cessans*) for the lender, or in modern terms, the opportunity cost of liquid funds, Antonine likewise points to the productive potential of money:

> I believe that anyone can claim compensation, not merely for the harm done him, but also the gain he might otherwise have obtained, if he be a merchant accustomed to engage his money in business. The same holds good even if he be not a merchant but have only the intention of investing the funds in lawful trade; but not if he be a man who hoards his wealth in his coffers. (Ibid.)

Herbert Johnson has suggested that this pre-modern understanding of capital is an application of the Augustinian doctrine of *rationes seminales* to money (1959, pp. 96–8).

Yet, despite these important counterexamples to the scholastic-money-capital-is-sterile thesis, Blaug still doubts whether scholastic writing has anything substantive to offer modern economists on the topics of money and interest – largely, it would seem, because of the dogmatic and metaphysical base to its treatment of usury. 'Ingenious apologists have found other nuggets in the literature', he quips, 'but on the whole it is analytically sterile' (Blaug, 1997, p. 31). Ekelund and Hebert, along with numerous other mainstream historians, would concur with Blaug's assessment:

> An absolutist position on economics would not accord medieval thought a high ranking. The Scholastics' discussion of utility and value was fragmentary and mainly adventitious. Their views on price control and their general condemnation of monopoly and price discrimination, outside of the link with theology, were not original. Greek and Roman sources were often much clearer on the nature and effect of controlled prices. Most critically, their ideas on value were normatively oriented. (1975, p. 28)

Usury has been a favourite target of positivist, rationalist and anti-Catholic polemicists. Three 19th-century critics, in particular, William Lecky (1887–90, 2, pp. 250–70), Andrew Dickson White (1896, 2, pp. 264–87) and Henry Charles Lea (1894, pp. 375–85) condemned the ecclesiastical prohibition against usury as a sulphurous residue of theological superstition and clerical oppression (see Noonan, 1957, pp. 398–400). Under the labyrinthine edifice of scholastic casuistry, boomed Lea, competition withered, the flow of credit congealed and interest rates soared (Lea, 1894, pp. 384–5). In a similar vein, the economist C.E. Ayres complained that 'a great deal of casuistry has gone into the formulation of the doctrine of capital, and we owe much of this to the master hand of the medieval church' (Ayres, 1955, p. 46). Chicago School economist, Frank H. Knight, assigned modern economics the accolade of being 'the leading phase in the development of Liberty and Liberalism', which finally liberated economics 'from its long confinement under priestly dictatorship' (Knight, 1955, p. 264). And, finally, even such an eminent historian as Raymond de Roover, a pioneer himself in the revival of scholastic economic research, spoke of usury as the Achilles' heel of scholastic economics, which eventually led to its decline and fall:

> The great weakness of Scholastic economics was the usury doctrine. Canon law, dating as it does back to the early Middle Ages when most loans were made for consumption purposes, defined usury as any increment demanded beyond the principal of a loan. Since this definition was part of Catholic dogma, the Schoolmen were unable to change it. As time went by, it became a source of increasing embarrassment. Tied to their definition, the Doctors were sucked deeper into a quagmire of contradictions. (de Roover, 1974, p. 318)

Usury is perhaps the most ridiculed, but least understood, idea in the history of economics.

The fundamental deficiency in almost every modern evaluation of usury is an insufficient understanding of and appreciation for the integrated nature of scholastic economics with metaphysics, dogmatics and the traditions of both canon and civil law jurisprudence. Modern commentators tend to isolate and abstract narrower, more specialized topics such as usury from their context within larger, intellectual systems, which they then proceed to evaluate on the basis of anachronistically construed canons of rationality. Once a topic like usury is severed from its metaphysical schema and broader intellectual tradition, the verdict of its incoherence and obsolescence is already sealed in the court of modern opinion.

An adequate evaluation of any topic within scholastic economics must also acknowledge that this tradition, like the traditions of natural law and natural right, has been deeply affected by the 'seismic' intellectual shift of the 14th and 15th centuries (essentialist/nominalist debates). 'That shift involved changes in the understanding of both the nature of nature and of the essence of law', relates the learned medievalist, Francis Oakley:

> and it was concerned with the very metaphysical grounding of natural law. It ensured that not one but two principal traditions of natural law thinking would be transmitted to the thinkers of early modern Europe. And it is necessary to take into account the continuing dialectical interchange between those traditions if one is to make adequate sense of what was going on intellectually in the array of natural law theories framed during the sixteenth, seventeenth, and even eighteenth centuries. (Oakley, 2005, pp. 25–6; see also Grabill, 2006, pp. 54–69)

If the import of Oakley's image of a 'profound geologic fault'[6] running across and beneath the conflicted landscape of the Western intellectual tradition is fully grasped, it will be impossible to treat scholastic economics historically and philosophically as an undifferentiated and homogeneous tradition with respect to its metaphysics (essentialism/ nominalism), anthropology (intellectualism/voluntarism), dogmatics (Protestant-Lutheran-Reformed-Anglican-Early English Reformation/ Roman Catholic-Franciscan-Dominican-Jesuit) or epistemology (discursive/self-evidence). The clear implication is that modern commentators should be much more circumspect in the blanket evaluations they make of it because historical and philosophical outliers will always foil their caricatures and generalizations.

THE DEBATE OVER THE PREHISTORY OF ECONOMICS

The positivist severing of economic ideas from their original historical and metaphysical contexts becomes especially pronounced in the contemporary debate over the prehistory of economics. Invariably, most mainstream economic historians identify the birth of modern economics to be in Adam Smith, the mercantilists and the physiocrats. For Blaug, the prehistory of economics begins with the 17th-century mercantilists and not, as the revisionists insist, with either the ancient Greeks or the 13th-century scholastics. He coins the term 'pre-Adamite economics' to methodologically define and restrict the era of prehistory to Smith's immediate and direct historical precursors: the 17th-century mercantilists, the physiocrats and the British free-trade writers of the 18th century. The broader question of whether the prehistory of economics should start in the 13th century or much earlier is, in Blaug's estimation, 'an afterthought' (1997, p. 29) – an afterthought, we might infer, which could presumably surface information that would challenge positivist assumptions about human behaviour and social cohesion, and one that will yield few, if any, new insights into quantitative methods and models. Where the scholastics analysed economic and commercial transactions as either ethical or legal matters involving the application of natural law to civil contracts, 'It was the mercantilists', contends Blaug:

> who, long before Adam Smith, broke with the canonical conception of market behavior as a moral problem and fashioned the concept of 'economic man' . . . They believed in the direct power of self-interest and in matters of domestic economic policy came near to advocating laissez-faire. Adam Smith was not the first to have confidence in the workings of the 'invisible hand'. Nor is it necessary to

appeal to Scholastic influences to account for his grasp of the determination of prices by demand and supply. (Blaug, 1997, p. 31)

Regardless of whether it is necessary to appeal to scholastic influences to explain how Smith, in particular, understood price and value to be determined, Blaug's assessment does not speak to the wider issue of whether such seminal figures in the history of economics as Bernardo Davanzati (1529–1606), Ferdinando Galiani (1728–87), Hugo Grotius (1583–1645), Samuel von Pufendorf (1632–94), Gershom Carmichael (1672–1729), Francis Hutcheson (1694–1746), Adam Ferguson (1723–1816), Jean-Jacques Burlamaqui (1694–1748), Auguste Walras (1801–66) and Léon Walras (1834–1910) were influenced by scholastic treatments of price and value. Or even, for that matter, whether Smith's entire system of thought remains intelligible, if the role he assigns to teleology, final causes, divine design and virtue is disregarded as merely ornamental (Alvey, 2004). In this wider respect, therefore, the modern quibble over scholastic influences in Smith is a red herring because, as Langholm attests,[7] it sidesteps serious historical investigation into the continuities and discontinuities between scholastic and modern economic ideas. And furthermore, it also has the convenient side-effect of downplaying the importance of teleology and natural theology in the thought of Smith himself and other 17th-, 18th-, and 19th-century political economists.

In fairness to Blaug, he readily acknowledges that 'Scholastic doctrines were transmitted to Adam Smith by way of the seventeenth-century natural-law philosophers, Hugo Grotius and Samuel von Pufendorf. Moreover, the writings of the physiocrats with which Smith was acquainted are replete with Scholastic influences: Quesnay often sounds like an eighteenth-century version of Thomas Aquinas' (Blaug 1997, p. 30). His principal concern, however, is not to dispute the point that 'the Schoolmen may have contributed ideas that passed through Grotius, Locke, and Pufendorf to Francis Hutcheson and Adam Smith' but rather to call into question 'Schumpeter's reduction of mercantilism to a mere by-current in the forward march of economic analysis' (ibid., p. 31).

So, with this in mind, let us assume that Blaug is correct about 'Schumpeter's reduction'. The question then becomes: what is lost or gained as far as the analytical contribution of scholastic economics is concerned? The answer, I think, is nothing. If Schumpeter did throw the proverbial baby out with the bathwater to make his point about scholastic influence, is it not also an over-reaction to use his indiscretion like a club to overshadow the legitimate criticism he raises of positivist historiography? Even if Schumpeter's glib assessment of mercantilism were to be struck from the record out of simple respect for Blaug's extensive research in mercantilist literature, the methodological question still remains of where to begin the prehistory of economics. On what reasonable grounds should scholastic influence on modern economics be considered discontinuous, if evidence can be presented that demonstrates lines of continuity extending from Aristotle and Aquinas that run through the Salamancans and the 17th-century natural-law philosophers to Smith, Galiani, Walras and beyond?

In light of the evidence revisionist historians have indeed surfaced, one is therefore justified in doubting whether recent work on mercantilism and the Scottish Enlightenment requires a reduction of the prehistory of economics to Smith's modern precursors. This position is the methodological converse of Blaug's historical starting point.[8] Moreover, as de Roover argues:

> to consider Scholastic economics as medieval doctrine is simply an error, and economists have bypassed a current of thought which runs parallel with mercantilism and reached out into the eighteenth century, connecting the *économistes* and even Adam Smith with Thomas Aquinas and the medieval Schoolmen. Traces of Scholastic influence still permeate eighteenth century economic thinking and sometimes appear in unexpected places, such as the *Encyclopédie* of Diderot and d'Alembert. (1974, p. 333)

Scholastic Economics: The Bogey Man of Economic History

'Scholastic', according to almost any contemporary definition, means 'arcane, abstruse, and dogmatic', and harkens back to an era when theological scholarship was allegedly tedious, opaque and sterile. Scholars who subscribe to this viewpoint generally find confirmation of their suspicions in the debates over usury and the barrenness of money. Mark Blaug, as we have seen, is no exception here and neither was John Locke, the 18th-century British nominalist (Milton, 1981; Oakley, 1999). Locke dismissed the scholastics as 'the great mintmasters' of useless and empty terms (Locke, 1690, III, x, 2). He lamented that 'sects of philosophy and religion' routinely coin new terms to support strange opinions and cover weak hypotheses. The sophistry of the schoolmen and metaphysicians, he wrote, 'remain empty sounds, with little or no signification, among those who think it enough to have them often in their mouths, as the distinguishing characters of their Church or School, without much troubling their heads to examine what are the precise ideas they stand for' (ibid.). Despite its apparent 'emptiness' and 'uselessness' as an intellectual movement, scholasticism (with its roots in Christian Aristotelian philosophy) extended from approximately 800 to 1700, with the 12th and 13th centuries representing the high water mark in the development of scholastic method. Some of the most prominent names in medieval scholasticism are active in this span of time: Hugh of Saint Victor (1096–1141), Bernard of Clairvaux (1090–1153), Peter Lombard (ca. 1100–60), Thomas Aquinas, Anselm of Canterbury (1033–1109), Roger Grosseteste (1168–1253), Roger Bacon (1214–94), Bonaventure (1221–74), Peter Abelard (1079–1142), John Duns Scotus (1265–1308) and William of Occam (ca. 1287–1347). From approximately 1150 to 1650 a modified Christian Aristotelianism dominated European educational curricula (Freedman, 1985, 1993; Kristeller, 1965; Schmitt, 1973, 1983; van Steenberghen, 1955), and was a vital current among Protestant and Roman Catholic theologians (Muller, 2003a, 1, pp. 360–405; Schmitt, 1983, p. 26) until it was unseated by the new philosophies of Cartesianism, atomism and rationalism that gained traction around the dawn of the 18th century.

Moderns attach diverse meanings to the term 'scholasticism'. First used in a derogatory sense by humanists (for example, Diderot (1713–84) said it 'was one of the greatest plagues of the human mind' (New Catholic Encyclopedia)) and historians of philosophy in the 16th century (e.g. C.A. Heumann (1681–1763) described it as 'philosophy brought into slavery to papist theology' (New Catholic Encyclopedia)), the term has come to be associated with a petrified and antiquated system of thought. Most commentators today mistakenly think that scholasticism refers to a body of doctrines, a philosophical system or some theological result. This misinterpretation is as much a problem in mainstream historical theology (Muller, 2000, 2001, pp. 45–64, 2003a, 1, p. 37, 2003b; Trueman and Clark, 1999; van Asselt and Dekker, 2001) as it is in the historiography of the social and natural sciences (Drakopoulos and Gotsis, 2004; Hayek, 1979, pp. 17–60). Originally, however, the term simply referred to teachers and authors who employed the scholastic method. According to J.A. Weisheipl, in his entry for 'Scholastic Method' in the *New Catholic Encyclopedia*:

> The Scholastic method was essentially a rational investigation of every relevant problem in liberal arts, philosophy, theology, medicine, and law, examined from opposing points of view, in order to reach an intelligent, scientific solution that would be consistent with accepted authorities, known facts, human reason, and Christian faith. Its ultimate goal was science (*scientia*), although frequently schoolmen had to be content with probable opinions and dialectical solutions. Its highest form, developed in the thirteenth century, was a positive contribution to education and research. In the sixteenth century the medieval method assumed the form of theses, proofs, and answers to objections to meet catechetical and apologetic exigencies. (vol. 12, p. 1145)

The ultimate goal of the schoolmen and the doctors was to use scholastic method in conjunction with the philosophy of Christian Aristotelianism to formulate a unified body of knowledge applicable to all areas of life.

Scholastic Economics is a Normative (and a Descriptive) Science

One reason why mainstream historians tend to regard scholastic economics as 'an afterthought' is to circumvent philosophical and historical counterexamples to the Enlightenment redefinition of economics along secular, descriptive and rationalistic lines. It goes without saying that the schoolmen and the doctors, like the philosophers of antiquity, thought political economy had an inescapable anthropological (normative) dimension that was integrated seamlessly into discussions of private property, public finance, money and exchange relations, commercial ethics, value and price, distributive justice, wages, profits, and interest and banking. Moreover, as Francisco Gómez Camacho shows in the case of the Spanish scholastics, in addition to the anthropological (normative) dimension of their thought there was also an intrinsic analytical (descriptive) dimension (Camacho, 1998b, pp. 506–14).

The Spanish scholastics clearly distinguished between the normative first principles of morality, which are abstract and immutable, and the socioeconomic cases to which they were applied, which are contingent and mutable. 'Abstract principles do not descend to the analysis of specific socioeconomic circumstances, and cannot be applied immediately and directly to the *case* defined by circumstances. Mediation between general principles and singular cases became the task that Spanish doctors would commend to *recta ratio* [or natural law]' (ibid., p. 509).[9] This meant that it was essential for the doctors to analyse and study the circumstances that define a specific case, and thus to the normative dimension of natural law was added an equally necessary analytical dimension. Likewise, as Schumpeter had discerned from his research, in late-scholastic thought 'the normative natural law presupposes an explanatory natural law' (1954, p. 111).

This *recta ratio* approach still held currency in the 18th century when Adam Smith assumed the chair of moral philosophy from his predecessor, Francis Hutcheson, at the University of Glasgow. In fact, as economist, James Alvey, points out, 'Even when [scholasticism] was replaced by more modern, natural law views (of Grotius and Pufendorf), the place of economics changed little. In the European universities of the 1700s economics was taught as part of moral philosophy' (1999, p. 111). This is an important recognition because it is possible to show the direct historical linkage of the late-scholastic theologians in Spain (e.g., Martín de Azpilcueta [1493–1586], Luis de Molina, S.J. [1535–1600] and Juan de Mariana, S.J. [1535–1624]) through Leonardo Lessio, S.J. (1554–1623) to Hugo Grotius and Samuel von Pufendorf and through them to Gershom Carmichael ([1724] 2002), Francis Hutcheson ([1747] 2007) and Adam Smith. 'In the case of Adam Smith', writes de Roover:

the ascendance which links him to Scholasticism passes through his teacher, Francis Hutcheson, Samuel Pufendorf, and Hugo Grotius. Smith's library contained copies of both Grotius and Pufendorf. Moreover, there is evidence that Adam Smith read Grotius at the age of fifteen when he was a student at Glasgow College. At that time, his teacher was using as a textbook a translation of Pufendorf's *De officio hominis et civis* by Gershom Carmichael (d. 1729), Hutcheson's predecessor in the chair of Moral Philosophy. (de Roover, 1974, p. 333; see also Bonar, 1966, pp. 78, 151; Gaertner, 2005; Mizuta and Bonar, 1967; and Young and Gordon, 1992, pp. 6–15)

In his economic analysis of the values and prices of goods and services, Pufendorf followed Grotius ([1625] 2005, II, p. 12) very closely in fundamental outline, but added a great deal of detail in his *Of the Law of Nature and Nations* (1703, V, p. 11). 'More particularly', as Terence Hutchinson insists:

> [Pufendorf's] chapter on value and price has a key position in the history of economic thought, not so much for its originality, but because it acted as authoritative transmitter of a long tradition of analysis of fundamental economic concepts concerned with value and price, the central element in which, the idea of scarcity, included the elements of the supply and demand framework, as well as a subjective concept of utility. (1988, pp. 99–100)

And it was through Gershom Carmichael ([1724] 2002, pp. 106–17) and Francis Hutcheson ([1747] 2007, pp. 3–5, 180–92) in Glasgow that Pufendorf's version of the basic, natural-law doctrine of the values and prices of goods and services passed on to Adam Smith. Alejandro Chafuen supports this judgment:

> In Germany, the Hispanic Scholastics had a great impact on the writings of Samuel von Pufendorf (1632–1694). Through Grotius, Pufendorf, and the Physiocrats, many late-Scholastic ideas influenced Anglo-Saxon economic thought, especially the 'Scottish School' consisting of Ferguson (1723–1816), Hutcheson (1694–1746) and Smith (c. 1723–90). (2003, pp. 15–16)

Whereas, in Geneva, through Jean-Jacques Burlamaqui (a near contemporary of Hutcheson) Pufendorf's ideas passed to Auguste Walras, and so to his son Léon, who became the father of the general equilibrium theory and one of the leaders (along with William Stanley Jevons and Carl Menger) of the 19th-century marginal utility revolution. 'Incidentally', observes Hutchinson:

> Auguste Walras was amply justified in complaining how neglected the natural-law concept of scarcity had become in the nineteenth century. In any case,

however, a writer [namely, Pufendorf] among whose intellectual grandchildren may be counted both Adam Smith and Léon Walras surely possesses a notable place in the history of the subject. (Hutchinson, 1988, p. 100)

Economic History is Inseparable from the History of Ideas

By methodologically constricting the prehistory of economics to the mercantilists and the physiocrats, as positivist historiographers commend, economic history congeals around such characteristically 'modern' concerns as the concept of 'economic man', self-interest, and the emancipation of economics from the so-called 'canonical concept of market behavior'. This arbitrary limitation of who and what ideas carry weight in economic history only serves to bolster 20th-century positivist assumptions, particularly those of value neutrality and *homo economicus*. *Homo economicus* is the assumption that humans act as rational and self-interested agents who desire wealth, avoid unnecessary labour and seek to order their decision-making exclusively around those goals. In the end, the modern reduction of the prehistory of economics to the 17th-century mercantilists can be put in the form of an Occam's razor-like question: why appeal to scholastic influences to illumine modern notions of money, value and price, when all the basic elements of classical economics are already embedded in mercantilism?

The most straightforward reply is that seminal ideas, which also encompass revolutionary economic ideas, never develop in intellectual, historical, religious, philosophical or geographical vacuums. 'Enlightened', secular reaction to the medieval church's temporal jurisdiction and to theology's intellectual hegemony as the queen of the sciences has created a modern milieu where scholars are no longer even aware of the historical influence that fundamental Christian doctrines have exerted in Western culture and university life. From very early times, Christian theologians assumed that the application of patterns of discursive reasoning (as in the scholastic method, which, as we have seen, was a 12th-century invention by Christian theologians) could yield an increasingly accurate understanding not only of God's word and moral will but also of the created order itself.

This all makes sense within the Christian Aristotelian framework because, as Rodney Stark points out in *The Victory of Reason*:

> The Christian image of God is that of a rational being who *believes in human progress* more fully revealing himself as humans *gain* the capacity to better understand. Moreover, because God is a rational being and the universe is his personal creation, it necessarily has a rational, lawful, stable structure, *awaiting increased human comprehension*. (Stark, 2005, pp. 11–12)

The dogmatic and essentialist underpinning to Christian Aristotelianism is succinctly expressed already in the writing of Quintus Tertullian (ca. 155–230), an early church father, who discerned the fundamental connection between the *Imago Dei*, human reason and the material world:

> For God is rational and Reason existed first with him, and from him extended to all things. That Reason is his own consciousness of himself. The Greeks call it *Logos*, which is the term we use for discourse; and thus our people usually translate it literally as, 'Discourse was in the beginning with God,' although it would be more correct to regard Reason as anterior to Discourse, because there was not Discourse with God from the beginning but there was Reason, even before the beginning, and because Discourse takes its origin from Reason and thus shows Reason to be prior to it, as the ground of its being. Yet even so there is no real difference. For although God had not yet uttered his discourse, he had it in his own being, with and in his Reason, and he silently pondered and arranged in his thought those things which he was soon to say by his Discourse. For with his Reason he pondered and arranged his thought and thus made Reason into Discourse by dealing with it discursively. To understand this more easily, first observe in yourself (and you are 'the image and likeness of God') that you also have reason in yourself, as a rational creature; that is, a creature not merely made by a rational creature, but given life from his very being. Notice that when you silently engage in argument with yourselves in the exercise of reason, this same activity occurs within you; for reason is found expressed in discourse at every moment of thought, at every stirring of consciousness. (Bettenson, 1956, pp. 162–3)

According to the hallowed divine ideas tradition – of which Quintus Tertullian, Augustine (354–430), Aquinas and a majority of the scholastics and natural-law philosophers were a part – there is an elementary correspondence between the archetypal knowledge God has in His own mind and the ectypal knowledge that is reproduced in human beings stamped in His image and that is, furthermore, insinuated into the very structure of the material world.

Christian divine ideas proponents held that God used the created order as the primary instrument through which to reveal this information to the human mind. In this sense, the world can be said to embody the very thoughts of God; but, as the Dutch Reformed theologian, Herman Bavinck, admonishes, that is only half of the equation:

> We need eyes in order to see. 'If our eyes were not filled with sunshine, how could we see the light?' There just has to be correspondence or kinship between object and subject. The Logos who shines in the world must also let his light shine in our consciousness. That is the light of reason, the intellect, which, itself originating in the Logos, discovers and recognizes the Logos in things . . . Just as knowledge within us is the imprint of things upon our souls, so, in turn, forms do not exist except by a kind of imprint of the divine knowledge in things. (Bavinck, 2003, p. 233)

The systematic application of reason to a variety of intellectual under-takings, including economic problems, led to increased understanding of the world and human affairs, and spurred efforts to formulate logical expla-nations of regular occurrences in nature. 'All things whatsoever observe a mutual order; and this is the form that maketh the universe like unto God', wrote Dante in the *Divine Comedy* (as quoted in Burtt, 1954, p. 20). It can be argued that the specific application of scholastic method to economic problems became the seedbed for innovative ideas that, after much dialecti-cal refinement, came to shape the world of modern economics. The truth of this statement does not rest on modernity's own understanding of its birth, development or future trajectory, but rather on the demonstrable 'internal interconnections and affinities among ideas, their dynamism or "particular go" (Lovejoy's phrase), and the logical pressures they are capable of exert-ing on the minds of those that think them' (Oakley, 2005, p. 9).

Assent to this claim, however, will require the positivist historian to reconsider not only the relationship between metaphysical schemata and intellectual traditions, which, in turn, will require an acknowledgement of the indispensable role of theological doctrines in the history of ideas (Courtenay 1984; Oakley, 1984, 1999, 2005, pp. 13–34, 2006), but it will also require an admission that the recent detachment of economics from morality is an aberration from a long-standing tradition within political economy itself (Alvey, 1999; Boettke, 1998; Crespo, 1998a, 1998b; Young, 1997). In Alvey's judgment:

> There are two major reasons why economics has become detached from moral concerns. First, the natural sciences came to be seen as successful, and the attempt was made to emulate that success in economics by applying natural science methods, including mathematics, to economic phenomena. Second, the self-styled economic science came to adopt positivism, which ruled out moral issues from science itself. (1999, p. 53)

It is the latter recognition, perhaps more than any other, that squares the revisionists off against the positivists in the debate over the prehistory of economics.

DISCOVERY OF THE SCHOOL OF SALAMANCA: THE TIPPING POINT IN THE REVISION OF ECONOMIC HISTORY

In the 16th and early 17th centuries, a small but influential group of theo-logians and jurists centered in Spain attempted to synthesize the Roman legal texts with Aristotelian and Thomistic moral philosophy. The movement began with the revival of Thomistic philosophy in Paris, where, as Camacho recounts, 'Pierre Crockaert underwent an intellectual conversion from nominalist philosophy to the philosophy of Thomas Aquinas' (Camacho, 1998b, p. 503).

Shortly before 1225, the year of Aquinas's birth, Aristotle's works on metaphysics, physics, politics and ethics became available in the West, and within the span of a generation, Aristotelianism, which had been brought to Europe by Arabic scholars, would be a serious contender in medieval thought. Thomas sought a rapprochement between the Greek philosophical tradition that Aristotle represented and the Christian divine ideas tradition that Quintus Tertullian, Augustine and Bonaventure articulated. In 1512 Crockaert published his commentary on the last part of Thomas's *Summa theologicae* with the help of a student, Francisco de Vitoria (ca. 1483–1546) (ibid.).

Approximately 200 years before Thomas was born, the *Corpus juris civilis* of Justinian had been rediscovered and had become the object of academic disputation. But the traditions of Roman law and Aristotelian and Thomistic philosophy existed in relative isolation from one another, at least until the early 16th century in Spain. 'In the sixteenth and early seventeenth centuries', states Camacho, 'a synthesis was finally achieved by that group of theologians and jurists known to historians of law as the "late Scholastics" or the "Spanish natural law school"' (ibid.). Schumpeter concurs with this judgment and adds: 'It is within their systems of moral theology and law that economics gained definite if not separate existence, and it is they who come nearer than does any other group to having been the "founders" of scientific economics' (1954, p. 97). 'And not only that', he continues in the very next sentence:

> it will appear, even, that the bases they laid for a serviceable and well-integrated body of analytic tools and propositions were sounder than was much subsequent work, in the sense that a considerable part of the economics of the later nineteenth century might have been developed from those bases more quickly and with less trouble than it actually cost to develop it, and that some of that subsequent work was therefore in the nature of a time- and labor-consuming detour. (Ibid.)

As a school of economic thought, these late Spanish scholastics are commonly referred to as the 'School of Salamanca'. This term has a distinguished history and attempts to designate that group of moral philosophers, moral theologians and jurists who either attended or lectured at the University of Salamanca and had been students of or colleagues with Francisco de Vitoria.[10] But not all historians accept the validity of the Salamancan designation and it is regarded as a 'point of dispute' in the literature (Moss and Ryan, 1993, pp. x–xxii). Even Schumpeter himself expressed some doubt about the claim that a school of thought centring on a single intellectual leader had been found in Spain, but admitted there was 'some justification' for it in his *History of Economic Analysis* (1954, p. 165). More than any other commentator, however, it was Marjorie Grice-Hutchinson, who after decades of painstaking research, convinced fair-minded observers that 'a definite group of theologians associated with the University of Salamanca wrote about issues of value theory and money with insight and originality. In addition, she applied her skills as a translator and linguist to present the world with the evidence required' (Grice-Hutchinson, 1993, pp. 23–9; Moss and Ryan, 1993, p. vii). Her translations of short excerpts from the Latin and Spanish texts of this group appeared in 1952 as part of her first monograph, *The School of Salamanca: Readings in Spanish Monetary Theory 1544–1605*.[11]

For over half a century, Grice-Hutchinson ably defended her thesis that, in the area of value and monetary economics, a genuine and incipient school of thought existed at Salamanca. This tradition began with Vitoria who brought Thomas's teachings to Salamanca from Paris, which he used to purge the curriculum of nominalist influence and to develop a great legal and philosophical system that addressed matters of international law, moral theology, politics, economics and business practices. His insights about money, markets and prices, reasoned Grice-Hutchinson, 'spawned a network of "colleagues . . . disciples and . . . principal continuators" such as Luís Saravia de la Calle, Domingo de Soto, Martín de Azpilcueta, Tomás de Mercado, Francisco García, Martín Gonzalez de Cellorigo, Luis de Molina, and Pedro de Valencia, who carried out Vitoria's "research programme", with dedication and accomplishment' (Moss and Ryan, 1993, p. viii). Over time Grice-Hutchinson has been successful in persuading unbiased observers within the professions of economics, the history of ideas and moral theology that 'something critically important to understanding the development of economic reasoning did happen in Salamanca in the sixteenth century' (ibid.).

CONCLUSION

The purpose of this chapter has been to show that the application of scholastic method by Christian moral theologians and jurists to economic problems resulted in revolutionary insights and new-found discoveries in economic thought. Over the course of several centuries these insights and discoveries eventually became refined into ideas that have exerted influence on the greatest economic minds of the early-modern and modern eras. In this sense, Schumpeter's ludicrous claim that economics first 'gained definite if not separate existence' (1954, p. 97) in the systems of Christian theology and jurisprudence is not as implausible as it may have seemed at first glance. I argue that the plausibility of Schumpeter's claim is first and foremost a matter of historical investigation and, thus, must be dealt with as a question of historical fact. That Christian moral theologians and jurists assumed a normative starting point in their analysis of commercial morality in no way diminishes or disqualifies their descriptive/analytic insights into the internal dynamics of economic phenomena such as inflation, subjective value, the price mechanism, currency debasement/exchange and a host of other topics. If this methodological plank of the argument has been sufficiently established, then it seems reasonable to expect the critics of scholastic economics to make a historical demonstration that proves otherwise.

3. Commercial order and the Scottish Enlightenment: the Christian context

Samuel Gregg

There is scarce, perhaps, to be found anywhere in Europe, a more learned, decent, independent, and respectable set of Men than the greater part of the Presbyterian clergy of Holland, Geneva, Switzerland, and Scotland.

Adam Smith, ([1776] 1904)

INTRODUCTION

Much contemporary and popular commentary on the 18th-century Scottish Enlightenment tends to present this movement as one that, while not as hostile to Christianity as the French late-Enlightenment, marked a radical break with the hitherto prevailing Christian intellectual culture. Invariably, much emphasis is laid upon David Hume's philosophical scepticism (and likely atheism) and Adam Smith's apparent deistic tendencies. Given the Scottish Enlightenment's unquestioned influence upon the modern moral case for commercial society and free markets, the widespread assumption of an implicit break with Christian moral thought has helped to proliferate the idea that the spread of commerce and the habits and institutions of economic liberty necessitates and even facilitates a cultural and intellectual break with Christian theology and morality.

Like most intellectual movements, the Scottish Enlightenment was not a monolithic formation. Unquestionably, Hume's philosophical and economic writings are seen by many as reflecting some of the most mature Scottish Enlightenment thought. Unfortunately there is a certain degree of a-historicism about this interpretation. First, unlike the French late-Enlightenment, the Scottish Enlightenment was never anti-Christian. Even in the work of a probable atheist such as Hume, we do not find the type of anti-clerical rhetoric and anti-Christian innuendo that we commonly encounter in the writings of Voltaire and Jean-Jacques Rousseau. Indeed, many Scottish Enlightenment luminaries, such as the leader of the Moderate Party in the Church of Scotland, William Robertson (1721–93), were not only convinced Christians but even favoured toleration of Roman

Catholic Christians. This marks them as very different men to those conti-
nental European *philosophes* whose political children sought to uproot
Christianity not just in France but in any country conquered by the
Revolutionary armies.

In this chapter, we focus our attention upon two scholars who might be
called the immediate fathers of the Scottish Enlightenment, including its
economic orientations, Gershom Carmichael (1672–1729) and Francis
Hutcheson (1694–1746). As the previous chapter of this book illustrates,
the intellectual case for economic freedom and its associated habits and
institutions had been made by Catholic and Protestant scholastic thinkers
over two centuries before Adam Smith's *The Wealth of Nations* ([1776]
1904). This chapter's attention to Carmichael and Hutcheson seeks to
demonstrate that it is an error to view the Scottish Enlightenment as
entailing a radical separation from the Christian intellectual and cultural
climate in which it emerged. While it is true that a number of Scottish
thinkers' reflections upon economic subjects suggest some distancing on
their part from Christian theology, our focus on Carmichael and
Hutcheson allows us to outline the case for a more nuanced, less 'secu-
larist' interpretation of this movement and its contributions to economic
freedom.

RELIGION, NEO-FEUDALISM AND THE EMERGENCE OF COMMERCIAL SOCIETY

No development in thought occurs in a vacuum, and the Scottish
Enlightenment is no exception. The Scotland of the late 17th and 18th centuries was above all a society that experienced a range of different tran-
sitions amidst a sea of continuity. For one thing, Scotland remained an
intensely religious society. Since the time of John Knox (d. 1572), Scotland
had been wracked by religious tensions. Roman Catholics, Presbyterians
and Episcopalians had struggled for religious supremacy. This conflict was
complicated by its association with inter-noble rivalry, the attempts of the
Stuart monarchy to impose bishops on the Church of Scotland, the emergence of militant forms of Presbyterianism and eventually conflict between
splintering Presbyterian churches and the established Church of Scotland
throughout the 18th century. Whatever individuals may have privately
thought about various elements of Christian doctrine or even the central
claims of Christianity itself, it was impossible for any Scot, intellectual or
otherwise, to avoid being shaped or affected by Christianity's prominent
place in Scottish society. There were reasons why figures such as Hume did
not display their atheism too publicly.

And yet change was occurring, most notably in the universities, and primarily as a reaction against the Covenantal anti-monarchical hyper-congregational theology espoused by many Scottish Presbyterian clergy that gave the Stuart monarchy such grief throughout much of the 17th century. With encouragement from William III of England (William II of Scotland), two Presbyterian clergymen, William Dunlop, the Principal of Glasgow University since 1690, and his brother-in-law, William Carstares, who became Principal of Edinburgh University in 1703, broke the radical Covenanters' control of the universities and the formation of Presbyterian clergy. They did so by appointing a series of regent professors who revised the curriculum of the universities, which came to embrace subjects such as law, botany, medicine, mathematics and natural philosophy. The point of these changes was not to 'secularize' the universities – or the Church of Scotland for that matter. Rather, it was to help move the Scottish clergy away from what some today would view as a type of fundamentalism; and to expose them to trends in continental European theology and philosophy (both Protestant and Roman Catholic) with the intention of integrating these insights into the Christian theology of the Church of Scotland.

Throughout this period, Scotland enjoyed an unusual relationship with its southern neighbour. Scotland's formal linkage with England had begun when Scotland's Stuart king, James VI, acceded to the English throne in 1603. This began a process of de facto political integration while also slowly opening up English markets to Scottish commerce. This situation was formalized through the Act of Union of 1707 when the two nations were unified under one Crown, though Scotland retained an independent church, judiciary and education system.

Establishing free trade between the two nations was one of the prime motivations underlying the work of the pro-Union party in Scotland. In the 20 years before the Union, a modern economy and social arrangements had begun to emerge in the overwhelmingly Presbyterian Lowlands. With free trade establishing access to English markets, a growing Scottish middle class was spawned, with strong commercial interests and a desire to partake of the social and political advantages of living in a more dynamic, numerically larger, wealthier and increasingly urbanized society.

Though these changes benefited large numbers of Scots, it took some time for a positive view of profit, interest-charging and commercial trade to emerge in Scotland. In Scottish intellectual circles, this was reflected in a long 18th-century debate about the merits of free trade and mercantilism (Fry, 1999, p. 57). Sir James Steuart (1713–80) and John Law (1671–1729) championed the mercantilist cause, while Frances Hutcheson and Adam Smith (1723–90) figured among the prominent supporters of free trade. In practical terms, the official monopolies, royal privileges and guild structures of Scotland's old pre-modern economy slowly collapsed. These were replaced by a system of corporate law that upheld strong commercially-oriented structures until the 19th century (ibid., p. 55). It was perhaps the financial disaster of the Company of Scotland's Darien scheme that convinced many Scots that their nation was too small to afford the luxury of mercantilist economics and ventures (ibid., p. 57).

Another source of resistance to commercial society in Scotland was to be found in the Highlands and much of Scotland north of the River Tay. Even late into the 18th-century, these regions of Scotland reflected a different socio-cultural configuration compared with the Lowlands (Herman, 2001, pp. 104–12). For one thing, these regions contained fewer Presbyterians, large numbers of Episcopalians and even a considerable number of Roman Catholics, especially among the nobility. In the Highlands, social and economic relations were primarily shaped by the almost feudal social structure attached to the clan. Contrary to contemporary legend, the Scottish clan had relatively little to do with blood relations. Instead, the extended, tribe-like vision of family at the heart of the idea of clan was one of different individuals owing almost feudal-like allegiance to a clan chief who held legal powers of life and death over clan members. In return for the almost absolute obedience of clan members, the clan chief gave his protection to them and also provided them with agricultural and shepherding work on his estates. In practical terms, the word of the clan chief was far more important than edicts from London or Edinburgh or even legal decisions and precedents established by Scotland's independent judiciary.

Despite these factors, the importance of clan structures and their influence steadily diminished throughout the Highlands throughout the 18th century. This process was accelerated by the British government's ruthless suppression of the second Jacobite Rebellion of 1745, which, among other things, stripped the clan chiefs of their legal powers. Many such changes opened up the Highlands to the economic opportunities experienced by the Lowlands. Observing the progress and growth in wealth occurring throughout the Lowlands, many Highland chiefs began changing traditional ways of managing their estates so as to share in the same economic progress experienced in the Lowlands.

The scale and impact of all these developments made a tremendous impression upon the minds of Scotland's emerging intellectual class; many – perhaps even a majority – were clergymen of the Church of Scotland. A considerable number of them occupied chairs of theology and moral philosophy at universities such as Edinburgh, St Andrews and Glasgow. Like many other European intellectuals of the time, they were conscious that the economic changes sweeping their country were part of a profound cultural transformation that was occurring throughout much of Western Europe. As the French political philosopher, Pierre Manent, writes:

> During the eighteenth century, in England, Scotland, and France, perceptive observers felt able to describe the workings of a new social bond, which went by the generic name of commerce, not rarely qualified as *doux commerce*. Commerce then is not just a human activity among a number of human activities; it connotes a new regime of human action itself, and its development aids the axis of human progress. The radical newness of commerce in this comprehensive meaning consisted in this, that people were now linked to one another without commanding each other, and without necessarily sharing a common way of life. (Manent, 1998, p. 222)

A common concern of Scottish Enlightenment thinkers – Christian or otherwise – was to investigate the deeper reasons for these changes. Many of these same scholars – again, Christian or otherwise – were also interested in ensuring that Scotland's emerging commercial culture did not degenerate into one dominated by naked greed and attitudes that would today be described as narrowly materialistic and consumerist. In many instances, these concerns were derived from Christian convictions. This was especially true of Gershom Carmichael and Francis Hutcheson. Not only did they teach many of the generation of Scots whose work was central to the Scottish Enlightenment but their work continued to be studied and referenced by the same generation long after Carmichael and Hutcheson's passing.

GERSHOM CARMICHAEL AND THE CHRISTIAN NATURAL-LAW LEGACY

Perhaps Gershom Carmichael's greatest contribution to the Scottish Enlightenment was to re-introduce the natural-law tradition, long dormant in Scotland since the Reformation, back into Scottish learning. While figures such as Hume reflected upon commercial society's emergence in ways that marked a break with Christian belief about human nature, most Scottish Enlightenment scholars – including, to a certain extent, Adam Smith – engaged in the same enterprise primarily within the context of the powerful theological and philosophical legacy bequeathed by the 17th-century Protestant natural-law tradition associated with figures such as Hugo Grotius (1583–1645) and Samuel von Pufendorf (1632–94). Taken together, the work of Grotius and Pufendorf involved the development of a social and political theory that sought to uphold the natural duties and rights they associated with human liberty and property. Grotius and

Pufendorf subsequently employed these duties and rights as the basis for defining the type of standards that ought to prevail in societies that were increasingly commercial in their orientation. This ranged from matters such as the importance and limits of religious tolerance to questions as economic and detailed as justice in exchange, price theory and interest rates. As noted in previous chapters, the work of Grotius and Pufendorf, like that of many Northern European scholars, was much influenced by the writings of 16th-century Catholic late-scholasticism, especially the writings of the Jesuit Francisco Suarez (Ferrater, 1950).

Within this Protestant early-modern natural-law tradition, we find the development and elaboration of medieval and late-scholastic insights into questions of price, value and scarcity. Grotius's *Mare Liberum* (1609), for example, made a powerful case for the liberty of all people of all nations to use the sea to trade freely (Grotius [1609] 2004, pp. 49–51) and is commonly regarded as one of the first early-modern arguments against monopolies. More generally, Grotius associated himself with the rejection of Calvin's doctrine of predestination articulated by his professor at the University of Leyden, Jacobus Arminius. For Grotius, freedom of the will had been given to man by the Christian God. Much of his political thought involved elaborating what this meant for a social order that facilitated human liberty, including economic freedom, without descending into anarchy. Widely regarded as one of Grotius's most prominent intellectual disciples, a considerable portion of Pufendorf's theological and jurisprudential writings were concerned with applying Grotius's schema to a range of then-contemporary issues. Thus, when it came to the question of economic value and price, Pufendorf argued that the determining factors were a good's relative scarcity and its subjective utility (Pufendorf [1673] 2003, pp. 140–45).

Grotius and Pufendorf might have remained somewhat marginal figures to the intellectual flowering of 18th-century Scotland had it not been for Carmichael. The son of a Presbyterian minister exiled to England for heresy, Carmichael studied at the University of Edinburgh and taught at the universities of Glasgow and St Andrews, before becoming a Presbyterian minister at the town of Fife. An instructor in philosophy at the University of Glasgow from 1694, Carmichael became its first professor of moral philosophy at the University of Glasgow in 1727 (Merikoski, 2001). Like almost all universities of the time, a number of subjects were taught under the rubric of moral philosophy in Scottish universities, including natural theology, ethics and economics. Hence the teaching of political economy was heavily embedded in instruction in natural religion and Christian natural-law moral reasoning. In part, this reflected the ongoing influence of the scholastic method of instruction. In Carmichael's case, however, it reflected his close attention to the work and method of Pufendorf.

Carmichael's work has been somewhat neglected by many contemporary scholars because he wrote almost exclusively in Latin and his professorial tenure at Glasgow lasted only two years, being suddenly curtailed by his death. His writings on natural rights, natural theology and logic do not, however, present God as simply a necessary postulate of philosophical reasoning. A certain degree of Scriptural reflection is integrated into rigorous philosophical analysis. Indeed, aspects of Carmichael's writings underline the importance and value of Christian asceticism on the basis of Scripture over and against what might be described as some of the more Epicurean and secularizing tendencies of Pufendorf's thought (Carmichael [1724] 2002, pp. 30–39). Carmichael also disputed Pufendorf's claim that natural-law reasoning had to occur in a manner that treats subjects such as the afterlife and the soul's immortality as irrelevant to such reflection (ibid.).

This disputing of aspects of Pufendorf's arguments did not, however, prevent Carmichael from drawing upon Pufendorf when it came to discussing the nature of government, human sociability and the character of property and contract. The Lowland Scottish society in which Carmichael was writing had clearly transcended the social and economic structures associated with feudalism, and Carmichael's commentaries on these subjects appear to reflect these developments.

This is especially apparent in Carmichael's treatment of property. Though much of this reflects the classic Roman law method of outlining different modalities of property, Carmichael's discussion begins with an essentially Thomistic explanation. Property, Carmichael states, is of divine origin. 'Surely', he writes, 'there is a purpose in God having given man a life which cannot be preserved without the use of external things' (ibid., p. 93). It is also, Carmichael writes, 'quite certain that external things are not assigned by nature to one man rather than to another' (ibid., p. 94). Thus far, this reflects traditional scholastic teaching about property. How humans are to organize the goods of the earth so that they serve humanity has, Carmichael makes clear, been left to humans to work out for themselves using their reason – a crucial faculty lacked, Carmichael notes, by animals. Carmichael goes on to state that there are many things that people cannot in most instances use without owning them (clothes, food etc.), and that ownership is essential if people are to plan adequately for their own and their families' needs and aspirations.

This second point is important because it chimes well with the *future*-oriented nature of commercial society. It is, of course, entirely consistent with the biblical injunction to subdue the earth and dominate it, in which we find much of the Christian justification for entrepreneurship and creativity. But then Carmichael introduces another thought of crucial importance for commercial order and economic freedom:

[T]he further expenditure of labour and industry which the interest of human society requires in the way of competition in cultivating the things of the earth, is likely to achieve a greater stock of a certain kind of thing than our own personal use requires. In return for these we can acquire, by the use of agreements, other things which are useful to us. This further fruit of our labour should not be taken from us, provided we got it without fraudulent and unfair oppression of others, who should always be left the opportunity to get what their own use requires under fair conditions. (Ibid., pp. 99–100)

Here Carmichael highlights the importance of competition in stimulating the human creativity that delivers a surplus of privately-owned goods that people can then trade via voluntary transactions, while simultaneously insisting that others should have the opportunity to enter the circle of exchange. The implication is that it is unjust and not in the interests of the common good to unreasonably restrict market exchange. This amounts to a Christian natural-law argument for the moral necessity of free trade – an argument that would have resonated throughout much of the Scotland of Carmichael's time.

Carmichael's discussion of property is immediately followed by his analysis of the institution of contract. The most remarkable feature of his analysis is the manner in which Carmichael largely affirms Pufendorf's view of the nature of economic value and its relevance for contract but proceeds to root it in explicit Christian natural-law reasoning. He underlines the subjective character of economic value by noting that, 'For a thing to have value, the first requisite is this suitability, either *real* or *imaginary*' (ibid., p. 107, emphasis added). Carmichael's insistence on this is more explicit than Pufendorf's and, if anything, closer to the late-scholastic emphasis on subjective value. Carmichael also specifies that this valuation occurs not only in the marketplace but also in 'an agreement between contracting individuals . . . unless a law of the commonwealth forbids it' (ibid.).

Another noticeable feature of Carmichael's analysis of contract is the manner in which he appeals to Christian theology to clarify a point about legitimately contracted debts. A person who acts as a surety (*fidejussor*) guarantees a debtor's debt. This is distinct from a substitute debtor (*expromissor*) who essentially takes on another's debt, which frees the original debtor from what he owes to his creditors. Theologians and jurists, Carmichael notes, have debated, 'whether, before the price of redemption had been paid, Christ our Lord had the position simply of a *surety* . . . or whether it was actually that of a substitute debtor'. 'The second alternative', Carmichael holds, 'has been proved by most lucid arguments to be correct' (ibid., p. 111). Carmichael's point is that Christ's divinity is better expressed by the concept of 'substitute debtor' than the idea of surety, because if Christ was simply the surety for the debt owed to God, then Christ could not have been God.

Carmichael's economic reflections are not confined to institutions such as property and contracts. He also focuses upon the motivations underlying commercial society. Carmichael's primary interlocutor here is Grotius, especially his attention to the social and economic benefits of what Carmichael calls, 'the harmless pursuit of self-interest'. Carmichael neither disputes these benefits nor suggests that there is something fundamentally wrong with people pursuing their self-interest. Rather, his concern is to suggest, 'that the claim of *harmless self-interest* should not be boldly advanced as a foundation of a perfect right unless there is also a claim of *necessity*. The latter is often sufficient in itself and is considerably strengthened by the former' (ibid., p. 75). Carmichael's emphasis upon the necessity that the self-interest be 'harmless' is directly derived from his interpretation of:

> that golden and universal rule taught by our Lord, *as ye would that men should do to you, do ye also to them likewise* [Matthew 7:12, Luke 6:31]. But this rule must be understood as tacitly limited by a twofold assumption of *similar circumstances on both sides* and a *right will conforming to reason*. It ought therefore not to be regarded as a principle from which, when applied to the individual actions of life, a sure distinction between right and wrong is to be deduced. Rather it should be regarded as an indication of an appropriate remedy to free the mind from the command of self-love and the assaults of the passions, to set it in equilibrium, and as it were, restore it to itself, so that it may be free to attend to the careful weighing of the importance of the arguments on either side. (Ibid., p. 75)

Carmichael's reasoning here is revealing. It effectively amounts to integrating the idea that right reason (i.e., natural law) frees us from blindly following unreasonable passions into the essence of Christianity's Golden Rule so as to (1) allow people to recognize whether or not their pursuit of self-interest is indeed harmless, and (2) assess whether there are any other considerations that they ought to take into account, even if their pursuit of self-interest is clearly harmless.

Much more could be said about the character of Carmichael's economic reflections but his approach to these matters is the same. He does not seek to tear down or undermine the motives and institutions vital to the growth of the commercial society then developing around him in Scotland. Rather, he draws upon early modern reflection that itself comes out of a Christian tradition, and actually modifies it where appropriate in order to *deepen* its explicitly Christian content, thereby correcting where he believed Grotius and Pufendorf had overly diluted the Christian content. A similar pattern appears in the economic reflections of Carmichael's student, Francis

Hutcheson, who generally affirms the growth of economic liberty, while emphasizing the importance of man's innate, God-given moral sense to ensure that commerce contributes to civilizing society rather than debauching it.

FRANCIS HUTCHESON: LIBERTY, TRADE AND HAPPINESS

The son of a Presbyterian clergyman, Hutcheson was a member of the Scottish diaspora in present-day Northern Ireland. He commenced his studies at Glasgow in 1711, studying for a masters degree in theology, before obtaining his licence to preach from the Church of Scotland in 1716. While in Glasgow, Hutcheson attended lectures given by its Divinity professor, John Simson (1667–1740). First, Simson was a strong proponent of natural religion, and presented a far more benign view of humanity and the world than the rather pessimistic vision hitherto conveyed by many Scottish Presbyterians. The world, according to Simson, was not characterized by dourness and evil. Instead, both humans and their world were stamped by the orderliness and symmetry of God's creative act. This world and human nature provided people with insight into the Divine *Logos*, who, far from being a God of wrath, was a God who loved and cared for human beings.

Such views had more in common with Grotius's neo-Arminianism and even Roman Catholic doctrine than Knox's Presbyterianism, and were immensely appealing to Hutcheson. Simson's positions concerning established Christian doctrines such as the nature of Jesus Christ and the Trinity, however, would have been offensive to believing Presbyterians, Anglicans and Roman Catholics alike. Simson appears to have denied Christ's divinity, and his ultimate vision of God appears to have more in common with deism than orthodox Christianity. This aspect of Simson's thought was anathema to Hutcheson.

There were, however, other influences operating upon Hutcheson. Apart from Carmichael, from whom Hutcheson learnt about the thought of Grotius and Pufendorf (not to mention Carmichael's qualifications of their ideas), Hutcheson was deeply impressed by the writings of Anthony Ashley Cooper, the third Earl of Shaftesbury (1671–1713). Shaftesbury ought to be seen more as an exponent of natural religion than a Christian. Though he did not rule out the possibility that the miracles reported in the Gospels happened (Shaftesbury [1711] 1999, pp. 231–8), Shaftesbury had difficulty imagining that a perfectly rational God would countenance miracles. He also disputed the view that the Scriptures were self-verifying (ibid., pp. 4–28). Shaftesbury was likewise critical of those forms of Calvinism that emphasized human sinfulness and articulated a strong doctrine of predestination (ibid., pp. 4–28, 163–230).

At the same time, Shaftesbury was deeply critical of Thomas Hobbes's theories concerning human nature, arguing that the selfish, even barbaric beings that appear in Hobbes's state of nature bear no resemblance to the reality of human nature, especially man's natural sociability (ibid., p. 287). Moreover, while Shaftesbury was a friend of John Locke (1632–1704), he later rejected Locke's social contract theory and was critical of Locke's failure to place his commentaries in a teleological context, claiming that this is to reduce the study of man to its parts rather than the purpose and design of the whole (ibid., pp. 70–162).

At the core of Shaftesbury's philosophy was his conviction that the world was created by a perfect God, and that any evil in the world was a temporary aberration and not reflective of God's infinite perfection. Human liberty was, to his mind, at the core of human civilization because it was naturally oriented to the human virtues, the attainment of which was the natural end of all humanity. Attaining virtue, Shaftesbury held, did not mean simply acting for the good but in a way that reflected one's own self-orientation to and consciousness of the good being attained. This means that the virtuous person serves not only the good of others but that of him or herself as well. And thus, to cite Shaftesbury, 'virtue and interest may be found at last to agree' (ibid., p. 167). One suspects that Shaftesbury believed that the fruits facilitated by this culture of virtue were beginning to appear around him, with London beginning to develop into a global centre of aesthetic and intellectual achievement, but also as a truly modern commercial city. Hutcheson was so impressed by Shaftesbury's thought and civilizational vision that, no matter how shaky Shaftesbury's Christian faith would have appeared to Hutcheson, the latter had no hesitation in dedicating his first book, *An Inquiry into the Origin of Our Ideas of Beauty and Virtue* ([1725] 2002) to Shaftesbury.

Upon succeeding Carmichael – though not without overcoming some resistance from the Kirk of the Church of Scotland – Hutcheson lectured on subjects ranging from jurisprudence, ethics, political economy and natural religion. In doing so, his students (including Adam Smith who studied under Hutcheson from 1747 to 1750) were exposed to an overarching view of man and human society that avoided a narrow specialization of education. Within this spectrum, Hutcheson had much to say about economics, as becomes apparent from close study of his posthumously published *System of Moral Philosophy* (1755). Here and in other works we find Hutcheson further refining economic ideas found in Grotius and Pufendorf, mediated through Carmichael, many of which anticipate theories subsequently developed in Smith's *The Wealth of Nations* ([1776] 1904).

Prominently featured in Hutcheson's economic reflections was his stress on the importance of the division of labour. Some of his early writings suggest that the division of labour is central to humanity's emergence from a rude state to achieve the conditions associated with commercial society. The desire to improve their living conditions, Hutcheson claimed, led people to divide their labour. The resulting surplus resulted in the need for barter, which in turn facilitated the tool of money as a means of exchange and measuring comparative value (Hutcheson [1725] 2002, p. 26; [1755] 2000, vol. 2, p. 56).

Figures such as Plato, Cicero, Bernard de Mandeville and Sir William Petty had already employed the concept of the division of labour to explain the development of economic life. Hutcheson himself suggested that it was worth reading and re-reading Cicero's *De officius*, which illustrated how the cooperation of many workers doing different things facilitated a whole range of material benefits for everyone, while also allowing societies to develop a variety of institutions, customs and rules, which, while serving different purposes, contributed to society's overall well-being (Hutcheson [1755] 2000, vol. 1, pp. 289–90).

Concerning value and utility, Hutcheson's analysis was virtually the same as Pufendorf (mediated via Carmichael), stressing the subjective dimension insofar as he defines utility as, 'any tendency to give any satisfaction, by prevailing custom or fancy'. He also noted, 'We shall find that the prices of goods depend on these two jointly, the *demand* on account of some use or other which many desire, and the *difficulty* of acquiring, or cultivating for human use' (ibid., vol. 2, p. 54).

It is, however, in Hutcheson's critique of Bernard de Mandeville (1670–1733) and his famous *Fable of the Bees* ([1714] 1970) that we see the Christian natural-law dimension in Hutcheson's thought emerging in reaction against the notion that the pursuit of selfishness (as opposed to rational self-interest) is at the root of economic well-being. Mandeville had suggested that it was actually through people indulging in luxury – widely understood in Christian circles of the time as a vice – that an economy grew prosperous. Like Carmichael, Hutcheson did not deny that many people worked hard in order to obtain luxuries (Hutcheson [1758] 1989, pp. 71–2). The activity of assessing the opportunity cost of one alternative over another was, Hutcheson believed, something engaged in by everyone and not morally offensive in itself. Hutcheson insisted, however, that economic prosperity was not ultimately driven by greed but rather by people who saved and were industrious. Hutcheson further noted that Mandeville's claim that even stealing served the prosperity of all (by creating a need for locksmiths) failed to account for the fact that, in the absence of theft, people might be willing to invest their capital in areas more profitable for themselves and others than the lock industry.

Much of Hutcheson's critique of Mandeville was economic but it was underpinned by moral outrage against Mandeville's casual celebration of the side-effects of human vice. This becomes clearer when we grasp Hutcheson's distinct vision of the moral life. Crucial to this was his emphasis upon what he called the 'senses'. These senses included self-consciousness, the 'internal sense' of beauty, a sense of honor, a public sense ('a determination to be pleased with the happiness of others and to be uneasy at their misery') and above all the 'moral sense'. This, Hutcheson argues, is not a product of society or culture. Rather, moral reasoning is innate to human beings. 'From the very frame of our nature', he writes, 'we are determined to perceive pleasure in the practice of virtue, and to approve of it when practiced by ourselves or others' (ibid., p. 63). This insight, which echoes the entire natural-law tradition back to Aristotle, is complemented by Hutcheson's emphasis upon love of neighbour as the source of all morality. Against Hobbes and Mandeville, Hutcheson insists, 'There is no mortal without some love toward others, and desire in the happiness of some other persons as well as his own' (ibid., p. 72). Here we see rational self-interest integrated with love of others, so that the two are indistinguishable. There is no question in Hutcheson's mind that this innate moral sense was grounded in human beings by the Christian God, which is especially apparent by Hutcheson's reference to love. Freedom was important, Hutcheson claimed, because it was only in liberty that people could freely follow the path laid out by the workings of right reason and love of others, and separate virtue from vice, love from selfishness. Thus, as Merikoski observes, Hutcheson:

> believed that divine grace and fostering the happiness of others lay at the heart of moral goodness. He also accepted the notion that life should be seen as a progress toward virtue and that individuals are capable of self-improvement. The best means for achieving progress consisted in following the disciplines of duty, faith, and virtue, incorporated with the lessons of human experience. For Hutcheson, moral philosophy was ultimately useful because it served to better not only the individual but also the quality of public life. (Merikoski, 2001, p. 13)

Material progress was good and to be valued but, in Hutcheson's mind, it needed to be accompanied by moral progress in the sense of growing virtue among the citizenry. Against Mandeville, Hutcheson proclaims, 'Thus may thine enemies triumph, O Virtue and Christianity!' (Hutcheson [1758] 1989, p. 100).

At this point, a number of commentators suggest (e.g., Copleston, 1985, p. 182; Herman, 2001, p. 71) that Hutcheson's famous maxim that the 'action is best, which produces the greatest happiness for the greatest number' (Hutcheson [1725] 2002, p. 212) foreshadows the development of utilitarianism as a philosophy – utilitarianism being normally understood as directly opposed to the Christian vision of morality. This may well be true in the sense of the formulation of the statement. But it is also true that Hutcheson's understanding of the content of happiness differs significantly from that of Bentham and Mill, who define happiness essentially in terms of pleasure maximization. Virtue *is* the summit of human happiness for Hutcheson, and utilitarianism is notoriously *uninterested* in the very idea of virtue.

FROM HUTCHESON TO THE MODERATE PARTY

Hutcheson was immensely influential for a whole range of Scottish Enlightenment figures. He is widely regarded as the father of the Moderate Party within the Kirk of the Church of Scotland, which included ministers such as Hugh Blair (1718–1800), William Robertson (1721–93) and Alexander Carlyle (1722–1805) as well as figures such as the mathematician, Matthew Stewart (1717–85). Also interested in Hutcheson's thought was the immensely influential lawyer, Lord Kames (1696–1782). Even David Hume (1711–76) corresponded with Hutcheson on questions of ethics, despite their very different theories about the origin and nature of morality.

Hume features as a key figure in this discussion, not least because he was a close friend and correspondent of Smith. Like many of his contemporaries, Hume was decidedly anti-mercantilist in his economic views and very optimistic about the progress unleashed by commercial society. His primary interest, however, was philosophy, and his *Treatise on Human Nature* (1739–40) is famous for postulating – *contra* Aristotle, Augustine, Aquinas, Suarez, Grotius, Pufendorf, Carmichael and Hutcheson – that 'reason is, and ought to be the slave of the passions' (Hume [1739–40] 1951, vol. 2, part 3, section III). In Hume's world, there is no virtue or vice. Societies simply learn by adaptation how to ensure that individuals, following their own arbitrarily-defined, passion-driven self-interest, can attain whatever it is they happen to want without hurting other individuals in the process. In this respect, Hume was neo-Hobbesian. Hence, we should not be surprised that Hutcheson reacted so negatively to Hume's moral theory, even going so far as to lobby to ensure that Hume never received a university appointment (Herman, 2001, p. 170). In Hume's schema, there is no innate moral sense or natural reason implanted in man by God – let alone a loving God. Instead, love is simply just another arbitrary passion with no content beyond what we arbitrarily decide to assign it, while morality is the product of evolutionary adaptation, though capable of being shaped by law so as to ensure that man's baser instincts were not given complete reign in a given society.

Then, as now, Hume's theory was subject to searing critiques, most notably by the Presbyterian minister and philosopher, Thomas Reid (1710–96). And yet for all its internal contradictions (such as the self-refuting exercise of a sceptic proposing scepticism as a truth knowable to the human mind), Hume's vision of the moral life was influential. Though, for example, Smith was influenced by Hutcheson's economic and moral theory, Smith's thought was also shaped by Hume's moral philosophy. This much is apparent from Smith's *Theory of Moral Sentiments* ([1759] 1982) and his *The Wealth of Nations* ([1776] 1904). In each text, Smith's treatment of self-interest (or what many Scots called 'self-love'), for instance, partly involves trying to reconcile Hutcheson (and Carmichael's) moral theory with ideas postulated by Hume.

These are important discussions. The difficulty, however, is the manner in which controversies about Hume, his influence on Smith and associated disputes about the place of God – and who He is – in Smith's writings have distracted attention from the continuing impact of Carmichael and Hutcheson's particular approach to commercial society upon other, presently less well-known, Scottish Enlightenment luminaries. William Robertson and Hugh Blair exemplify such figures.

The son of a clergyman, Robertson himself became a minister in 1743. Educated at the University of Edinburgh, Robertson was appointed chaplain of Stirling Castle in 1759. Eventually he rose to become principal of the University of Edinburgh in 1762, before his election to the influential position of Moderator of the General Assembly of the Church of Scotland in May 1763.

Robertson was extremely open to the new learning. Indeed, though he disagreed with much of Hume's thought, Robertson was quietly active in ensuring that Hume was not prosecuted for heresy on account of his apparent atheism. Robertson's passion was history and, in his various historical writings, commerce is invariably treated favorably. In his *History of the Reign of Emperor Charles V* (1769), for example, Robertson enthusiastically described how commerce's spread throughout Western Europe was reconfiguring the cultural tone of large communities. 'In proportion as commerce made its way into the different countries of Europe', Robertson wrote, 'they successfully . . . adopted those manners, which occupy and distinguish polished nations' (Robertson [1769] 1996, vol. 3, p. 21). Civility, in short, was both necessary for commercial society as well as a by-product. It embraced a range of characteristics such as self-restraint, politeness, self-confidence and charity. Robertson also stressed that civility helped to diminish some of commercial society's sharper edges. Robertson was not afraid to acknowledge that an element of self-interest was involved insofar as such behaviour made life more pleasant for everyone and facilitated a greater ease and predictability in commercial transactions. Moreover, Robertson was confident, as Bernard Aspinwall writes, that 'a reasonable Christian morality would inform the new Enlightened order' (Aspinwall, 1999, p. 156). In Robertson's view, man's mind is 'formed for religion' (Robertson [1794] 1996, p. 304), and the benefit of true religion – by which Robertson meant the type of Christianity associated with Carmichael and Hutcheson – is that it gives people, 'a standard of perfect excellence, which they should have always in their eye, and endeavour to resemble, it may be said to bring down virtue from heaven to earth, and to form the human mind after a divine model' (ibid., p. 308). It is not difficult to see the parallels here between Robertson and the path laid out by Carmichael and Hutcheson (Smitten, 1992).

A similar optimism and style of reasoning pervades the sermons of another member of the Moderate Party of the Church of Scotland, Hugh Blair (1718–1800). His father was once Merchant Burgess of Edinburgh, and Blair himself was the University of Edinburgh's first Regius Professor of Rhetoric and Belle Lettres. Like Hutcheson, Blair rejected the theory of total depravity and was also a committed anti-Hobbesian. Licensed as a minister of the Church of Scotland in 1741, Blair was appointed to Edinburgh's most prominent parish, St Giles, the High Kirk, in 1758.

A regular preacher, Blair's sermons, most of which were addressed to his Edinburgh congregation of merchants and other well-to-do citizens, focused upon the application of Christian morality to the type of practical matters encountered by people in commercial society. Blair warned against the temptations of affluence but at no point condemned the rise of commerce and the material progress it facilitated. Indeed, Blair emphasized on several occasions the virtues that he believed were both efficacious in preventing economic decline and advantageous for success in business. Here he laid special emphasis upon the need for thrift, a prudent approach to matters of finance, as well as the central place of sound time management (Blair [1777] 1819, vol. 1, p. 296).

Reflecting more broadly on the human condition, Blair presented a reasonable and enlightened Christianity, commercial order and a refined education as key ingredients for true human progress. Virtues were important for Blair, not simply because they helped society to grow in a material and civilizational sense, but also because they helped people's consciences remain steady. In the final analysis, Blair believed that a commercial society that took seriously the life of virtue needed theological grounding in revealed rather than simply natural religion. In Richard Sher's view, Blair 'defined Christianity chiefly in terms of virtue or benevolence grounded in a faith in Christ' (Sher, 1985, p. 182). This contrasts profoundly with Hume's tendency to associate commercial society with atheistic utilitarianism and philosophical egoism but resonates strongly with what might be called the Christian stoicism espoused by Hutcheson and Carmichael.

CONCLUSION

Not all Christians living through the Scottish Enlightenment agreed with the economic changes flowing from commercial society and Scotland's integration into wider economic markets. Though not unmindful of the material benefits of commercial society, Adam Ferguson (1723–1816) presented commercial order as resulting in society's general coarsening and eventual corruption (Ferguson [1767] 1978). Indeed by the late 19th and early 20th century, large numbers of Scottish Presbyterian clergy were beginning to embrace decidedly non-market-oriented views of economic affairs.

These developments, however, mask and obscure the important influence of Christian scholars and ideas upon the emerging complex of ideas in 18th-century Scotland that was to reshape the world's political and economic history. Moreover, Robertson, Blair and other members of the 'Moderate Party' that dominated the workings of the mid-18th-century Church of Scotland were able to shape in a positive way much of the religious reaction to Scotland's emergence from relative poverty to relative wealth in a short period of time, its gradual embrace of commercial culture and the new economic thinking exemplified by Smith's *The Wealth of Nations* ([1776] 1904), much of which was foreshadowed in Carmichael and Hutcheson's writings. Perhaps more importantly, the consciousness of these clergy of the Church of Scotland that they were at the core of the rising elites of the new Scotland ensured that Christian contributions to the shaping and intellectual understanding of the changes in economic life and thought were not marginal to the discussion but rather at its very centre.

4. Christianity's post-Enlightenment contribution to economic thought

Paul Oslington

INTRODUCTION

The relationship between Christianity and economics since the Enlightenment is a vast, mostly unexplored territory. Assessments of the strategic importance of this terrain vary, with scholars of religion devoting a lot of attention to it but economists and historians of economic thought not showing much interest until recently. Signs of growing interest among economists include the recent History of Economics Society Annual Conference at George Mason University in Washington DC, where the number of papers on religious aspects of economics (including the Presidential Address on the secularization of American economics) led one participant to jest that the theme of next year's conference ought to be atheist economics to redress the balance. The major journal in the field, *History of Political Economy*, devoted its most recent annual conference to religious influences on economics. Theologians and scholars of religion have tended to be more interested than economists in exploring the connections, but lack of knowledge of economics has limited their engagement with the discipline. For the last two years at the American Academy of Religion annual meeting, there have been well-attended sessions on theology and economics, with scholars from both disciplines participating.

It remains a puzzle why there has been so little progress in the area.[1] The scale and complexity of the issues are illustrated by the work of two of the most distinguished explorers of the historical connections between theology and economics, Jacob Viner and Anthony Waterman. Viner was described by Lionel Robbins (1970) as 'the greatest authority of the age in the history of economic and social thought' and by Mark Blaug (1985) as 'quite simply the greatest historian of economic thought that ever lived'. Viner began writing in the 1920s about the theological dimensions of Adam Smith's work (Viner, 1927), and then spent most of the second half of his professional life on 'an intellectual history of the economic aspects of Christian theology from the Fathers to modern times' (correspondence in Viner papers). However, even a scholar of Viner's capacities found this task beyond him; the work was never completed and we have to be content with a posthumously published set of lectures (Viner, 1972), four unfinished chapters of the projected book edited by his PhD students, Donald Winch and Jacques Melitz (Viner, 1978) and the correspondence and unpublished manuscripts among his papers at Princeton. Viner's devotion to understanding the theological context of early economics is especially significant given his distinctly sceptical personal attitude to religion, and the large investment required in teaching himself theology to equip himself for the work.

Anthony Waterman, one of a small number of scholars with formal qualifications in both economics and theology, has devoted a large part of his professional life to the historical relations between these two key parts of Western culture. Waterman, a Canadian Anglican priest who studied economics at Cambridge, was sent by his bishop to acquire a PhD in economics at the Australian National University in order to better advise the Canadian Church on economic matters. Economics and the church's social ethics tradition don't often mix well, and he turned increasingly to intellectual history, partly to understand why this is so:

> If I am right in my belief that economics has gradually ousted theology from the discourse of politics over the past two centuries, and if I am also right in thinking that this is the most significant intellectual mutation ever to occur in the political life of the civilized world, then the point of such a history is obvious. We want to know when it happened, why it happened and how it happened. (Waterman, 2004, p. 13)

Like Viner, he saw the 18th and early 19th centuries as the crucial period in shaping relations between economics and theology. His work (including Waterman, 1991b and essays collected in Waterman, 2004) has greatly enriched our understanding of the alliance and eventual separation between economics and theology. Yet he writes 'That story has yet to be written. This book is nothing but a straw in the wind' (Waterman, 2004, p. 14). Even with a substantial discount for modesty, this statement illustrates the difficulty of the task, albeit for a rare individual who has focused his scholarly energies for several decades on a small subset of the questions for a particular period for a particular country.

Many scholarly lives will be spent before we can claim anything like a comprehensive and robust understanding of the relations between economics and theology. However, we must not be put off the task. History combined with philosophical analysis is the best strategy for learning about the relationship, and especially about what might be helpful and unhelpful strategies for relating economics and theology today. As

Quentin Skinner (1969, p. 53) says, we 'learn from the past – otherwise we cannot learn at all'.

The aim of this chapter is to survey what we know about the contribution of Christian theology to economic thought since the Enlightenment, and to draw lessons where appropriate for contemporary discussions of the relationship. The contribution of Christianity to economic thought will be taken to mean historical influence, for good or ill. Economics includes economic theory produced by economists, policy discussion and public understanding of the functioning of the economy. It is worth noting that professional economists are a fairly late arrival on the scene, with the first chairs in political economy created in British universities in the early 19th century and the public awareness of an object called the economy arising rather later. I will concentrate on post-Enlightenment Britain and America. Continental Europe and important figures such as J.B. Say and Bastiat will be excluded, apart from some brief comments on the Roman Catholic social encyclicals beginning with *Rerum Novarum* in 1891. Also excluded are contemporary Asia and Africa where the vitality and different cultural situation of the church is generating some challenging new perspectives on economics. I will not discuss the influence of religion on economic behaviour, such as Weber (1905) or the recent literature on the economics of religion (Iannaccone, 2002).

BRITAIN

We know relatively more about the contribution of theology to British economic thought, partly because it has been the focus of the work of historians of economics such as Jacob Viner and Anthony Waterman, and partly because of the rich parallel literature on the relations between theology and science in Britain (for instance, Brooke, 1991), together with discussions of economics by theologically sensitive historians of the period such as Hilton (1988), Winch (1996) and Clark (2000).

Political economy in 18th-century Britain emerged out of moral philosophy, then a deeply Christian enterprise. It was much stimulated by Scottish Enlightenment writers such as David Hume, Adam Smith and Dugald Stewart. Some Scots would claim that the genesis of political economy was an almost entirely Scottish affair (Dow, Dow and Hutton, 1997) and find the notion of an English Enlightenment hilarious, but this stretches things too far. In terms of theology, recent writing on Adam Smith suggests that substantial amounts of theology were embedded in the political economy the Scots passed on (for example, Hill, 2001; Long, 2006 but contested by Fleischacker, 2004).

Even without the Scots, it is likely that political economy would have emerged as a distinct body of thought in England some time in the 19th century partly through the process of specialization within moral philosophy (hastened in the area of economics by new problems connected with industrialization), and partly through a desire to emulate other successful sciences. Of course, in the 18th century, emulating other sciences in no way meant distancing from theology, as the sciences were part of a larger natural theological project. As Robert Young (1985) has put it, natural theology was the common context of intellectual inquiry in 18th- and early 19th-century Britain. This was a project of reading God's nature from creation, a project in which most of the major figures in what we would now call British science participated, including Francis Bacon, John Ray, Robert Boyle and Isaac Newton. The extension of the natural theological project to the social world from the 18th century is described in Oslington (2005 and forthcoming). Natural theology legitimated political economy, shaped economic theory and provided a common language for economists and theologians through this period.

William Paley exemplifies the process of specialization within moral philosophy as well as the natural theological context of the emerging discipline. Paley was a central figure in the British tradition of moral philosophy and worked out his economics in the context of his theological utilitarianism. His *Principles of Moral and Political Philosophy* (Paley, 1785, based on 1766–76 Cambridge lectures) became a hugely influential Cambridge textbook, admired by Malthus, Charles Darwin, J.M. Keynes and others. It was the first part of a project of explaining and defending the Christian society then existing in Britain, a project that included his *Evidences of Christianity* (1794) and culminated with his *Natural Theology* (1802). Paley's economics is mostly contained in the lengthy Chapter XI of Book VI 'Of Population and Provision'. It was only lightly influenced, it seems, by Adam Smith's *Wealth of Nations* ([1776] 1904) although published almost ten years later. Waterman (1996) discusses the details of Paley's fairly sophisticated growth model but the question of most interest for our purposes is the extent to which Paley's theology contributed to his economics.

In the end I believe the most we can say is that his commitments to natural theology, utilitarianism and individualism, and positive view of the growth of wealth and population, created space for economic investigation. His method involved 'combining the conclusions of reason, the declarations of scripture, when they are to be had, as of co-ordinate authority, and as both terminating in the same sanctions' (Paley, 1785, p. x) but emphasized that 'whoever expects to find in the Scriptures, directions for every moral doubt that arises, looks for more than he will meet with' (ibid., p. 5).

This is a key methodological move, also made by other 18th-century British moral philosophers interested in economic matters, including Butler and Josiah Tucker.

The links between the theology and the economics are perhaps clearer for T.R. Malthus, one of the 'joint founders of the science' of political economy with Adam Smith (Winch, 1996, p. 373). The *Essay on the Principle of Population*, published in 1798 as a refutation of the perfectibilist ideas of William Godwin, brought Malthus to national attention.

Just as for Paley, Malthus's natural theological commitments cleared the ground for economic investigation. He states that 'it seems absolutely necessary that we reason from nature up to nature's God and not presume to reason from God to nature' and goes on to speak of 'the book of nature where alone we can read God as he is' (Malthus, 1798, p. 220). It could be objected that Malthus does not consider at length the argument from design and other staples of natural theology, but he explains in correspondence that he considered Paley to have dealt sufficiently with these and assumed his own works would be read in this context.

The core economic argument of Malthus's *Essay* was that population tends to grow more rapidly than the food supply, with any discrepancy corrected by the checks on population of vice and misery. Policies such as more generous poor laws would thus increase population without increasing the food supply, increasing vice and misery rather than improving life for the poor. In the second edition of the *Essay* published in 1803, Malthus added an additional check, moral restraint (essentially delaying marriage), which could operate as an alternative to vice and misery in restraining population. Adding the check of moral restraint softened the harsh implications of the theory, so that human choice along with divine design was responsible for vice and misery. The struggle to reconcile Malthus's economics with the goodness and omnipotence of God – in other words to construct an economic theodicy – is the subject of Waterman (1991b).

Is there a link between Malthus's economic analysis and his theology? John Pullen (1981) has argued that Malthus's theological ideas (which Pullen helpfully elaborates in the categories of contemporary theology) are 'an essential component of his system of thought' and the 'Essay without its theology would be a very different work' (p. 51). The difference in Pullen's view is that the seemingly pessimistic economic analysis must be read in the context of an optimistic theology, so that the work overall is an exploration of feasible and infeasible policies for progress. Pullen's argument about the inseparability of the economic and theological aspects of Malthus's work suggests the theology influenced the economics and vice versa. Recognizing Malthus's optimistic theological framework also makes sense of his enthusiastic acceptance of Adam Smith's providential account of markets.

Another example (suggested by Winch, 1996, p. 349) of how Malthus's theology contributed to his economics is the argument that the surplus accruing to English landlords in the form of rents was a 'bountiful gift of providence' (Malthus, 1815, p. 16) and hence justified. If the price of output is determined by costs of production on the least productive land, then owners of more productive land who receive the same price for their product earn a surplus rent. Malthus asks rhetorically:

> Is it not . . . a clear indication of a most inestimable quality in the soil, which God has bestowed on man – the quality of being able to maintain more persons than are necessary to work? Is it not a part, and we shall see further on that is an absolutely necessary part, of that surplus produce from the land which has been justly stated to be the source of all power and enjoyment? (Ibid., p. 16)

Ricardo and others had similar theories of rent but very different theological commitments. Malthus also saw that large rents to landlords and their consequent luxury consumption had a function in maintaining the general level of demand and guarding against gluts (or recessions in modern terminology). Malthus's theology led him to a different use of the rent theory than Ricardo, who saw providentialism as nonsense.

If we accept Quentin Skinner's (1969) interpretative rule that 'no agent can eventually be said to have meant or done something which he could never be brought to accept as a correct description of what he had meant or done', we must take account of the theological context and this makes it impossible to separate the economics of Smith and Malthus from their theology. If so, many historians of economic thought and contemporary economists who quote Smith and Malthus without recognizing the theological framework are at grave risk of misleading their readers.

In the 19th century, the theological economics of Smith and Malthus was developed by J.B. Sumner, Richard Whately, Thomas Chalmers, William Whewell and others (as described by Waterman, 1991b). Whately, for instance, amplifies Smith's providential account of markets: 'Man is, in the same act, doing one thing by choice, for his own benefit, and another, undesignedly, under the care of Providence, for the service of the community' (Whately, 1832, p. 94) and praises Smith as a greater natural theologian even than Paley. For Chalmers, 'The greatest economic good is rendered to the community . . . by the spontaneous play and busy competition of many thousand wills, each bent on the persecution of his own selfishness, than by the anxious superintendence of a government, vainly attempting to medicate the fancied imperfections of nature' (Chalmers, 1833, p. 238) and this 'strongly bespeaks a higher Agent, by whose transcendental wisdom it is, that all is made to conspire so harmoniously, and to terminate so beneficially' (ibid., pp. 238–9).

Theology contributed not just to the formation of economics in Britain but to its eventual separation from theology. Forces of specialization and professionalization operated to separate all the sciences from theology during the 19th century (Brooke, 1991). Specifically for political economy I have argued (Oslington, 2005) that two tensions fatally damaged British natural theology, destroying the framework that linked economics to theology: first, tension between the static design arguments that dominated early-19th-century natural theology and the dynamics of classical political economy; and second, problems of theodicy created by extending the natural theological project to the economy. Waterman, in his work, emphasizes the damage done to natural theology by the publication of Darwin's *Origin of the Species* in 1859, but in my view this overstates the tension in the 1860s between evolutionary theory and theology (see Moore, 1979) and concedes too much to T.H. Huxley's tale of a war between science and theology, in which Darwin fired the decisive shot on the scientific side.

Whatever consensus emerges about the causes of the separation, the process was well advanced by the later decades of the 19th century. Keynes (1933) identified the 1860s as 'the critical moment at which Christian dogma fell away from the serious philosophical world of England, or at any rate of Cambridge'. An economist like Phillip Wicksteed, whose economics arose from an underlying religious vision (Steedman, 1994), did not consider it appropriate to deploy theology in support of his economics or discuss the relationship of his economics to theology. Alfred Marshall, who set the tone of British economics well into the 20th century, introduced his *Principles of Economics* with the statement that 'the two great forming agencies of the world's history have been the religious and the economic' then makes little reference to religion, dealing with what he sees as the separate realm of economics.

But although theology retreated from or was pushed out of mainstream economics, economic questions could not be avoided in the church. In England, an influential strand of the continuing church discussion of economic issues was the Christian socialism of F.D. Maurice, Charles Kingsley and others (see Norman, 1987). Others in the established church attempted to bring theologians and economists together to discuss policy – for example, the Oldham groups and Oxford Conferences of the early 20th century – but the growing gap between the ways theologians and economists viewed the world made such gatherings less and less fruitful.

CONTINENTAL EUROPE

In the 18th century, political economy was an international affair; developments in France, the Netherlands and Italy were important, and all had strong theological connections. The French Revolution dampened this. Moving to the 19th century, J.B. Say and Frederic Bastiat offered theologically-based defences of the market in France, but the dominant strands of European economics in the second half of the 19th century were sceptical at best about markets. Much European discussion of economics in the churches ran parallel to the Christian socialist movement in Britain.

Catholic social teaching from Leo XIII's 1891 encyclical *Rerum Novarum* is a strong and distinct tradition. It stood apart from British classical political economy, being influenced somewhat by European political economy, but more so by the earlier scholastic natural-law thinkers and the emerging personalist tradition. It offered an anti-modern or at least non-modern alternative, with a different philosophical framework and different anthropology, and asked different questions. The key papal texts may be found in O'Brien and Shannon (1992) and the background discussed by Waterman (1991a), Dorr (1992), Charles (1998), Yuenguert (1999) and Barrera (2001) among others. Fruitful questions were asked about the relationship between this tradition and contemporary economic theory by a series of writers, including de Roover (1955), Noonan (1957), Dempsey (1958) and Lonergan (1999, 2002). Bernard Lonergan's work began in the 1930s and continued until his death in 1984, and is in my view particularly significant. It is hard to identify significant contributions to economic theory, but this tradition certainly influenced policy, and public understanding of economics.

AMERICA

The Enlightenment in America tended to be allied with religion, in contrast to the sceptical tone of the English Enlightenment, and the outright hostility to religion of the continental European Enlightenment (May, 1976). Scottish common sense philosophy was perhaps the most important philosophical framework in 19th-century America, and common sense philosophy, together with the economics of Adam Smith and a large measure of optimism linked to the growing economy were the ingredients of most early American political economy.

The 19th-century clerical economists such as Francis Wayland, Alonzo Potter and John McVickar have been analysed by Marsden (1973), Noll (2002) and Davenport (forthcoming). In this period, economics was often part of a capstone course in moral philosophy taught by the college president or another figure of sufficient moral standing. The clerical teachers and textbook writers regarded Adam Smith's economics as harmonizing perfectly with their theological commitments and disseminating it to be a religious task. Confidence in the robustness of this harmony allowed them to investigate economic questions, just as had Smith, Paley and Malthus in Britain. For instance, Francis Wayland, Baptist minister, President of Brown University and author of one of the most popular textbooks of the period, *Elements of Political Economy* (1837), argued 'economical questions on economical grounds' and 'has not thought it proper to intermingle them with moral philosophy and theology' (Wayland, quoted in Marsden, 1989, p. 31).

Clerical laissez-faire was dominant in 19th-century America but had difficulty coping with the changed late-19th-century American economy. Marty (1969) and Marsden (1989) have argued that a gradual and mostly unintentional process of secularization was going on in this period. Francis Wayland expressed his theological reasons for putting theology and moral philosophy to one side when considering economical questions, but neglected the theological framework leading to a wholly secular economics. It is similar to Max Weber's (1905) argument that capitalism was formed in a particular Calvinist theological framework but, as this framework had been discarded, only an 'iron cage' remained. A remark by the late-19th-century advocate of laissez-faire, W.G. Sumner, also captures something of the spirit of the secularization of American economics: 'I never consciously gave up a religious belief . . . it was as if I had put my beliefs into a drawer and when I opened it there was nothing there at all'.

The often-told story of the religious foundation of the American Economic Association in 1885 (Coats, 1985; Bateman and Kapstein, 1999) is not the beginning or in my view the most important religious contribution to American economic thought. Instead it is better seen as an attempt by Richard Ely and economists associated with the Social Gospel movement to legitimate their version of economics, against critics like Simon Newcomb. Bateman (forthcoming) argues that the collapse of the progressive movement after World War I was the decisive event in the secularization of American economics, and is sceptical about the creeping, unintentional secularization argument of Marty and Marsden. Bateman's argument seems to me to work if the Social Gospel movement was the dominant theological influence on American economics, but this does not seem to be the case when we look at the earlier history.

A popular tale of this period, which must be rejected, traces the secularization of American economics though J.B. Clark. The tale opens with the early Clark basing his economics on religious sentiment in *The Philosophy of Wealth* (1886), then abandoning this for secular scientific reason in *The Distribution of Wealth* (1899). Alongside Clark's own change is a transformation of the American Economic Association as Ely and his supporters are displaced. However, close examination of Clark's transformation by Everett (1946) and Henry (1982) does not support this tale. There seems to be little change in Clark's theological commitments, his anthropology or view of private property – just his attitude to competition. Many of the differences between the two books are of rhetoric rather than substance, as Clark accommodates his style to the different situation of the 1890s where appeals to religion are less persuasive. If the tale is false, then so too the moral of the tale that is so much a part of the self-identity of American economists: that religious influences are inevitably cast aside in the march towards good economics.

It is undoubtedly true that the gradual process of secularization that Marty and Marsden describe removes explicit reference to theology, but this is not the only way theology can contribute to economics. There are also the implicit influences of the Christian theological frameworks of economics in a deeply religious culture and these are harder to detect. Even identifying such influences in one's own work is difficult. Great scholarly skill and persistence is needed – we need more work like that undertaken by Ross Emmett on Frank Knight (e.g., Emmett, 1994 and his forthcoming book on Knight).

There is another type of contribution if we accept the argument of Robert Nelson (1991, 2001) that all economics is religious, irrespective of whether explicitly religious language is used, and irrespective of the personal faith commitments of economists. Nelson's emphasis is on the religious functions of economics rather than theological content, but Milbank (1990) argues that all social theory, including political economy, is deformed theology.

As in Britain, the separation of professional economics from theology did not end discussion of economic issues in the churches. 'Social ethics' has arisen as a church alternative to mainstream economics. This literature does not attract much attention from economists and it is difficult to think of any substantial contribution it has made to economic theory or policy, or any deep engagement between economics and theology that tends to generate contributions.

AUSTRALIA

Australia's Enlightenment (Gascoigne, 2002) was not dominated by imported Scottish common sense philosophy, but instead by the non-religious utilitarianism of Jeremy Bentham and his followers. This utilitarianism provided a congenial framework for economics to grow in Australia, as it did with great distinction but with little connection to theology. Australia's universities, unlike their British and American counterparts, excluded theology and this limited the capacity of theology to participate in Australian intellectual life and contribute to economic thought in Australia.

It is interesting to read Scott's (1990) history of the Economic Society of Australia alongside the reports of the founding of the American Economic Association. Its objects were limited and practical – there is no trace of an overarching religious vision for the economics profession that drove the American founders.

The standard histories of Australian economic thought, Goodwin (1966) and Groenewegen and McFarlane (1990), give little hint of religious influences. They are probably right for explicit religious influences, but possible influences through the religious backgrounds of important individual economists have not been investigated. And a Nelson-type argument that economics functioned as some kind of alternative theology probably has more force in Australia than elsewhere as, for instance, in the Australian debates of the 1980s over the supposed intellectual dominance of 'economic rationalism'. All this is speculation and our ignorance of connections between religion and economics in Australia remains profound.

RECENT DEVELOPMENTS

A way of trying to understand the dearth of work in the 20th century connecting economics and theology is to look at the incentives facing professional economists and theologians. Professional economists, particularly academic economists, are rewarded for publishing research in a well-recognized set of journals. Specialization and heavy personal investment in particular techniques are the usual paths to these journals. Not all specializations though are equal, and we have seen the marginalization of specializations like the history of economics that have the potential to engage with theology. Papers in the history of economic thought are no longer published in the top journals, nor are historians of economics found in the elite North American departments that lead professional opinion. Philosophy of economics, another of the specializations that can engage religion, has fared a little better. It remains to be seen whether the economics of religion, which has grown rapidly as a subfield and won professional acceptance in recent years, will evolve in ways that engage more deeply with theology. There are extremely weak incentives for economists to engage with theology, or to acquire the training in theology that makes deep engagement possible.

The situation facing the professional theologian or scholar of religion is similar, with specialization and heavy sunk cost investments in technique required in particular subfields. By their nature, theology and religious studies ask a broader range of questions than economics, and so there has been some space in the major journals and conferences for discussion of economics. The main problem is that there is no incentive for scholars of religion participating in discussions of economics to inform themselves about economics. Their colleagues in religious studies who assess discussions of economics are similarly ill-informed, and we observe a low equilibrium level of discussion of economics – to put it kindly.

Besides incentives in the particular disciplines, there is the question of incentives for interdisciplinary work. This has seemed an almost permanent flavour of the month among higher education policy-makers and university administrators, but reality for interdisciplinary scholars in the theology or economics job markets, especially at the junior level, is grim.

Despite the lack of incentives in the mainstream of the disciplines of economics and theology, we have seen a remarkable revival from the mid-1970s of discussion of relationships between theology and economics. Reasons are complex – the interest in Christian critiques of economics coincided both with a larger crisis of confidence in economics and with a revival of interest among evangelicals in social issues. Some of this has occurred in segments of the profession distanced from the incentives facing mainstream economists, such as the US Christian colleges.

I will briefly mention two parts of this revival. First, in the Roman Catholic Church it is fair to say that the tradition of social teaching stemming from *Rerum Novarum* was losing its way in the 1970s. Beginning about then has been a vigorous reassessment of the role of markets in the Catholic traditions, exemplified by the work of Michael Novak (1981, 1982, 1993), John Paul II's encyclical *Centesimus Annus* and more recently the work of the Acton Institute for the Study of Religion and Liberty in the United States.

Second, in the Reformed tradition, especially that part of it stemming from the work of Abraham Kuyper, we have seen a series of works about the theological nature of economics (Cramp, 1975; Vickers, 1976; Goudzwaard, 1979; Storkey, 1993) and a long-term project centred at Calvin College in the United States to reconstruct economics on Christian foundations (Tiemstra et al., 1990, 1994). This work in the Reformed tradition has stimulated evangelical writers such as Kim Hawtrey (1986) and Donald Hay (1989). Organizations such as the Associations of Christian Economists in the United Kingdom and United States, and the Zadok Institute in Australia, all founded in the 1970s, reflect this revival.

It is interesting that both share a natural-law background. Aquinas and Calvin in their own ways are natural-law thinkers (Grabill, 2006) and thus the Roman Catholic and Reformed traditions have more in common with each other than they do with the utilitarian and empiricist philosophical framework of mainstream economics.

Alongside these revivals, the Christian Socialist tradition remained influential in Britain up until the 1980s, producing a steady stream of church documents and reflections – for instance, Preston (1983). Mainstream Protestant social ethics continued to generate vast volumes of material, especially in the United States, without producing much of lasting value or influence in relation to economics. It remains to be seen whether the current interest in public theology will amount to anything more than a new marketing slogan for this type of work.

Nor has religious economics been without its critics, among whom are included Anderson (1984), Bauer (1984), Heyne (1994), Richardson (1994) and Coleman (2002).

CONCLUSION

There can be no doubt that theology has contributed to the development of economics since the Enlightenment. In the 18th century, theology shaped and legitimated the new discipline in Britain, and greatly influenced early American economics. Natural theology was a framework that made the development of political economy possible. Much theology was built into economic theory and remains with us. And theology had an important role in the defence and popularization of economics. Without theology (if this counterfactual is conceivable) we might not have modern economics, and if we did it would be a very different discipline.

As well, there is a continuing contribution of theology to economics through a number of channels – most obviously, but perhaps least importantly, from Christian economics. Writers who identify their work as Christian economics are a small and probably biased sample of the Christian contributions. The nature of this larger contribution is extremely hard to identify, and we need more studies of the connection between the theologies (and anti-theologies) of major economists. Finally, if we accept the arguments of Robert Nelson and John Milbank that all economics is ultimately religious, then the religious contribution becomes overwhelming.

What lessons can be drawn from this history? First, that good economics and theological influences are not mutually exclusive, although recent history has been less encouraging in this regard than periods such as 18th-century and early 19th-century Britain. Second, we need an adequate intellectual framework for linking economics and theology – natural theology has operated this way in the past, but may not be the best framework for contemporary circumstances. Third, for deep and fruitful interaction we need institutions and incentives that make for good scholarship across the disciplinary boundaries.

PART II

Christianity and economic theory

5. Christian theology and economics: convergence and clashes

Geoffrey Brennan and Anthony M.C. Waterman

Until the end of the 18th century what was then called 'political œconomy' was taken to be wholly compatible with Christian theology. The appearance of T.R. Malthus's *Essay on Population* (1798, 1803) almost immediately destroyed that assumption (Waterman, 2004, Ch. 7). Robert Southey's (1803) maledictory review of the second *Essay* inaugurated what (the Victorian) Arnold Toynbee called 'the bitter quarrel between economists and human beings' (Winch, 1996, pp. 402, 418). By the end of the 19th century, Christian theologians in England were allied with Romantic writers and artists as self-appointed spokesmen for the human beings (Waterman, 2003). The legacy persists. Many theologians in the English-speaking world take it for granted that economics is hostile to true religion and therefore, we may suppose, to Christian theology.

It is our purpose in this chapter to analyse the relation between economic theory and Christian theology so as to throw some light on the compatibility or otherwise of the two. We begin with definitional matters, for this is a semantic minefield. Next we attempt a taxonomy of the various modes of coexistence possible. Finally, we take a closer look at two central theoretical conceptions, 'rationality' and 'scarcity', on which much of our analysis turns.

DEFINITIONAL MATTERS

According to an aphorism familiar at least to economists, economics is 'what economists do'. By extrapolation, we might suppose that (Christian)[1] theology is what theologians do.

As a way of delineating areas of enquiry, this approach to definition might at first seem unpromising. Both economists and theologians do many things that in no way identify their professional concerns. They eat, sleep, make love, sing, and so on. We need to modify the formulation to exclude these 'irrelevancies'; but if we do so in the most natural way – so as to make the aphorism read: 'economics (theology) is what economists (theologians) do when they are doing economics (theology)', the whole exercise becomes hopelessly self-referential. No such definition can be informative unless we have a prior notion of what economics (theology) is.

Still, the approach has something going for it. It tells us where we might look in trying to see what economics and theology are – namely, in the literature that practising economists and theologians take to be 'core material' for their respective areas of enquiry. So, in the economics case, in the pages of the leading journals and in the mainstream textbooks – and for theology, in analogous places.

This is, of course, to conceive of economics and theology as intellectual enterprises, each taking place within a specific 'knowledge community' whose members recognize one another to be engaged in the same enterprise and committed to the same specific rules of discourse. In the case of theology in particular, such a conception may well appear contentious. In defence of our approach here, two things should be borne in mind. First, it is possible to draw a distinction between the *intellectual* enterprise of theology, on the one hand, and the *spiritual* enterprise of 'working out one's salvation with fear and trembling' on the other. The former admits of specialization within a broader epistemic division of labour; whereas there are limits on specialization and exchange within the latter enterprise. It needs to be conceded, though, that to the extent that the spiritual enterprise admits an intellectual component – one is called to 'love the Lord with all one's *mind*', among other aspects of one's person – the spiritual and the intellectual enterprises are connected. This is an important distinguishing feature of theology in the present context. Although one can operate in the 'real world' economy with no knowledge at all of economics (as one can drive a car with no knowledge of mechanics), it is doubtful whether one can live a spiritual life without any knowledge of theology. For though St Augustine said, 'A man supported by faith, hope and charity, with an unshaken hold upon them, does not need the Scriptures except for the instruction of others' (Augustine of Hippo, 1958, *Doct. Christ.* I, p. xxxix), this presupposes a community in which the relation between the 'theological virtues' and Holy Scripture is understood, studied and taught. So while the distinction between the intellectual and the spiritual has some bite, it is not a clear-cut one. Moreover, there is no analogous distinction in the case of economics: the fact that most Christians ought to take theology seriously makes theology different from economics in one significant respect.

On the other hand (and this is our second line of defence), we do not need to think of theological reflection as the monopoly of specialist professionals in order to make the point that the activities of the specialists can be instructive in informing us as to what theology as an intellectual enterprise consists of. And that is the central purpose of this section.

Thinking about economics and theology in this way allows us to conceptualize the relation between them in somewhat similar terms to the relations between other, more or less well-defined disciplines in the academic arena. So in principle, the relation is similar in kind to that between, say, economics and philosophy, or economics and political science, or for that matter theology and philosophy.

In this sense, it is important to emphasize the features that economics and theology, so understood, share. Both are committed to what passes within their respective knowledge communities as the standard rules of rational discourse – to terminological precision and logical coherence – and to intra-community agreement as to what counts as relevant 'evidence', and what counts as appropriate respect for that evidence once it is established. In both cases, the approach taken – the 'method of thought' practised – is a kind of heuristic apparatus, formulated with the intention of 'finding out' something about that part of human experience identified as relevant. This apparatus emerges collectively from the interactions among mutually recognized practitioners over time – as a gradual process, proceeding by trial and error, in which the identification of 'errors' is itself part of the process of collective enquiry. But what is 'discovered' is likely to be shaped by the apparatus of enquiry. Enquirers tend to see the things they are looking for, partly because cases in which what is sought is absent tend to be less salient.

Equally, the idioms and vocabulary of the two conversations will differ between communities. And what counts as relevant evidence may well be very different. These features will make communication difficult. But we reject any extreme theses of necessary mutual incomprehensibility. Observers from either side can recognize that a game is in play, and have the rules explained, even if that game is one that the observer could never play – and perhaps never wish to play. Indeed, if economics and theology are to be seen, as we do see them, as elements in a larger division of intellectual labour – one to be rationalized on the grounds that time, energy and creative imagination (the inputs into intellectual enquiry) are limited – then communication between the enterprises must at some level be possible if that division of labour is to be justifiable.

One aspect of this 'division of intellectual labour' picture is that each of theology and economics will put into the background – and perhaps abstract from entirely – elements that the other regards as central. Both deal with aspects of human experience; but it is a kind of analytic necessity that neither can capture the *whole*. Accordingly, one possible area of tension between economics and theology lies in the conception of human nature – or as the economist might put it, the 'model of man' – that each deploys.

Christian theology conceives man as a damaged and somewhat defaced *Imago Dei* – with the damage a naturally ineradicable feature of the human condition, remediable only by the direct redemptive action of God through Jesus Christ. Economics conceives of man as a rational individual, pursuing relatively stable ends (the objects of relatively stable preferences) subject to the constraints imposed by scarcity. Are these pictures compatible? Are they reconcilable in terms that would be mutually agreeable to general practitioners in both camps? Does the exercise of trying to limit tension between the two conceptions suggest a distinctive sub-field of Christian economics – or perhaps of economic theology? These are matters we shall want to take up in greater detail below.

In the meantime, we need to offer some more detailed remarks about exactly how we think of economics. Many, probably most, recognized economists understand their intellectual enterprise in terms less of its subject matter than of its approach – in terms, that is, of what Paul Heyne (1991) has called 'the economic way of thinking' in his admirable book of the same title. If we were to examine the content of the mainstream economics journals it would immediately become apparent that economists see their explanatory domain as extending across the entire range of social phenomena. There is no self-imposed limit to subject matter that might conventionally be thought of as 'economic'. There are, for example, lively sub branches of the discipline dealing with politics (so-called 'public choice theory' or 'rational actor political theory'); law (the 'law and economics' enterprise is now a standard piece of legal education across the Anglo-American world); sport (including what Robert D. Tollison (1990) refers to as 'sportometrics'); the arts and even so-called 'religious behaviour' (Iannaccone, 1998). There are attempts at an 'economic theory of the family', an 'economic theory of suicide', an 'economic theory of the caste system', an 'economic theory of esteem', an 'economic theory of military tactics'. McKenzie and Tullock (1975) devised an introductory textbook some years ago purporting to illustrate the range, including a chapter on the 'economics of sex'. Not all these applications have struck the economics profession as completely successful, but for the most part they have been recognized as legitimate attempts to apply what is basically the economic method. Of particular relevance to this chapter, a recent contribution analyses *The Economics of Sin* (Cameron, 2003). The ever-increasing explanatory ambition of economics has brought it into conflict – sometimes quite vigorous – with neighbouring disciplines. Attempts at colonizing other territory have not always been hospitably greeted by the original inhabitants. So while economists might assent in principle to an intellectual division of labour, they have seldom respected the boundaries such a division might imply. That is a fact about economics that needs to be borne in mind.

Both theology and economics involve 'positive' and 'normative' elements. The distinction is more emphasized in economic than theological circles, and economists have sometimes been criticized for making the distinction in tendentious or philosophically problematic ways. But for all its difficulties, the distinction is useful and important, and some separation of positive from normative elements in analysis – if only in a comparative sense – seems worthwhile. When economists claim that the quantity of any good demanded is a diminishing function of price, they are making a positive claim – one that can be falsified by empirical evidence. When they claim that rent control is a bad idea and should be abolished, they are making a normative claim. Such normative claims in economics do not always operate as ethical primes. The assessment of rent control, for example, is typically grounded in positive claims about the effects of rent control on the supply (or quality) of the housing stock. In other words, claims of the kind: 'X is good (ill)' can typically be decomposed into two separate claims: 'X has consequence Y'; 'Y is desirable (undesirable)'. Of course, the claim that 'Y is desirable' may appeal to considerations of a more basic kind – and these considerations will often involve further claims about the consequences of Y for something yet more ethically basic. Eventually, however, we come to something in the chain of reasoning that for purposes of the exercise can be taken to be self-evidently a good or an ill. This final claim, on the economist's reading, is a *purely* normative matter. Everything else in that backward chain is a *derivatively* normative matter and appeals to some kind of positive claim, usually about the consequences of actions or policies. Arguably, the positive/normative distinction is best thought of as a continuum ranging from claims that are distant from the purely normative to claims that are very close. Note that this approach accommodates the idea that what sometimes looks like a purely 'positive' claim – 'X leads to a net additional 1 million deaths', say – can be virtually a 'normative' claim if a net additional 1 million deaths is self-evidently an ill, at least *pro tanto*. The mere grammatical form of a sentence – whether it has an 'is' or an 'ought' form – does not always settle the issue.

Economists are fond of insisting that proper normative analysis incorporates an ineluctable positive element. And this is almost certainly true for the kinds of normative questions with which economics is primarily interested – such questions as: what policies should be enacted? Or which market institutions are best? Or whether aid or trade is better for third world countries? Whether the same is true of theology is a more open question. On the face of things, 'This is my body, given for you' is a positive proposition; whereas 'we ought at all times to acknowledge our sins before God' is a normative one. The latter is indeed normative in the same sense as that in which one might say that 'City Council ought to abolish rent control': as an instruction for achieving a desired end. If we wish to be forgiven by God, then we *ought* to acknowledge our sins. But it is doubtful whether propositions of the former kind can be thought of in purely positive terms. In the context in which they are made, such propositions make claims upon our willingness and ability to exercise the theological virtue of faith that merely empirical claims do not. It would appear that normatively charged 'definitions' abound in theological contexts, and the positive/ normative distinction is much harder to draw. Nevertheless, expressly normative claims in theological settings do often depend on a substructure of positive claims – that God *desires* of humans that they acknowledge their sins, perhaps – that it is often useful to expose and interrogate. Moreover, *Christian* theology at any rate is supposed to rest on a body of evidence respecting 'the mighty acts of God', as recorded in Old and New Testaments, for which witnesses are claimed to have existed.

LIVING TOGETHER

In light of what we have said so far, we can catalogue the possible relations between theology and economics into four broad categories: *independence*; *dependence*; *convergence*; and *clash*. Although these possibilities are expressed as mutually exclusive categories, it is better to think of them in continuous terms, because issues of relation are unlikely to be settled by purely logical a priori considerations. What the relations are in practice, and whether claims broadly accepted in one field sit entirely happily with claims broadly accepted in the other, whether the analytic styles of the two enterprises are similar or dissimilar and whether such differences in style are in any way important – are all matters that have empirical content. And the empirical story is unlikely to be identical across all the matters that fall under the scope of economics and theology. Relations are matters of degree – and the degrees may differ across different aspects of the interaction.

But it is nevertheless useful to begin with 'ideal types', and we examine the four possibilities in turn.

Independence

Consider two intellectual enterprises – say, musicology and ornithology. For the most part, these proceed without reference to each other. Matters that interest the one are of no interest to the other. This is not to deny that there may be people who are interested in both at an amateur level – birdwatchers who like music, say; nor that there may be some smaller number who are professionals in one area and have amateur interests in the other.

But whether a musicologist is interested in birds or not is unlikely to exercise much influence, if any, on her competence as a musicologist or on the sort of musicology she does. Of course, we can *imagine* the musicologist of a rather technical stripe whose expertise lies in the mechanisms of the human voice and ear; and who is interested in the possible analogies with the ways in which birdsong is made and accessed by other birds. But such an overlap of interests is hardly mainstream within either group.

It could be that the relations between economics and theology are essentially of this kind. If this were so, each could properly go its own way without need to refer to the other. Theologians will of course operate as participants in the economy – buying and selling and saving for their old age and so on – and may be interested in what the stock market is doing, or whether interest rates are likely to rise. And economists may be Christian, and see theological matters as broadly relevant to some aspects of their spiritual lives. But the same thing might be said of Christian materials-scientists or Christian foresters: they may well be vitally interested in theology, but not expect theology to make any contribution *within* their professional intellectual enterprise.

Richard Whately, Drummond Professor of Political Economy at Oxford and subsequently (Anglican) Archbishop of Dublin, famously argued (1832) that the Bible transmits 'religious knowledge' but not 'scientific knowledge'. The latter, he thought, is to be discovered by observation of 'nature'. In that sense, scientific knowledge can throw no light on religion, and equally, theological methods can throw no light on science. In Whately's view, political economy was a science. Since modern economics is directly continuous with 19th-century political economy, the relation between economics and theology is essentially the same as the relation between chemistry and theology – total independence in each case.

With somewhat similar effect, it has been argued by Leszek Kolakowski (1982) that 'science' and 'religion' are non-intersecting, non-competing Wittgensteinian language games: no clash, no convergence – the two enterprises are totally orthogonal.

Dependence

The foregoing picture can be challenged at a number of levels. One kind of interdependence occurs when one or other enterprise claims epistemological sovereignty over the other. One might, for example, offer an account of theology that emphasizes the institutional processes whereby the allocation of grant monies affects the agenda of theological scholarship – a kind of 'economics of theological enquiry'. A Marxian account of the history of thought exhibits something of this character; and Marx was first and foremost an economist, who learned much of his craft from Ricardo and Adam Smith. Although Marxian economics is widely (and often somewhat ill-informedly) rejected by most contemporary economists, the explanatory agenda of the Marxian enterprise is in many ways not so very far from that of, say, the modern Chicago School.

An attempt along similar lines from the theological side might also be conceived. It might be held, and indeed sometimes is held, that the Bible contains a 'complete' and thorough-going presentation of all principles from which a 'true' economics can be constructed – and that the secular alternative is ontologically defective in not being based on Scripture. Economic 'creationists' are not quite as common as their biological counterparts. But some attempts to construct a distinctively 'Christian economics' seem very close, especially within the Dooyeweerdian, Neo-Calvinist School associated with the Free University of Amsterdam and its North American offshoots (e.g., Vickers, 1975, 1976; Tiemstra, 1990). It may be noteworthy that these endeavours have usually emanated from economists rather than from theologians.

More plausible than either of the foregoing extremes is the notion that although economics and theology are independent over a wide range, they overlap or are mutually informing in relation to some aspects of their respective enterprises. Here there are prospects of both convergences and clashes – and indeed of both convergence and clash operating simul-taneously in different aspects. Let us offer some examples of each.

Convergence

One familiar point of intersection arises in relation to natural theology. If God is the 'author of nature', our study of the natural order can inform our understanding of the divine. Most famously, Newton's *Principia* was written for this purpose. For most 18th-century thinkers, science informed theology. Sometimes the relation can run the other way: a prior theological commitment can inform science. It is said that Einstein's commitment to the *general* theory of relativity was based largely on quasi-theological prin-ciples. 'God does not play dice with nature', Einstein is said to have affirmed.

In the spirit of Newtonian natural theology, it has sometimes been argued that the self-regulating properties of the market order demonstrate the existence of a benign and providential God. This is perhaps to interpret Adam Smith's 'benign deity' less metaphorically than Smith himself would have thought proper, but his use of that metaphor has certainly encouraged this interpretation – from Carey (1837) and Bastiat (1850) to Hill (2001). Still, what is at stake in any such exercise is to harness what are essentially positive (though often contested) claims about the operation of the market order to an exercise in theological induction.

A related attempt at a kind of convergence arises in relation to theodicy – the attempt to explain how it is that a God who is both benign and omnipotent could allow evil in creation. A particular solution based on the supposition that *moral* evil is allowed so as to permit a greater good to emerge requires an analysis of the consequences of certain 'vices' (psychological dispositions) as they apply in relevant conditions. Here too essentially positive claims about the properties of the market order are used to show how 'cupidity' may be harnessed to benign ends. On some readings, modern economic analysis began in this way – under the appropriation of Augustinian theodicy by the Jansenists, Pierre Nicole and Jean Domat. Their pupil, Pierre de Boisguilbert, constructed the first more-or-less complete account of the interdependent processes of the free market from this starting point (Faccarello, 1999). In a somewhat similar move, Anglican theologians in the 19th century harnessed Malthusian population dynamics to the task of constructing a theodicy of the *physical* evil of scarcity (Waterman, 1991b).

In many ways, the now common economics assumption of predominant self-interest is congruent with theological conceptions of Sin and the Fall. In this respect, a central feature of theology and a central feature of economics come together and are seen as mutually reinforcing. Empirical evidence that agents are predominantly self-interested, and/or analytic results showing that apparently altruistic actions can be more or less fully explained by self-interest assumptions, stand as empirical evidence in favour of a particular view of the sinful human condition – the essentially '*crooked* timber of humanity' in Kant's phrase (authors' emphasis). Certainly there seems to be a basic consistency between the economic picture and the claim that humans fall short of common ideals of virtue. Whether, and to what extent, there is also consistency between the economistic emphasis on the 'redemptive' powers of the free market order and the theological insistence on the necessity of external divine intervention is less clear. This brings us to one aspect of the possibility of clash.

There is one notable possibility of 'convergence' operating directly within the intellectual division of labour: in the normative analysis of public policy when economics is supposed to supply the 'positive' element and theology the 'normative' element. In this way, economics and theology are married in a way somewhat analogous to the relation between demand and supply in the determination of market outcomes. Theology delivers the Christian principles that speak to pure normative questions of what ought to be desired; and economics delivers the constraints arising from the world as it is, which set the bounds on what is feasible. Economics is taken to be 'autonomous in its own sphere' as *Quadragesimo Anno* (Pius XI, 1931) put it, but that sphere is restricted to strictly 'positive' questions about the workings of the economic order. William Temple's classic *Christianity and Social Order* (1942) was based on this conception of the relation between the two disciplines. Economists have long paid lip service to the idea of economics as a pure science that cannot authorize them to offer 'a single syllable of advice' (Senior, 1836). But in practice, they have rarely been able to resist making policy recommendations of all sorts – recommendations that necessarily commit them to underlying normative foundations. As one influential moral philosopher has put it, thinking of economics as it is actually practised, 'economics is a branch of ethics' (Broome, 1999): a judgment with which Sidgwick and Marshall may have concurred.

It is worth emphasizing that if one accepts a picture of this kind, then economics and theology will be mutually indispensable in policy analysis. Like demand and supply (or preferences and opportunity sets), one cannot cut without both blades of the scissors. This observation suggests one possibility for a more acceptable 'Christian economics' than that proposed by the neo-Calvinists; and which could be regarded as alternative to that branch of economics traditionally referred to as 'welfare economics'. Of course, it can be questioned whether theology *does* deliver a clear ethical position of the kind that would be useful in normative analysis, and if so whether it is really distinct from conventional 'secular' ethics, indebted as secular ethics in the West are to a long history of broadly Christian influence. But it should not simply be assumed that there could be no place for a 'Christian economics' of this kind.

Clash

The foregoing immediately suggests one possibility of clash – namely, in relation to the normative foundations under which normative economics operates. Economists will routinely make policy recommendations about the foolishness (undesirability) of rent control or minimum wage laws or tariffs – appealing (often implicitly) to normative foundations that theologians might well be inclined to find unacceptable or at least highly contestable. So this is one issue worth exploring in somewhat greater detail. Simply put, what are the normative foundations of welfare economics? And how do they appear, viewed through a more or less standard theological lens?

But of course, this is not the only point at which conflict might emerge. As we noted earlier, both economics and theology are 'human sciences', or 'moral sciences' to use Hume's term. Both deal with an aspect of human experience; both appeal to a conception (in the terms of economics, a 'model') of man. And it is an open question whether these conceptions are really compatible.

It is important to note that this is not the same question as whether the conceptions are the *same*. On our picture, such conceptions are necessary abstractions, backgrounding aspects that are of less relevance in favour of aspects that are more relevant. And the issue of 'compatibility' itself is an unhelpful one if it is formulated in strictly logical terms, because the logical formulation accommodates a simple 'yes/no' response. It is in our view better to conceptualize the issue as one of 'tension', which can be greater or less. Alternative 'models' of human nature can sit side by side relatively comfortably if they are conceived as models – tools of analysis, in which the particular abstractions made are helpful for the purposes to which the analysis is to be put.

But this kind of epistemic modesty does not seem to be one that either economists or theologians find congenial. Economics, as we have already noted, is an imperialist beast, claiming the relevance of its general approach – including specifically its model of man embodied in the (predominantly selfish, entirely rational) *homo œconomicus* – to a very wide range of human activities. And theology, with its transcendent, cosmic aspiration, is no less inclined to consider its picture of the human condition as definitive and metaphysically prior. In other words, theology might accept *homo œconomicus* as a possibly useful abstraction in certain contexts but not concede that the Christian conception of the human condition is a 'model' in the same way. Overall, there is clear scope for tension over issues of how human activity is to be conceived, and what factors in such activity are most 'significant' – and what the relevant test of 'significance' might be.

It is also worth noting that tensions can arise in relation not so much to subject matter as to style. Two examples of tensions of this kind occur to us especially.

The importance or otherwise of exegesis

Although economists sometimes talk metaphorically of particular works being the 'bible' for economists, there is nothing in the economics discipline that approaches the status of the Bible as a fundamental theological text. The Bible is normative for theologians, and its exegesis and interpretation play a central role in theology totally unlike anything in economics circles. Indeed, economists are notorious for being disrespectful of their own past. It is the contents of the 'latest journals' that command most, indeed almost exclusive, attention. Moreover, the last 30 or 40 years have seen a declining professional interest in history of economic thought (HET), so that HET plays almost no role these days in the training of professional economists. Such HET specialists as remain tend increasingly to throw in their lot with intellectual historians more generally, or with 'science studies'. The effective intellectual presence of HET in leading centres of economics is therefore small and declining.

This fact gives economics a very different 'feel' from theology, for the latter cannot depart too far from its biblical roots. It is interesting to note in this connection that historians of economic thought seem disproportionately represented among self-styled 'Christian economists'. Exegetical skills seemingly do double duty! Perhaps the theological context of pre-industrial economic thought especially attracts the attention of theologically informed practitioners.

In terms of disciplinary style, however, the point remains that economics is largely a-historical and is so self-consciously. HET enjoys the same sort of status in economics as history of physics plays in physics. Theology is quite different in this respect.

The notion of intellectual progress
Relatedly perhaps, economists and theologians have rather different attitudes to the idea of intellectual progress. As the analogy with physics suggests, economists hold to a thoroughly 'modernist' attitude to knowledge, and many incline to the view that the progress of economics is a gradual march into all (economic) truth. Anything worthwhile in earlier writings is seen to have been absorbed into mainstream doctrine, so that reading the economics of the past is an exercise more of piety towards professional heroes than of serious economics. One possible contrast here is with philosophy. There, Plato and Aristotle, Hume and Locke, Hobbes and Kant are often taken to be more or less contemporary interlocutors. To engage in philosophy at all is to enter a conversation that includes great thinkers of the past. There are self-proclaimed Aristotelians, Thomists, Kantians, Humeans, Lockeans, all of whom claim to be applying the insights of their respective name-bearers to a new range of issues or defending positions earlier established against new-found 'heresies'. The situation in theology is much the same, though with one distinctive, extra gloss. Earlier theologians are sometimes identified as possessing a *special* authority, which contemporary contributors do not have. Thomas Aquinas and Augustine of Hippo, for example, having attained 'sainthood' status and been officially recognized as 'Doctors of the Church', are for that reason objects of pious deference in the present age.

These two considerations do not give rise to direct confrontation between economics and theology. But they are very significant differences of approach and 'posture' that make communication especially difficult. Indeed, in some ways direct confrontation between the disciplines might be recognized as an intellectual accomplishment, since genuine disagreement can only emerge on a platform of prior propositions to which contestants are agreed. Often, however, the experience of conversation between theologians and economists is that of people talking past one another; and this is partly because basic attitudes towards epistemic and methodological issues are so different.

OF RATIONALITY AND SCARCITY

Rationality

As we have already noted, one source of possible substantive disagreement revolves around differing assumptions about human nature. In the case of economics it is useful to distinguish two features of so-called 'economic man': the assumption of rationality; and the assumption of predominant self-interest. The former concerns the *structure* of preferences; the latter concerns the *content* of preferences.

Before proceeding with rational self-interest, we must note the most controversial aspect of the economist's construction: their usual assumption that all individuals are basically the *same*. David Levy and Sandra Peart (2005) have shown that 'analytical egalitarianism' was a standard feature of the economists' approach to social explanation in the 18th and 19th centuries, and it brought them into conflict with an odd variety of bedfellows: eugenicists, conservatives with their belief in natural 'orders of men', and moralists. For moralists it seemed clear that even if 'all have fallen short', some had fallen shorter than others. The distinction between 'good' people and 'bad', between the virtuous and the vicious, appears to have been something that neither theologians nor moral philosophers were prepared to relinquish. The economists' standard simplifying assumption seemed to many to destroy any scope for the moral distinctions they deemed indispensable.

However, it is doubtful whether either motivational uniformity or predominant self-interest lies deep within the Lakatosian 'hard core' of the economists' research programme, though both are widely practised simplifications. The idea that some people might be more trustworthy, more benevolent or more creative than others would do no great violence to economic models – especially if trustworthiness, benevolence or creativity could be shown to have some place within the division of labour. And provided economic actors have *some* preference for their own individual well-being, the economistic doctrine that 'incentives matter' in social affairs would not disappear. Economic incentives would still play a significant role in altering behaviour 'at the margin'.

But though neither predominant self-interest nor motivational homo-geneity is indispensable, the same cannot be said for the assumption of rationality. Rationality, for the economist, is 'core business'. As understood by economists it comes in a variety of forms and performs a variety of tasks. Most forms derive from a Humean conception in which there are three basic categories: action, desire and belief. An agent is said to be rational if his actions are such as to maximize the satisfaction of his desires, given his beliefs. So action can be thought of as pursuit of agents' purposes (things most desired). In practice, desires are usually aggregated and repre-sented in terms of *preferences*; and the language of economics mostly pro-ceeds in terms of 'preference satisfaction'. Moreover, the role of beliefs is usually backgrounded in the economics story, though it is presumed that agents will acquire 'rational' amounts of information: amounts that reflect the expected benefits and costs of (further) acquisition.

Furthermore, rationality is interpreted to impose a certain structure on preferences: that they be complete, transitive and convex. Thus, for any choice options X and Y, *completeness* requires one of: X is preferred to Y; *or* Y preferred to X; *or* the agent is indifferent. Incommensurability is excluded. *Transitivity* requires that if X is not preferred to Y, and Y is not preferred to Z, then X cannot be preferred to Z. Finally, *convexity* implies that if the cost of X in terms of Y forgone increases, one will consume less X: demand curves 'slope downwards'. It is this third assumption that does most of the predictive work in economics: changes in relative prices (incen-tives) lie at the core of economists' explanations of changes in behaviour.

It is worth noting that these are *structural* conditions on preference. They make no supposition as to what the Xs and Ys are. That latter issue is a matter of the 'content' of preferences. And though income (or material well-being) may be one obvious possible X, rationality does not strictly require this. Moreover, these structural properties could be in place without there being any connection between action and desire. Suppose, for example, that A was to choose his consumption bundles according to B's preferences, and B was to choose his according to A's preferences, with both preferences having the stipulated properties. Aggregate behaviour would follow all the standard predictions. All the predicted responses to relative price changes would be observed. But neither A nor B would be getting the bundles of goods that best satisfied his own true preferences (or purposes or desires).

It is worth noting these things because rationality in the Humean sense is not strictly required for much of the economists' predictive work. But rationality in that sense *is* necessary for something else that economists often do: namely, supplying a normative defence of liberal institutions such as markets and democracy, where the fulfilling of agents' preferences is assigned normative weight. Rationality is implicated in the economists' presumptions in favour of the principle of consumer (more generally, individual) 'sovereignty', because if agents are fully rational then they will be perfect judges of their own interests/purposes/desires. They will routinely choose options that they believe will make their lives go best for them, given their beliefs about the consequences of their actions.

This idea seems alien to Christian notions of human nature. Theologians may therefore accept the assumption that human action exhibits a certain kind of abstract structure (rationalized as maximizing a 'utility function') but flatly deny any presumption that the fulfilment of individuals' desires/purposes has any normative weight at all. The position of theology is surely that humans are not 'rational' at all in our sense. They do not do what they have most reason to do. Their desires do not reflect their true interest. Their actual behaviour has no presumptive normative authority. Man is sinful. Agents know what they *ought* to do, but they do something else. And although human ability for self-deception is not to be underestimated, agents are aware of this. As St Paul puts it: 'That which I would not, that I do. And that which I would, I do not!'

The most natural way of construing the theological picture in 'utility function' terms is by reference to meta-preferences and weakness of will. But though these have played some role in economics from Adam Smith to Frank Knight and Amartya Sen, the idea is decidedly non-mainstream. The standard formulation of the 'fundamental theorems of welfare economics', for example, implies full rationality on the part of all.

One might, to be sure, defend liberal institutions on the safer ground that although agents' actions are far from a perfect reflection of their true interests, individuals are better judges of those interests than politicians, bureaucrats or even theologians. Moreover, even if this were not the case, the impossibility that any ruler or government could obtain the information necessary to implement its putatively benevolent designs must count strongly against all paternalistic policy.

These considerations can produce a genuine clash between economics and theology. Proponents of the latter are justifiably sceptical about human rationality. Proponents of the former are justifiably sceptical about human knowledge.

Scarcity

Rational choice implies scarcity. We have to choose A rather than B because we can't have both. 'Political œconomy', once the science of wealth, gradually mutated in the century after Malthus into 'economics', the science of scarcity. By the 1930s it had become 'the science which studies human behaviour as a relationship between given ends and scarce means which have alternative uses' (Robbins, 1932). Though some economists such as Whately and James Buchanan, following Adam Smith, have preferred to think of the science as 'catallactics', exchange itself implies scarcity. We give up some of our B in order to get more of your A because for us (though not for you) B is less scarce than A.

Scarcity is thus the relation of *resources* to *wants*, and because of the latter is inescapably subjective. It is very often open to us to deal with scarcity simply by reducing our wants. Saints of many religions have taught that happiness lies therein. Nevertheless, because we inhabit a finite world, some choices always have to be made by all. And as economists have long recognized, some of these are 'tragic' in the sense that they can only be a choice between evils. Scarcity is thus a cause of physical or moral evil, or both (Walsh, 1961).

Scarcity may result not only from the inordinate wants of some, but from the moderate wants of many. In Malthus's original formulation, scarcity becomes a major social problem because of increasing population and relatively fixed food-producing resources. Poverty for some is therefore inevitable. Malthus's proposal to ameliorate this by voluntary restriction of procreation was the original cause of the 'bitter quarrel'.

Many theologians are uneasy with the economists' conception of scarcity for at least three reasons. First, scarcity is a nasty example of the 'problem of evil'. Why did God create a world in which many, perhaps most, of his creatures are doomed to a Darwinian 'struggle for existence'? Malthus's partial solution had always appeared blasphemous to some; and a learned Dominican (Barerra, 2005) lately constructed a theodicy of scarcity that completely ignores population control as a remedy for world poverty.

Second, the success of the early-19th-century Anglican economists' theodicy of scarcity was achieved at the cost of a bland acceptance of inequality, which they justified as a necessary incentive to socially useful behaviour. This offends the sensibilities of many present-day theologians, for whom inevitable poverty and a permanently stratified society are inconsistent with the Christian Gospel.

Third and most seriously, ineluctable scarcity in human affairs is an affront to a central Christian conviction: that the new life in Christ transcends all the limitations of time and space in which we now exist. When Christ fed the multitude with a few loaves and fishes he taught thereby that God has liberated us from scarcity, or at any rate will do so very soon. This world *ought not* to be a place in which we are constrained by physical limits. The economists' untroubled acquiescence in scarcity, and their elaborate calculus of our rational response to it, has outraged Christian Romantics from the first. As Wordsworth put it: 'High Heaven rejects the lore/Of nicely calculated less or more'. Romanticism has been described as 'a revolt against the finite' (Lovejoy, 1941, pp. 263–4); and though by no means all Christian theologians are or have been Romantic in the modern period, the hope or belief that scarcity can and will be transcended is an important determinant of every theologian's 'angle of vision'. An influential American theologian has written of *The Beauty of the Infinite* (Hart, 2003).

Since the economists' angle of vision necessarily excludes the infinite, there must always remain – at some levels of discourse – an unavoidable clash between economics and Christian theology.

6. Economics as identity

Gordon Menzies

Events in the closing decades of the 20th century – notably the political success of the Reagan and Thatcher administrations and the end of the Cold War – provided a boost to market economics[1] in academia. Out on the street, market economics has become – along with democracy and sexual freedom – the ideology of choice for the masses.[2]

Yet support for market economics is not universal. The opponents of globalization and microeconomic reform are always on the lookout for adverse outcomes for particular groups – the invisible workers of the Third World, the Western unemployed and the culturally dislocated. This is partly due to their perception that the benefits of economic change are not shared around. Or, to put it the way an economist might, they suspect that potential Pareto improvements are not routinely turned into actual Pareto improvements.[3]

Important as economic outcomes are, however, it would be a mistake to suppose that they are the sole cause of the residual unease with market economics. Like all social arrangements that organize consumption and production, market economics has an *identity-moulding* function. Any economic system can potentially provide us with the table, chairs and coffee to be with our friends. But it will also influence how we think and talk about ourselves – our identity – when we are with our friends. Could it be that some unease with market economics comes from a resistance to being pressed into the mould of 'economic man'?

Some economists ignore identity because they admire the scientific objectivity of behaviourism. This is the branch of psychology that explains behaviour by response to external stimuli ('conditioning'), rather than beliefs, emotions or intentions. Behaviourism has the supposed scientific advantage that stimuli are objectively observable in a way that beliefs, emotions and intentions are not. A concept like identity is not easily observed and is therefore easy for admirers of behaviourism to dismiss.[4]

Other economists are not so sure. Akerlof and Kranton (2000) point out that branches of psychology, sociology, political science, anthropology and history have all adopted identity as a central concept and ask why economics could not do the same. They suggest that group identity might have significant explanatory power for economic analysis.

An alternative way to put identity centre stage in economics is to consider the possibility that economic theory might influence personal identity, either directly or indirectly, through the uptake of market economics. The direct effect of market economics on identity is most likely to be felt by those who undertake training in economics. Although it is cast in terms of behaviour rather than identity (as is inevitable, given the behaviourist-envy of economists), Frank, Gilovich and Regan (1993) find that training in microeconomics teaches people to be less cooperative.[5] Economics encourages the view that people are self-interested, which leads people to believe that others will not cooperate in social settings. This, in turn, encourages people not to cooperate if they believe others will not. A qualifier is that economists do not necessarily see conflicts as 'zero-sum games' (the gains of one person must equal the collective losses of all other parties), and so economists may be more enlightened problem-solvers in fact.[6]

An indirect effect of market economics is flagged by Becker (1981, p. 303): 'If I am correct that altruism dominates family behaviour perhaps to the same extent that selfishness dominates market transactions, then altruism is much more important in economic life than is commonly understood'. If Becker is correct, a society that substitutes market production for household production – as Western society has done over the late-20th century – will experience a greater orientation towards selfishness. Again, it is hard to imagine an economist thinking of selfishness in terms of identity but it is not that hard to do.

Unlike economics, social contract theory has described the dangers of absorbing too much of 'economic man' into identity. Gauthier (1986) is a staunch advocate for the model of economic man and his 'morals by agreement' is based on enlightened self-interest. Yet even he is concerned about the prevalence of economic identity:

> In so far as the idea of economic man is part of our way of understanding ourselves, part of our idea of what it is to be human . . . then the rational bonds of morals by agreement may be too weak to hold us. We need exorcism [of economic man] in addition to argument. But that I have no power to provide. (Gauthier, 1986, p. 317, cited in Evans, 2004, p. 278)

In view of the above, it does not seem unnatural to me to assert that the ascendancy of market economics, both in academia and on the street, could itself explain some perceptions of human identity in market economies.

This chapter seeks to clarify what 'the idea of economic man' – the economic identity that Gauthier is so afraid of – looks like. Since I am writing as a Christian, I compare the identity of economic man with a model of Christian identity.

Fortunately, there is a natural way to make the comparison. Both economics and Christianity have a long-standing tradition of representative agents. The representative agent in economics is 'economic man', invented by John Stuart Mill (1844). The Bible also has its representative agents, an example being the Apostle Paul's reference to each human person being 'in Adam' or 'in Christ' in 1 Corinthians 15.[7] Let me therefore arrange a meeting between 'theological man' and Mill's 'economic man'.[8] The rest of the chapter takes the form of a Platonic dialogue about their respective identities.

SCENE 1: ECONOMIC MAN AND THEOLOGICAL MAN INTRODUCE THEMSELVES

Economic Man is sitting on a bench. His appearance is androgynous. He is reading John Stuart Mill (1844) 'On the Definition of Political Economy'. A woman comes and sits down on the bench: she is Theological Man.

Theological Man: Hello – er – that looks like an interesting book.
Economic Man: Yes, it was a birthday present.
Theological Man: I see (*pause – she is confused by his androgynous appearance*). If you don't mind my asking . . . how old are you?
Economic Man: I was born in the Enlightenment. By the way, my name is Economic Man.
Theological Man: Nice to meet you (*they shake hands*). My name is Theological Man.
Economic Man (*taken aback*): Well . . . I mean . . . you don't look like a man.
Theological Man: Neither do you.
Economic Man: I'm not supposed to; I am a construct whose attributes are applicable to either gender. I am completely rational, my preferences never change and I thrive on mathematical calculation.
Theological Man: Are you *sure* you're gender neutral? Anyway, I'm fictitious too. I am a theological model based on Scriptural statements but I'm not androgynous. 'Human beings exist in an irreducible duality of male and female; there are no generic human beings, only male and female human beings' (Volf, 1996, p. 183).[9]
Economic Man: It *does* sound a little old fashioned to use a gender-inclusive 'man', so I would find our conversation a little more . . . er . . . modern if we could do something about our names. John Stuart Mill made me up, so why don't you call me John?

Theological Man: Fine. There are plenty of Marys in the Bible; why don't you call me Mary? (*John nods,*) Why don't you tell me about yourself, Econ . . . er . . . John?
John: I was introduced by John Stuart Mill in 1836:[10]

> What is now commonly understood by the term 'Political Economy' . . . makes entire abstraction of every other human passion or motive except those which may be regarded as perpetually antagonizing principles to the desire of wealth, namely, aversion to labour, and desire of the present enjoyment of costly indulgences. . . . Political Economy considers mankind as occupied solely in acquiring and consuming wealth; and aims at showing what is the course of action into which mankind, living in a state of society, would be impelled, if that motive, except in the degree in which it is checked by the two perpetual counter-motives averted to, were absolute ruler of all their actions . . . Not that any political economist was ever so absurd as to suppose that mankind are really thus constituted, but because this is the mode in which science must necessarily proceed. When an effect depends upon a concurrence of causes, those causes must be studied one at a time, and their laws separately investigated, if we wish, through the causes, to obtain the power of either predicting or controlling the effect . . . With respect to those parts of human conduct of which wealth is not even the principal object, to these Political Economy does not pretend that its conclusions are applicable. But there are also certain departments of human affairs, in which the acquisition of wealth is the main and acknowledged end. It is only of these that Political Economy takes notice. The manner in which it necessarily proceeds is that of treating the main and acknowledged end as if it were the sole end; which, of all hypotheses equally simple, is the nearest to the truth . . . This approximation is then to be corrected by making proper allowance for the effects of any impulses of a different description, which can be shown to interfere with the result in any particular case . . . the conclusions of Political Economy will so far fail of being applicable to the explanation or prediction of real events, until they are modified by a correct allowance for the degree of influence exercised by the other cause.

Mary: Let me see if I understand this. You are, if I may say so, a fictional construct – Mill states plainly it would be absurd to think otherwise. But you exist in order to understand only those parts of human conduct whose end is primarily the accumulation of wealth. To use Blaug's (1993) phrase, economic man 'abstracts twice': all those actions not connected with the pursuit of money income are outside your domain; and the other motives in 'money-making' activities are ignored so that the effects of your acquisitiveness – checked by your love of current consumption and your dislike of work – can be isolated.
John: That's right. Mill wrote before the development of econometrics, or experimental economics, so he lacked these more recent means of controlling other factors in a scientific investigation.
Mary: But Mill didn't have the last word, did he? Robbins (1932) veered away from what he called a *classificatory* definition of economics – such

as Mill's income maximization subject to wanting leisure and current consumption – towards what he called an *analytic* definition of economics. The analytic definiton 'does not attempt to pick out certain kinds of behaviour, but focuses attention on a particular aspect of behaviour, the form imposed by the influence of scarcity' (Blaug, 1993, pp. 16–17). Robbins describes 'economic science' by four statements: first, humans desire various ends; second, the time and means of achieving these ends are limited and capable of alternative application; third, ends have different importance; and fourth, the economist studies the disposal of scarce means to achieve competing ends (ibid., pp. 12–13).

John: This debate to define the proper limits of economics continues to this day and it has a dynamic relationship to the way in which the literature unfolds. I like Mill's observation that the definition of a science usually follows the creation of science itself: 'Like the wall of a city, it has usually been erected, not to be a receptacle for such edifices as might afterwards spring up, but to circumscribe an aggregate already in existence'.[11] So I need to tell you about two people who tried to move the wall even further out than Robbins did. Friedman (1953) argued that the test of a good model is its ability to predict, even if the assumptions appear unrealistic. Friedman's idea allows theorists to use me in an astonishing variety of contexts, which would have been ruled inappropriate by Mill, so long as the model predicts something. One example you might be interested in, Mary, is an economic explanation of the Protestant Reformation by Ekelund, Hebert and Tollison (2002)[12] (*Mary raises her eyebrows*). Alongside Friedman is Gary Becker (1981). He won a Nobel Prize for extending economic applications into areas such as marriage, divorce and child-bearing. His economic methodology, namely, 'maximizing behaviour, market equilibrium, stable preferences, used relentlessly and unflinchingly' (Becker, 1976) could, in his view, be applied to *any* area of human endeavour. So some later thinkers disagree profoundly with Mill, who was relatively humble about the scope of economics.

Mary: In fact, I noticed at the end of the quote from Mill that he said any economic analysis should involve a correction of the 'approximation' before it has any hope of explaining a real event. That is even more humble.

John: But if my motives are the most important ones in a given situation – and he said that political economy should not be applied otherwise – then an explanation *is* offered, albeit an approximate one, by *only* considering what I would do.

Mary: Do you think a classificatory definition still holds sway?

John: The winner of the 1984 Nobel Prize in Economics, Sir Richard Stone, seems to have used it when he said, 'The three pillars on which an analysis of society ought to rest are studies of economic, socio-demographic and environmental phenomena' (Stone and Corbit, 1997, p. 5). Environmental phenomena are affected by scarcity, so why would he have separated it from economic phenomena if he were using Robbins's wide–ranging definition? Most public servants use Mill's definition too. Everyone knows that an *economic* policy department is one that concerns itself with Mill's concerns. A department of arts and culture would not normally be called an economic policy department. Going more broadly, I think Mill is alive in the popular consciousness (*Mary looks puzzled*). What I mean is that different kinds of behaviour are observed in situations involving money transactions compared with situations involving ethical norms. There is some research into switching between monetary and ethical valuations and it goes by the name of 'motivation crowding'. Gneezy and Rustichini (2000) noted that when a crèche in Israel introduced a fine for parents who were late in collecting their children, the number of late collections increased markedly. The interpretation they gave was that the institution of a payment for late collection changed the attitudes of the parents. Previously, late collection had been understood to be bad behaviour but once there was a price the parents worked to a different calculus. Frey and Oberholzer-Gee (1997) found that the willingness of Swiss citizens to accept the location of a nuclear facility in their neighbourhood fell sharply once compensation was offered. The point of these studies is that introducing prices changes the frame of reference by which behaviour is determined.[13]

Mary: But why should academic economists care about the opinions of ordinary people!? Most ordinary people don't understand Einstein's relativity theory.

John: I thought you admired Mill's humility! (*Mary looks uncomfortable.*) I am not saying that academics have to believe uncritically everything ordinary people say. What I am saying is that ordinary people are the *objects of study* of social scientists. And if their beliefs lead to actions, social scientists are obliged to explain these actions as best they can. If the change in frames – between a price-dominated one and an ethical one – is a real social phenomenon, it ought to be of interest to at least one branch of the social sciences. And the most natural science for this purpose is economics. That is, economics conceived of in the way that Mill did.

Mary: Can we move to another point? You said earlier that you were always rational, and I've heard other people say that you maximize 'utility'. What do these terms mean?

John: At a minimum, they mean that I can hold a preference over two states of the world, *x* and *y*, and consistently reveal that preference through

time. My personal utility is then defined as simply a numerical representation of this preference – a mathematical function – assigning a
higher utility index to a preferred alternative (Sen, 1977).

Mary: With this set of definitions, you can hardly escape maximizing your
own utility.[14] If you are consistent, then 'no matter whether you are a
single-minded egoist or a raving altruist or a class-conscious militant,
you will appear to be maximizing your own utility in this enchanted
world of definitions' (ibid., p. 323).

John: I can see your utility function has many arguments. But I've talked
long enough; why don't you tell me about yourself?

Mary: Before I do, I want to ask you something important.

John: What is it?

Mary: What would a world look like if it was entirely composed of people
who had your identity?

John: Well, if we use the definition of Robbins, Friedman and Becker, it
would look pretty much as it is now. Since everyone is, by definition,
maximizing utility, everyone has my identity. Perhaps it would be a more
stable place than it is now, since people do seem to violate the assumption of stable preferences.

Mary: Might be a bit boring, I suppose, but anti-globalization protesters
or the opponents of microeconomic reform can hardly be so scared of
becoming more . . . er . . . stable.

John: Many of these people use Mill's definition, I think, and his horror
expressed in the phrase 'Not that any political economist was ever so
absurd as to suppose that mankind are really thus constituted'. A world
where people were only concerned about money-making is the world
they want to avoid. But, anyway, I've answered your question, and I
won't let you avoid telling me about yourself any longer.

Mary: Alright, you began by quoting Mill, so I am going to start with some
biblical texts. I hope you don't mind, but because there is a double
meaning of Adam in Genesis – a single man and mankind – I will use
the English 'man' sometimes to mean mankind (*John acquiesces by
nodding*):

Genesis 1:26–28
26 Then God said, 'Let us make man in our image, in our likeness, and let them
rule over the fish of the sea and the birds of the air, over the livestock, over all
the earth, and over all the creatures that move along the ground.'
27 So God created man in his own image, in the image of God he created him;
male and female he created them.
28 God blessed them and said to them, 'Be fruitful and increase in number; fill
the earth and subdue it. Rule over the fish of the sea and the birds of the air and
over every living creature that moves on the ground.'

Genesis 2:7
[T]he LORD God formed the man from the dust of the ground and breathed into his nostrils the breath of life, and the man became a living being.[15]

Man is a special animal. On the one hand, he is firmly part of the natural world – formed from the dust. That is one reason why the sciences that emphasize continuity with the animal kingdom work as well as they do – medical science being the best example. But man is also made in the image of God, so that 'man cannot be understood or explained completely in terms of categories taken from "the world"' (John Paul II, 1979).

John: I've heard the phrase 'image of God' before but I don't understand it.

Mary: On a common sense level, obvious differences between humans and animals could possibly indicate what the image might be. Things like sophisticated language, self-awareness, ability to enter relationships and highly developed feelings could all be part of the story. But Gunton (1992) disputes this approach, arguing that the image of God is to be understood relationally, rather than in terms of fixed characteristics like reason or will.[16] Sherlock (1996) says a similar thing, and focuses on relationship 'upwards' to God, comprising obedience and praise, and the relationship 'downward' to the rest of creation, comprising dominion and the task of gaining sustenance. Evans (1979) focuses on the epistemological and existential dependence on God that this image implies. Though human images are used in Scripture to describe God (for example, in Genesis 2 or the phrase 'heavenly father'), an adequate understanding of man proceeds from an adequate understanding of God, not vice versa. Man is God's creation. Not only does he originate with God but God sustains him moment by moment (Colossians 1:17). Without God, man is literally nothing. Another key idea is that, under God, man is supposed to care for the creation – this is the theme of stewardship that features prominently in the economic principles of Hay (1989).[17]

John: But if we understand humanity by understanding God, how do you explain the moral lapses of humanity – for example, environmental degradation?

Mary: The Fall is a key doctrine here. The judgment for disobedience is a kind of 'un-creating' – humanity suffers a broken relationship with God, with other human beings (for example, Cain killing Abel in Genesis 4) and with the environment.[18] Through physical death, man unravels and returns to the dust (Genesis 3:19). It might even be conjectured that fallen man is closer to nature – to dust – than he would have been without the Fall, and so the more cynical views of humanity (present company included) may have greater explanatory power than they would otherwise have. Incidentally, the Fall illustrates that man has the ability to choose between good and evil, to some extent,[19] and that humans are held accountable for their actions – theological man is a responsible agent.

John: This is a long way from where I am coming from, but before we debate some points, you had better spell out any other relevant features of theological man.

Mary: OK, there are two in particular. First, humans are members of a *mishpaha* (Hebrew: *family*). Family can be as wide as a nation or as small as the immediate family. It can be contemporary or through time. The communal nature of human life is a strong biblical theme, without which a book like 1 Corinthians would not make sense.[20] The communal nature of human life means that we are all implicated, in some mysterious way, in cinema-scale evil such as the Inquisition or the Holocaust.

John: And I thought economics was the 'dismal science'! What was the last thing you wanted to say about yourself?

Mary: Crucially, the whole of the New Testament is devoted to the reversal – partly present, partly future – of the Fall. This reversal – it is called redemption – occurs when individuals choose to make Jesus their Lord and Saviour. The biblical account of redeemed man is that they have been granted a new stature due to the activity of Christ. Sherlock (1996) sees this new man as being caught up in the divine initiatives of Christ's reconciliation of man to God, his reconciliation of all nations, classes and genders and his reconciliation of the whole material universe to God. These are yet to be completed but have begun with the coming of Christ. While waiting for the completion of God's plans, Christians are to witness the crucified and risen Christ, and live a life worthy of their new status (Ephesians 4).

John: I'm not sure I understand all of this but let me ask you: what would the world look like if everyone had your identity?

Mary: Well, I'm afraid that's a little hard to answer. As you might have gathered from what I said, the work of Christ in creating a new humanity (or 'man' if you will) does not apply to everyone automatically. There are really two types of people – those in Adam, who have not entered a relationship with God, and those in Christ, who have. A world where everyone is 'in Adam' is described by Paul in Romans 1 (18ff.); and a world where everyone is in Christ is the future hope of Christians – the resurrection to a new humanity.

John: I see. Your anthropology really contains two types then (*Mary nods*). I'll have to keep this in mind as we dialogue.

SCENE 2: THEY BEGIN A CONVERSATION

Act 1: Is John a Behaviourist?

John: You've told me a lot about yourself, Mary, even though I don't pretend to understand it all. I suggest we ask each other some questions to try to get at our essential identities.

Mary: Alright, I want to ask you about how economics relates to behaviourism. You will recall that this is the branch of psychology that explains behaviour as a response to external stimuli ('conditioning'), rather than beliefs, emotions or intentions. What is really interesting to me is how this focus on external observable phenomena, and this discarding of mental events, seems to lurk within economics.[21] Listen to Becker (1981) sidestep the whole question of motivation for altruism in *A Treatise on the Family*:

> Since an altruist maximizes his own utility . . . he might be called selfish, not altruistic, in terms of utility . . . I am giving a definition of altruism that is relevant to behavior – to consumption and production choices – rather than giving a philosophical discussion of what 'really' motivates people. (Becker, 1981, p. 279)

The quotes around 'really' are striking; the implication is that motivation per se is imponderable, or even meaningless. It's the sort of thing a behaviourist would say. Even a highly innovative article on identity displays the same tendency (Akerlof and Kranton, 2000). When talking about their utility function that incorporates identity, they say that the opinions of others are revealed through actions. Why don't they admit the possibility of hearing opinions through speech! Behaviourist-envy again . . .

John: Why do you care about this?

Mary: Within a theological framework, the deep thoughts of people are significant – in fact eternally so, for they will be one of the criteria used in God's judgment. And the important biblical notion of the 'heart' is connected to thought.[22] Listen to Mark 7:21: 'for from within, out of the heart of men, proceed evil thoughts, adulteries, fornications, murders, thefts, covetousness, wickedness, deceit, lewdness, and evil eye, blasphemy, pride, foolishness'. These real phenomena include both inward attitudes (e.g., pride) and outward actions (e.g., adultery). It is impossible to square the seriousness given to motives and thoughts in the Scriptures with their supposed irrelevance within behaviourism and, by implication, economics.

John: But you have misunderstood modern economics! Rational choice theory (assuming agents have consistent preferences) *does* have a role for mental events. My consistent ordering of alternatives – my preferences – could very well be a function of the kind of mental events that behaviourists dismiss.

Mary: Alright, I admit rational choice does make a step in the right direction here. It is not as bad as classic behaviourism.

John: Thanks.

Mary: But I am afraid that I am still not satisfied (*John rolls his eyes*). The presumption that the most useful scientific explanations of personal action can be found without ever asking the agents concerned seems very odd. The economic assumption is that people choose what they want (they 'maximize utility') and nothing more is gained by asking them about their actions. Sen (1977) argues persuasively that a lot could be gained from delving into motivation. In particular, he argues that sometimes people act against their interests due to their commitments. This point is lost on economists because of a linguistic sleight-of-hand with the word 'preference':

> The characteristic of commitment with which I am most concerned here is the fact that it drives a wedge between personal choice and personal welfare, and much of traditional economic theory relies on the identity of the two. This identity is sometimes obscured by the ambiguity of the term 'preference', since the normal use of the word permits the identification of preference with the concept of being better off, and at the same time it is not quite unnatural to define 'preferred' as 'chosen'. I have no strong views on the 'correct' use of the word 'preference', and I would be satisfied as long as both uses are not simultaneously made, attempting an empirical assertion by virtue of two definitions. (Sen, 1977, p. 329)

John: So, given this tendency towards behaviourism, what do you think of my identity?

Mary: It reminds me of the story about the economist who was put in charge of an orchestra. He sacked the 2nd violins because they already had 1st violins, and then he cut out all the repeats in music because he put a dollar value on all the 'wasted' time by the audience. That story is usually told to emphasize the obsession of economists with efficiency but it also says something about the kinds of interests a quasi-behaviourist has. Someone who trivializes beliefs, emotions or intentions is hardly likely to 'get' what constitutes human culture.

John: I think we are back to the question of the proper limits of economics. The narrower its goals, the less it may matter if theorists 'get' human culture in a deep way.

Mary: I agree with that.

Act 2: Can Mary Live in the Modern World?

John: I want to ask you a question now, Mary. What do you think of the Enlightenment – I mean the whole social science enterprise? All the stuff you quoted earlier is pretty ancient and . . . well, a lot has happened in the last few hundred years. I guess I want to know if your 'in Christ' identity turns you into a Luddite![23] Can you live in the modern world?

Mary: Theologians try not to be taken up with the latest fad – they don't dismiss all thinking prior to the Enlightenment. Stott says tradition '[gives] votes to the most obscure of all classes, our ancestors'. He then quotes Harry Blamires: 'If you accept the "one man, one vote" principle for the Christian church, the pollsters will have to do most of their sampling in heaven' (Edwards and Stott, 1988, p. 84)[24] (*John looks offended at all this*). But I am not opposed to science – just because I value pre-Enlightenment thinking doesn't mean I despise post-Enlightenment thinking. Since all truth belongs to God (Holmes, 1977), I value it wherever I find it.

John: But that doesn't answer my question; what criteria are you using to decide if a social science is providing you truth? Isn't it right that you have an overriding commitment to theological truth? Doesn't that mean that you wouldn't accept sound scientific judgment if it conflicted with what you believed the Scriptures said?

Mary: It's interesting the way you phrased the question; the implication is that I would find quite frequently that my worldview was being thrown into question by science. Religious believers are by no means the only thinkers with loose ends and unanswered questions. If you were to be honest, you'd admit that economists have a few too.

John: We do not!

Mary: Really? Imagine saying that it doesn't matter if assumptions are wrong as long as a model predicts well (Friedman, 1953). So you believe in Ptolemaic astronomy, do you!?

John: (*grudgingly*) Well, the Copernican system predicted some things better, which is all that Friedman required. But I do see your point – it is odd to regard a theory as being *completely* untainted by assumptions you know to be patently untrue (Hay, 1989).

Mary: Rather than presuming I would have lots of conflicts with 'sound scientific judgment', I think it would be better to talk about what constitutes such judgments. You're right that I'm not an uncritical fan of the Enlightenment.[25] I think it burdened Western thought with a particularly narrow conception of what real knowledge is, which can be summarized by two theses. 'Scientism' says that science gives us *ultimate* truth about *all* reality, and the 'unity of science' thesis defines science in a very narrow sense, namely, there is *one genuine scientific method* and it consists in giving us *impersonal* causal explanations, which lead to *testable propositions*. Here is how Evans (1979) breaks down scientism and the unity of science theses into four propositions:

Scientism
1a   Science gives us truth about the whole of reality.
1b   Science gives us ultimate truth about those realities it describes.

Unity of science thesis
2a   There is one method that all genuine sciences employ.
2b   This method consists of giving impersonal causal explanations, which are empirically testable (positivism).

You're correct that revelation has an impact on my general approach. In particular, I cannot accept all these propositions bundled together. To accept scientism, I would need to define theology as a science (thereby rejecting the unity of science thesis). Or, to accept the unity of science thesis, I would have to limit the scope or ultimate nature of science (thereby rejecting scientism). This is all because I regard biblical revelation as real; and even though my theological theories are imperfect models of it, I take them very seriously. Evans says I can be a *limiter* of science by rejecting 1a or 1b or a *humanizer* of science by rejecting 2a or 2b.

If I reject 1a, I am saying that there are some 'off-limit' areas for economics. This could mean that I accept a classificatory definition, like Mill, and completely discount what it says of, say, the Protestant Reformation. If I reject 1b, I am saying that economics may give us some truth about everything but maybe not ultimate truth. I could say that an economic analysis of the Protestant Reformation might have some value, without a prior commitment that it has *much* value.

If I reject 2a, I am saying that the positivistic account of science is appropriate for some sciences but not others. Surely you would be the first to agree with me that economics *is* different to physics and chemistry? It is one thing to ask for impersonal explanations of chemical reactions but quite another to ask for impersonal explanations of persons! But I would go further than you. I would want to allow for revelation to inform some issues that lie close to core Christian doctrines. So, if I went down this path, I could accept scientism (1a and 1b) but I would have to claim theology as a science. By the way, this needn't mean a wholesale transformation of all received scientific wisdom. I agree with Holmes (1977, p. 51): 'not all matters are equally closely related to central issues of Christian belief or unbelief. Mathematics is more remote than political science, political science than ethics and ethics than theology. Within each of these disciplines, likewise, there are degrees of proximity to central issues'.

In my opinion 'economics' deserves the same ranking as 'politics' in the above quote – the corpus of economics is generally less impacted by biblical revelation than ethics is (or should be) but economics should be more impacted by biblical revelation than pure mathematics.

Finally, if I reject 2b, I am saying that the positivist account doesn't even work for the physical sciences (Blaug, 1993). So, you might find that I accept your 'sound scientific judgment' quite often, though there will doubtless be times that I won't.

John: Can you give me an example of something you'd reject?

Mary: Your sound scientific judgment includes embracing Hume's fact/value distinction, which is loosely the positive/normative split in economics. The idea is that positive economics tells you what 'is' (say, what the level of gross domestic product [GDP] is and how it could be increased) and normative economics tells you what 'ought' to be the case (how high GDP *should* be). I want to criticize the fact/value distinction along two dimensions. First, Blaug (ibid.) says all facts are theory-laden to some extent. To use GDP as an example, the original national accounting schemes were strongly influenced by Keynes's writing, which in turn focused on aggregate expenditure because he was concerned about high unemployment. Had Keynes written in an era where environmental degradation was seen to be more important than unemployment, it is likely that the national income measures would have included environmental externalities, and been very different as a result. On the second dimension, when you move closer to core Christian doctrines, you are moving into a realm where ethical, spiritual and relational 'facts' have prominence, so the Enlightenment distinction is in error, perhaps badly so. The personal or social goal of increasing command over resources[26] is potentially idolatrous, according to Scripture. It follows from this 'fact' that those 'in Adam' will easily find themselves worshipping it. If you want to use economic language, you could say that they chronically overvalue the benefits, to the detriment of their families, the environment and, most importantly, of their relationship to God. Why doesn't this 'fact' find its way into the positive analysis? After all, it is part and parcel of the fabric of reality. And while we're on this subject, why can't I assert 'too many people in Africa are destitute' as a fact? If people are bearers of the image of God, doesn't that imply the basic dignity of material sustenance and, if we are created for community, doesn't it imply that we have real factual responsibilities to these people (van Til, 2007)?

John: I'm sorry, Mary, but you just don't understand the fact/value distinction. Its whole usefulness in economics is just to separate the analysis of possibilities, with its attendant policy menu, from decisions about what you do with those choices.

Mary: Well, use that language then! You have to admit that calling something a fact gives it an objective, indubitable edge over a mere value.

John: You haven't convinced me but I just want to clarify something from your discussion about GDP. Don't you care at all about economic efficiency?

Mary: It's true that it doesn't even rate a mention in the biblical narrative (Hay, 1989) but it could be justified under the heading of care for the creation; the flip side, inefficiency, is waste of some form. But if I may be permitted to misquote Jesus, GDP was made for man, not man for GDP.[27]

Act 3: Is John Anti-social?

Mary: John, we need to talk about relationships (*John gets out his pad and starts drawing indifference curves*).[28] Mill did talk about man 'living in a state of society', and that does imply relationships.

John: (*preoccupied*) So?

Mary: One of the casualties of Hume's distinction is that things intrinsic to relationships – values, trust, mutuality – do not really pass as 'facts', and so do not relate to the 'real' or objective world. The Christian point here is that relationships existed prior to any material creation, in the guise of the Trinity (Gunton 1992). So, if relationships are more fundamental even than matter, Hume's distinction starts to look odd.

John: (*looking up*) But what has this got to do with economics?

Mary: Doesn't it strike you as odd that a *social* science has no truly adequate theory of the social? Just look at the articles in the *American Economic Review* on the loss to the economy of gift-giving (Waldfogel, 1993 and Solnik and Hemenway, 1996). These authors compare the recipient's valuation of the gift with the giver's cost and, if it is lower, announce a loss. But gift-giving is a much more complex phenomenon and, to truly understand it, you need to understand relationships. You could even understand giving as a kind of consummation of relationship. C.S. Lewis put it well when describing the eternal rewards of being a follower of Christ:

We must not be troubled by unbelievers when they say that this promise of reward makes the Christian life a mercenary affair. There are different kinds of reward. There is the reward which has no *natural connexion* with the things you do to earn it, and is quite foreign to the desires that ought to accompany those things. Money is not the natural reward of love; that is why we call a man mercenary if he marries a woman for the sake of her money. But marriage is the proper reward for a real lover, and he is not mercenary for desiring it. (Lewis, 1942, p. 1)

So, gifts are more than utility-maximizing trades, and economic analysis is not the best way to understand them.

John: I want to take you to task on this, Mary. Aren't you mixing up an *ideal* world with the *real* world? I mean, you even said yourself that man is 'fallen'. Isn't it possible that gifts *could* be more than trades but they often *are* just trades? If I get another pair of socks from Aunt Harriet, I shall scream.[29]

Mary: That's an important point. My 'in Adam' person could indeed become like this. That makes you a subset of my anthropology in some instances. So, I have to grant you legitimacy for discussing the way the world often is, regrettably, as opposed to the way the world ought to be. This is important, not only for the sake of truthfully describing the world, but also from the point of view of designing wise policy – after all, Jesus did say we should be as wise as serpents and as harmless as doves.[30] Part of being wise like a serpent is seeing motives in a fallen world realistically.

John: All that stuff about the way the world is and ought to be sounds a bit like Hume's is/ought distinction!

Mary: (*sighs*) Alright, I could put what I just said in terms of Hume's distinction. But I still think you're anti-social.

SCENE 3: INTEGRATION IS DISCUSSED

John: Mary, I've been doing some calculations (*he shows her the pad*) and I think we should get married.

Mary: John, it's kind of you to ask . . . but there's a problem.

John: (*puzzling over the diagrams and mathematics*) I . . . I don't think so.

Mary: I'm afraid I've read the literature on the economics of the family. It starts off with Becker espousing altruism but then degenerates into selfish bargaining games (Menzies and Hay, 2007).

John: I'm still not getting it.

Mary: John, I'm sorry. Let me try to explain it this way. Even though I'm prepared to use you, I find you, well, offensive in many ways.

John: We could use each other! It's utility maximizing. Will you, Mary, promise to maximize utility relentlessly and unflinchingly (Becker, 1976) . . .?

Mary: Sorry, no. We'll have to stick to theorizing. After all, you *are* androgynous (*both exit*).

PART III

Christianity and modern business

7. Business as a moral enterprise

Michael J. Miller

When one thinks about business it is rarely within the context of a positive view of the moral life. If morality is discussed, it tends to be focused on scandal and corruption in business or seen as something antithetical, irrelevant or even humorous. Rarely do we hear praise of business as a moral good or as playing a role in the development of one's moral life.

Business is often viewed as a necessary evil, something required to live but generally sullying to the soul, an obstacle to a rich moral life, rather than a constitutive part of it. 'Do business if you must but be wary of its corrupting effects', is a common view shared by Christians and non-Christians alike. In some ways this is understandable given recurring business scandals and the hazard to the soul that the profit motive can be. The Gospels give a clear warning of the dangers of riches, with St Paul going so far as to declare the 'love of money is the root of all evils' (1 Timothy 6:10). Add to this the negative portrayals of business people in television and media, and scandals such as Enron and WorldCom, and it is no wonder that business and morality are seen as incompatible. In his study of Hollywood, Michael Medved showed that since 1970 business people have consistently been portrayed as the villains in movies and television (Lapin, 2002, p. 35). Yet it is not only the media. Even many of the approaches to business ethics and corporate social responsibility (CSR) taught in business schools tend to perpetuate this image by viewing business with suspicion and in need of restraint.

In this chapter I will argue that business not only can be performed in a moral manner but that it is essentially a moral enterprise, a good for society and an opportunity for virtue – even at times heroic virtue. Business benefits society in a myriad of ways, is replete with opportunities for moral growth and plays a role in developing a flourishing human life. Like any moral good, it can be corrupted but it is essentially a worthy undertaking – one in which most people spend a majority of their lives. When one hears about business ethics it is often in the context of 'negative' regulative moral norms – for example, what not to do, or extrinsic activities such as corporate volunteering or donations as promoted by the CSR movement. 'Negative' norms are a necessary element, of course, but rarely does one hear about the moral dimension of business itself. I will attempt to illustrate the moral value of business in both its objective and subjective senses, that is, its economic and social contribution to the common good and the important role it plays in natural human flourishing.

THE PURPOSE AND LEGITIMACY OF BUSINESS

In order to discuss more fruitfully the moral value of business, it will be helpful first to examine the purpose of business. One of the most well-known statements of the role of business comes from the late Milton Friedman who argued that the social responsibility of business is to make profits for shareholders (Friedman, 1970). While the role of shareholders is important and cannot be overlooked, I would argue that Friedman's vision of business is insufficient and one-dimensional. A richer definition has been provided by Peter Drucker, considered the father of management and who was also a Christian. Drucker argues that the purpose of business is to create a customer (Drucker, 1973, p. 61). At first glance, this definition may seem crassly utilitarian but, in light of Drucker's other writings, the notion of creating a customer becomes clearer. It is tied to meeting the needs of others, which requires that the business person be 'other directed' (Sirico, 2001, p. 21). An eminently self-centred business person focused on his own profit would be oblivious of the needs of others and so would be unable to create a customer (see Novak, 1982, 1996; Sirico, 2001). Drucker argues that profit is actually irrelevant to the purpose of business; it is merely a measure of success. This is an important distinction, since profit is the indicator of whether a business is producing goods that meet human needs in a way that utilizes and allocates capital and human resources in an efficient manner. If a firm does not do this, people will not pay for its product and this will force it to adjust in order to meet expectations.[1]

Still, the notion of creating a customer does not sufficiently do justice to the moral nature of business. While Drucker did not ignore the relational, interpersonal and inter-subjective elements of a business, a richer definition of business from an explicitly Christian source that includes these elements and is reflective of the larger Christian tradition can be found in John Paul II's *Centesimus Annus* where he writes:

> [T]he purpose of a business firm is not simply to make a profit, but is to be found in its very existence as a community of persons who in various ways are endeavouring to satisfy their basic needs and who form a particular group at the service of the whole society. Profit is a regulator of the life of a business, but it is not the only one; other human and moral factors must also be considered, which in the

long term are at least equally important for the life of a business. (John Paul II, 1991, 35)

This approach is interesting because it emphasizes a multi-dimensional view that includes the communal and relational aspects. John Paul II places business within a larger context of the human person as a moral agent, and his discussion of business as a 'community of persons' is an important point that has repercussions on the way one views the legitimacy of business in society. His idea is rooted in the natural right of free association found in Leo XIII's *Rerum Novarum* (1891) and in St Thomas Aquinas. This approach is markedly different from the CSR approach, which sees business as receiving its legitimacy from society or the state.

While Catholic social teaching is but one example of Christian reflection on these issues, I have decided to draw from John Paul II for several reasons: his writing is deeply rooted in Scripture and the overall Christian tradition that is accepted by most serious Christians, his role as leader of the Catholic Church gave him a certain stature and authority even among non-Catholic Christians who may disagree on various doctrinal approaches, and finally, because his analysis of work and business are perhaps the most recent systematic reflection by a world-regarded Christian authority.

The Christian tradition views business as a manifestation of a natural right of persons to form an association to achieve some common end. John Paul II sees business as a type of what de Tocqueville ([1835] 2003) called an 'intermediary institution' or what is commonly called civil society. In business, man has the opportunity to live out his freedom and responsibility and to take care of himself and his family while also serving society. It is important to note that the importance of profit is not denied. 'The Church acknowledges the legitimate *role of profit* as an indication that a business is functioning well. When a firm makes a profit, this means that productive factors have been properly employed and corresponding human needs have been duly satisfied' (John Paul II, 1991, 35, italics in original). But it is also emphasized that profit cannot be the only regulator. The fact that one can make a profit from a particular endeavour does not by itself provide sufficient moral legitimacy, nor do decreasing profit margins always justify the laying off of workers or moving a factory. For example, the fact that one can make a profit by selling pornography in no way justifies engaging in such business.

While profit is a legitimate and important factor it is not the sole factor in making business decisions. This is precisely because a business is more than just a profit-making venture; it is a 'community of persons'. John Paul II's discussion of profit and business is one element of his analysis of the market economy in general. He recognizes the value of the market economy but rejects a libertarian view that would idolize choice as the determining factor. A market can produce and distribute goods and services more efficiently and equitably than any other economic system but efficiency and equality are only certain values among others and must be measured within the context of the human person and the backdrop of basic moral goods:

> All of this can be summed up by repeating once more that economic freedom is only one element of human freedom. When it becomes autonomous, when man is seen more as a producer or consumer of goods than as a subject who produces and consumes in order to live, then economic freedom loses its necessary relationship to the human person and ends up by alienating and oppressing him. (Ibid., 39)

This vision of rooting economic freedom in human freedom and the nature of the person is reiterated when he asks whether capitalism is the model that developing countries should adopt. He says that if capitalism means 'an economic system which recognizes the fundamental and positive role of business, the market, private property . . . as well as free human creativity in the economic sector' then the answer is yes; though importantly, he notes it would be more accurate to call this a 'business economy', 'market economy' or 'free economy'. On the other hand, if capitalism means a system in which freedom in the economic sector is not placed 'at the service of human freedom in its totality, and which sees it as a particular aspect of that freedom, the core of which is ethical and religious, then the reply is certainly negative' (ibid., 42).

John Paul II's emphasis on the 'business economy' or 'free economy' is illustrative. He rejects the Marxist terms 'capitalism', which was focused on structures, 'labour' and 'capital' in favour of a vision of economics that is centred on the person. The focus shifts from a mechanistic vision of man where the state plans the economy to a vision of individual persons and groups meeting their own needs through creative private initiative. This creates space and freedom for businesses and other intermediary institutions, thus setting the stage for a flourishing civil society.

There is a tendency when one thinks of civil society to limit it to nongovernmental organizations or private charities, and to exclude business firms or corporations. Businesses, however, are examples of civil society par excellence – private, voluntary associations of persons organized toward a specific end, which also provide a means to satisfy the needs of workers. All of this is of central importance to understanding business as moral enterprise and can have profound practical implications for management and business ethics.

THE ROLE OF BUSINESS IN SOCIETY: BUSINESS AND THE COMMON GOOD

Business makes significant contributions to the common good in several ways. The most obvious is, of course, creating economic value. Businesses not only supply goods and services, they also provide technological innovation that spreads beyond individual firms to other industries, including medical care and agriculture. Entrepreneurship and innovation, both technical and managerial, spur economic growth, create new opportunities and enable more dignified standards of living. Business provides the means for employees to raise a family, save, purchase a home, educate their children, invest in valuable cultural and leisurely pursuits, and generously help the less fortunate (see John Paul II, 1981, 10).[2] Investors in these businesses help create social cohesion by bearing risk, thus enabling salaried workers to think long term, both economically and socially, and become rooted in their communities. All of these things are clearly moral benefits. By creating the wealth necessary to live beyond subsistence, business also contributes to the cultural good of society. The late German philosopher, Josef Pieper, wrote that, 'leisure is the basis of culture' (Pieper, [1948] 1998). However, this leisure can only be attained in an economy where basic needs are met and business is the primary force in accomplishing this.

Yet even these seemingly evident contributions are under-appreciated. Too often people tend to see business through the lens of the economically fallacious zero-sum mentality, which assumes that one person's success and material gain is another person's loss. But this, as the reality of economic growth demonstrates, is clearly not the case. Take the famous example of Bill Gates who made literally billions of dollars producing software that enabled millions of individuals to start companies or save time for other economically productive, cultural or leisurely pursuits. Gates's wealth did not cause poverty; on the contrary, his products created benefits for others. In a commercial society with a proper understanding of abundance, people tend to see others as cooperators, not as threats or combatants for limited resources the way they do in socialist or oligarchic regimes (see Gregg, 2007). A commercial society where business and entrepreneurship are appreciated and widely accessible can help reduce the occasion for envy. Instead of seeing a wealthy person as an object of envy and disdain, people are instead inspired to achieve the same level of success through work and enterprise. The zero-sum fallacy is pervasive even in business schools and especially in the CSR movement with its insistence that businesses need to 'give back' to their communities as if they took something away in the first place. It is ironic that this seems to apply predominantly to business and not to other professions. One rarely hears the call for professors or doctors to give back, though one could argue that professors have more of a debt to society especially if their education was funded by public tax dollars.

While economic value is important, it is only one dimension of the moral nature of business. Just the act of participating in business requires a whole set of virtues that can have positive effects on the soul and be 'transferable' to other parts of life. The ability of business to help people 'grow up' and become responsible members of society is something almost taken for granted, which is why when we see a young man causing trouble we often hear the remark: 'that guy needs a job'. The successful business person will need to develop habits of collaboration, focused attention, punctuality, honesty, dedication, patience, internal discipline and self-control. He or she will need the four cardinal virtues: courage to assume risk and prudence to know how much to risk and when, temperance, fortitude and even the three theological virtues of hope, faith and love especially when dealing with co-workers and customers. Thus, when people learn to work with others at their jobs, it can help them be more collaborative with their families and friends.

Business can be a school of virtue, especially in a market economy where there is competition. This is especially true with the cardinal virtue of prudence, which can be defined as seeing the world as it is and acting accordingly (cf. Pieper, [1966] 1990, pp. 4–8). In a competitive market, if one does not develop the virtue of prudence, he or she will soon be out of business. Business history is replete with examples of people whose imprudence, or inability to diagnose the situation accurately, led to financial loss and even ruin. Prudence in one area of life does not necessarily mean prudence in others, but business does act as a life-teacher, which benefits both the individual and society.

Another important life skill that business teaches is the ability to collaborate. Collaboration can be an occasion for genuine inter-subjectivity, the ability to see another person as a subject, another individual with hopes, wants and needs (cf. Buber, [1923] 1970; Wojytla, 1994). This is a necessary element for the development of a healthy personality and its presence, or lack thereof, has profound impacts on family life, friendship and social stability.

Collaboration contributes to the common good in an intangible manner that is hard to measure but without which society would be worse off. Hittinger uses the example of raising children to illustrate this point. He asks: if it could be shown that the state could raise children better than families, would it be wise for society to institute policies requiring that this be done? Hittinger contends that, if we think instrumentally, the answer might be yes, but if we approach the question in terms of the broader common good, then the answer would be no. If the state took this role, society would lose many intangible benefits to the common good that derive from the fact that parents have to work together to solve their difficulties in an agreeable manner while discovering the best way to train each child. All this would be lost, as would the benefits children receive by having to get along with their siblings and parents. This multitude of interactions contributes, albeit intangibly, to the common good and additionally prepares individuals to contribute as citizens. Hittinger argues that by expanding our analysis beyond the realm of instrumentality we are able to see a myriad of positive contributions to the common good that would otherwise be ignored (see Hittinger, 2003).

This is relevant to the nature of business. Business requires individuals to come out of themselves and 'collide' with other persons from many different backgrounds and nationalities. It requires adaptation, negotiation, compromise, synergy, empathetic listening and seeking to understand the other (see Covey, 1989). All of these skills and habits lead to maturity, and when properly ordered they can have positive effects on personal and family life and play a foundational role in maintaining cohesion and stability, which are so necessary for a healthy society. Business in a global world further helps promote understanding of different cultures and ways of life by putting a human face on others.

It is important to note that all of these benefits – both those to the individual and the common good – are not *extrinsic* to the work of business. In other words, they are not part of a social outreach or CSR programme, but are *intrinsic* (or natural positive externalities) to the nature of doing business. This fact is missed even by many business people who tend to see themselves as contributing to society only when they are engaged in activities extrinsic to the business such as charitable work – or worse, see their charitable work as a type of atonement for their everyday work in business. Charitable work is a good that should be commended and encouraged, but it should be seen as an additional contribution to society, not as their only one.

Many of the contributions of business tend to be overlooked partly because of the propensity to assume that business is essentially a dishonest profession that breeds corruption. While some of this is due to a zero-sum mentality, more is involved. Even Adam Smith, the great promoter of free market economics, had a negative view of the business person (Smith, [1776] 1904, p. 145).[3] Yet Smith's caricature ignores the virtues needed for business and the importance of trust and honesty for long-term success.[4] While moral evil does occur and there are many potential dangers to the moral life, for a corporation to be sustainable in the long term, virtuous, skilful and honest employees are necessary. While dishonest behaviour may provide short-term benefits, in a competitive and transparent economy, the firm will suffer in the long run as the fate of companies like Enron and WorldCom has illustrated.

Aristotle wrote that politics was the noblest profession because it helped the common good and provided the greatest opportunity for both virtue and vice. A similar thing could be said about business with its temptations for easy profit and opportunities for heroic virtue and its ability to serve the common good. It may not be the case that each individual business owner or employee is thoroughly cognizant of all that is occurring both within him or herself and in society when he or she is working (though some are). Still, doing business is a morally good act that generates a host of positive fruits.

WORK IN SCRIPTURE: THEOLOGICAL REFLECTIONS

In the Christian tradition, business has unique moral and spiritual value because it is a type of human work and an element of vocation of the human person. The ability to work belongs to man alone. It is 'one of the characteristics that distinguish man from the rest of the creatures . . . only man works, at the same time by work occupies his existence on earth. Thus, work bears a particular mark of man and of humanity, the mark of a person operating within a community of persons' (John Paul II, 1981, Introduction). While it is commonly believed that the need to work is a result of the Fall, Scripture reveals that work existed in the Garden of Eden.[5] Man is called to tend the garden and be fruitful and multiply. 'Man is the image of God partly through the mandate received from his Creator to subdue, to dominate, the earth. In carrying out this mandate every human being reflects the very action of the creator of the universe' (ibid., 4). Work is a constitutive element of man's personhood; a means by which he lives out his humanity.

Thus, in the first book of the Bible, a central element of man's vocation is laid out before him – to be fruitful and multiply – not only in the procreative sense of raising children but in the sense of taking dominion and stewardship over the earth. Man is called to transform the earth and rule it, not as tyrants, but as 'benevolent kings and queens' (Richards, 2007, Introduction). Man is called to use his intellect to harness the resources of creation and to put it at the service of humanity. He is called not only to transform material resources, but also to use his intellect to create value through better use of information and human resources.[6] Much of the value created by modern business comes precisely from innovations in organization, management, operations and technology. In the modern information economy, much of the wealth is immaterial – it is rooted in knowledge, further reflecting the image of God and the call to take dominion.

The importance and moral significance of hard work is found throughout the Old and New Testaments. The Proverbs are filled with exhortations to be diligent in work. They are filled with praise not only for work in general but for commerce, ingenuity and what today we would call entrepreneurship. They commend the industrious man as wise and warn against sloth, which leads to poverty.[7]

The Gospels further stress the value of work. Jesus says, 'as the father is working so I am working' (John 5:17). Jesus's own life as a carpenter reveals the dignity of labour and he praises work in its many dimensions and uses examples of work to illustrate his teaching. He speaks of the faithful servant 'whose master finds him working when he returns' and, in the oft-quoted parable of the talents, Jesus praises the virtue of diligence, hard work and entrepreneurship. To the servants who were diligent the master says: 'well done, my good and faithful servant. Since you were faithful in small matters, I will give you great responsibilities. Come, share your master's joy' (Matthew 25:21). While this is not the only possible interpretation of this parable, we nevertheless see in the Gospels evidence of Jesus acknowledging the value of work and its ability to build virtue that can be used in both small and big things alike.[8]

The Epistles too are filled with exhortations to work. St Paul, a scholar and a tent-maker, writes that the disciples worked day and night so they would not be a burden. He exhorts the thief to 'no longer steal, but instead do honest work with his own hands so that he has something to share with those in need' (Ephesians 4:28). He encourages the disciples to 'work quietly so they may eat their own bread' and goes so far as to say, 'if anyone is not willing to work, he should not eat' (2 Thessalonians 3:10). The toil of work also plays an important role in sanctification and salvation. Man is called to earn his living by the 'sweat of the brow' and this is to be embraced as part of the Christian understanding of taking up one's daily cross. Work provides an occasion for the person to attach his (or her) successes and his failures, his struggles and tiredness to the redeeming work of Christ for the sanctification of himself and the world (see Escriva, 1997 and Plancher, 2005, p. 281).

I am in no way suggesting a type of 'prosperity gospel' or 'name it, claim it' interpretation of Scripture. While the Bible praises work, it is also filled with stern warnings against attachment to riches and turning money into an idol. 'No one can be a slave of two masters, since either he will hate the one or love the other. You cannot serve both God and Mammon' (Matthew 6:24). The Psalmist says: 'Unless the Lord builds the house those who labour, labour in vain . . . In vain do you get up early and stay up late eating food earned by hard work; certainly he gives sleep to the one He loves' (Psalm 127:1, 2). Work alone does not make man whole and it can easily become an idol. Rest, too, is necessary for a flourishing life. God commands man to observe the Sabbath – a day of worship, a holy day (holiday) whereby man reflects and gives honour to God. The young rich man, who was called by Jesus but who went away sad because he had too many possessions, provides a warning of the dangers riches can be to moral life and salvation. Jesus warns that it is easier for a camel to pass through the eye of a needle than for a rich man to get to heaven. The rich man who tore down his barns in order to build bigger ones was called a fool and told that his life would be taken from him, and the examples go on. Notice, however, that in all of this, neither work nor business and commerce are condemned in themselves, not even when Jesus drives the money-changers and merchants out of the temple. What is condemned is attachment to riches and dishonesty and corruption.[9]

What we see emerging is a dignified and balanced vision of work that neither idolizes nor disdains it – one that recognizes its moral value and importance for human flourishing. Work is an important element of man's life, sanctification and salvation but not the ultimate end of life itself. In this sense, work is similar to other goods of creation and must be put in its proper order. This concept of work has implications for management and for the market economy. Studies have shown that firms that recognize the importance of rest, honesty and treating workers in accord with their dignity are more successful and sustainable in the long run than those who ignore or reject these principles.[10]

The picture in Scripture is quite different from the vision portrayed by proponents of the 'social gospel' who tend to see business as morally suspect and tend to praise poverty as a virtue in itself. This departs from the Scriptures and the Christian tradition, which do not praise poverty per se but praise the poor in spirit and an attitude of detachment toward material things. The renunciation of worldly goods to follow Christ is lauded and indeed encouraged, and there is a deep concern for the poor and powerless throughout Scripture. Some people are called to live the evangelical counsels of poverty, chastity and obedience – as it appears that the rich young man was. But nowhere do the Scriptures condemn business and commerce outright as immoral. Rather, God calls business people as He does all people to obey the moral law, be honest in all their dealings, to be generous to the poor and to take care of the widow and the orphan.

The Judeo-Christian understanding of work and business is also dramatically different from pagan and secular visions, which tend to either glorify or disdain it. To the ancient Greeks, for example, most work was something contemptuous and unworthy for an aristocrat. Both manual labour and commerce were viewed as demeaning and something to be done by slaves in order to provide leisure for the upper classes. A similar position was taken by French aristocrats who were by law unable to engage in business since it was seen as something beneath them. With the Enlightenment we see a range of divergent views on work. Rousseau envisioned a state of nature before civil society with man as a 'noble savage'. Work was a product of civil society and thus a scourge on natural man. The utilitarian approach, on the other hand, made utility the highest value with its focus on progress, technology and efficiency. Marx's materialist philosophy was preoccupied with work and the organization of labour, and the economic system was the determining factor for the rest of society and culture.

These various approaches present markedly different visions of work than the Judeo-Christian tradition, which attaches great human and moral significance to work, but always within the context of other moral virtues and the need for rest and worship.

WORK IN THE CHRISTIAN TRADITION

The Christian tradition, both Catholic and Protestant, has spent a considerable time reflecting on the moral value and importance of work as part of God's economy of salvation. While there are differing degrees of appreciation of markets and commerce, there is a general appreciation of business throughout the tradition. Nor is this limited to Calvin and the Puritans, as Max Weber posited. Weber both misread Calvin and ignored entire elements of the Christian tradition on work, commerce and markets (see Gregg, 2003; Stark, 2005). While it is true that Calvin had a generally positive vision of business (while warning against attachment), he was not the only one. We see an affirmation of commerce and business throughout the tradition. Referring to the unfaithful servant in the parable of the talents, St John Chrysostom acknowledges the duty of developing all the virtues including fulfilling one's duties to one's neighbour in business writing 'in that instance, the man's virtue was in every point unimpaired, and there had been nothing lacking, but forasmuch as he was slothful in his business, he was rightly cast out' (Chrysostom, 2007). St Thomas Aquinas affirmed private property, free exchange, free association and market pricing. The late-scholastics, specifically the School of Salamanca, applied moral theology to questions of business and economics.[11] Francisco de Vitoria affirmed free exchange between peoples of different countries as natural to man and part of the eternal and natural law (Chafuen, 2003,

p. 74). Albornoz argued that, 'by buying and selling the world is united, joining distant lands and nations, people of different languages, laws, and ways of life' and 'without these contracts some would lack goods that others have in abundance and the common good would be worse off' (ibid., p. 75).

Though Martin Luther was more suspicious of business and markets than others in the tradition, he did not condemn commerce outright. The Puritan reformer John Baxter, quoting St Paul,[12] urged people to support the church and commonwealth by their labour: 'man, being a sociable creature, must labour for the good of the society to which he belongs'. He lauded the importance of work as vital for health, as an avoidance of temptation and mortification of the flesh and as 'God's appointed means for getting our daily bread'. Baxter spoke of various trades and merchants as supporting the public good and made the distinction between gaining riches and making them 'your chief end' (Baxter, 2005, pp. 278–85). John Wesley (1760) in a famous sermon exhorts his listeners to 'make all you can, save all you can, give all you can, do all the good you can, by all the means you can'. Throughout the Christian tradition, we see this same type of praise for work and the moral necessity of using one's talents wisely, but always within a proper order. Business and commerce are legitimate activities that benefit the common good and the individual person but like any earthly good must be approached with care so as not to become an idol. Business is a moral good but business will not save you, and there are higher goods than creating wealth. With this brief overview providing a context, we can now turn to analyse work from the 'inside' as a moral act of the human person.

BUSINESS AND PERSON: THE INTRANSITIVE MORAL DIMENSION OF HUMAN WORK

From a Christian philosophical perspective, work has a distinct moral value because it is an act of the human person. For an act to be in the moral realm it must be performed by a free and rational agent – a person. A moral act has both objective and subjective effects on society and the person. We have already discussed many of the objective effects of business on the common good. In this section I examine work as a moral act, specifically its subjective and intransitive value for the human person, focusing on the thought of Thomas Aquinas and John Paul II. Again, while John Paul is not the only Christian thinker to reflect on these issues, his encyclical letter *Laborem Excercens* (1981) provides a synthetic approach to work that is rooted in the broad Christian tradition.

Aquinas on Moral Action

St Thomas Aquinas (b. 1225–d. 1274) provides a framework for the analysis of human action that is helpful in understanding the moral dimension
of work and that can be applied to business or any human endeavour.
St Thomas distinguishes between *actus hominis* (acts of man) and *actus
homanus* (human acts). *Actus homanus* would include things such as diges-
tion and breathing, which are acts that man performs but which do not
engage the will or the intellect. *Actus hominis*, on the other hand, are those
voluntary actions that involve the intellect and the will. Aquinas distinguishes between involuntary, voluntary and non-voluntary action to
further clarify the moral aspects of human action (Aquinas, 1948, 2.1, q.
6). For our purposes we will focus on voluntary actions.[13]
Voluntary actions are actions that a person willingly and knowingly
chooses to perform. They involve the intellect and the consent of the will
and thus are part of the moral sphere. This would include all sorts of
actions such as study, helping one's neighbour, brushing one's teeth, prayer
and all types of work. This understanding of human action demonstrates
the moral significance of human work and why business – and all types of
work – have moral importance. In this light even the most seemingly
insignificant action can have moral value (see Grisez, 1993). Now this is not
to say all work is good merely because it is work, just as it is not the case
that all voluntary actions are morally good. Murder, theft and adultery are
all voluntary actions that are morally evil just as some types of work are
morally evil, such as prostitution or pornography. But viewing work and
consequently business from within the philosophical framework of *actus
hominis* enables them to be seen in a whole new light. All the aspects of
business life – from arriving on time, to working diligently throughout the
day, to getting along with others and carrying out one's job with honesty –
have moral value and play a role in shaping the soul toward virtue or vice.
This can have profound consequences on a manager's method of dealing
with his or her employees and on employee attitudes to their co-workers
and customers.

John Paul II: The Subjective Dimension of Work and Human Flourishing

Rooting his analysis in St Thomas's understanding of human action, John
Paul II's investigations into the objective and subjective dimensions of
human labour further illuminate the moral value of business and its
significant role in the development of human personality and moral life.[14]
John Paul II goes so far as to say that the subjective sense of work is most
important. 'Independently of their objective content, these actions [of

work] must all serve to realize this humanity, to fulfil the calling to be a person that is by reason of his very humanity' (John Paul II, 1981, 6). Even the biblical concept of 'dominion' has its deepest meaning in the subjective sense since:

> [It is the] subjective dimension that conditions *the very ethical nature of work*. In fact there is no doubt that human work has an ethical value of its own, which clearly and directly remains linked to the fact that the one who carries it out is a person, a conscious and free subject . . . a subject who decides about himself. (Ibid.)

The Judeo-Christian view of work eliminated the ancient prejudice against manual labour and commerce. All work had value because it was performed by persons. 'This does not mean that, from an objective point of view, human work cannot and must not be rated and qualified in any way. It only means that the primary basis of the value of work is man himself' (ibid.). It is legitimate for a market to place different values on different types of work. What is illegitimate is to make economic value the only value when dealing with human labour, because unlike products and services, labour is not merely a commodity; rather labour presupposes the human person.[15] Here again we see John Paul rejecting both Marxian and libertarian materialist conceptions of work. Man is not merely an instrument of production or a cog in an economic machine. Man's value is not primarily economic, though his labour, skills and know-how may have economic value (see ibid., 6–7). 'In the final analysis', John Paul writes, 'it is always man who is the purpose of work' (ibid., 6). The act of work then, in any field, is imbued with moral significance. All work including the myriad of different work that one finds in the realm of business is morally valuable because it is done by persons.

APPLICATIONS FOR TODAY: A CRITIQUE OF CORPORATE SOCIAL RESPONSIBILITY

This dimension of work further illustrates the moral nature of business, no matter how rudimentary or complex. Business should not be disdained because it is thought to be vulgar or because it deals with common products instead of art, music or philosophy.[16] Business is a moral good because persons engage in it. This is often lost, especially in the CSR movement, which seems to have appropriated a type of ancient disdain for business. It attempts to redeem business from the 'outside' as it were, by adding additional 'requirements' that firms need to fulfil to be considered good members of society. Much of this disdain is rooted in deficient anthropology and an inability to recognize the subjective dimension of work. While a full analysis of the CSR movement cannot be addressed in this chapter,[17] I think it is worth comparing it briefly with the vision of work given to us by the Christian tradition. CSR is perhaps the most common approach to business ethics today and favoured in the media and academic journals and widely adopted by major and smaller corporations alike.

While perhaps well intentioned, I would argue that CSR is ultimately confused about the nature, role and purpose of business in society precisely because it misses its moral dimensions. Much of this is due to its relativist ethical underpinnings, which present a number of problems for ethical analysis. First, a relativist vision does not enable one to attach authentic moral significance to human actions. Second, it precludes any serious analysis of moral issues. This perhaps explains CSR's tendency to promote fashionable social policy instead of providing a coherent framework within which to make difficult business decisions. It shifts the focus away from the firm's internal activities toward external charity or programmes often unrelated to the work of the individual firms.[18]

The relativist underpinnings also preclude any serious consideration of how charity should be approached or where corporate donations should be allocated. Thus, we see many donations going not to the economically disadvantaged[19] but to groups with political or social influence[20] or to organizations that engage in highly questionable moral activities or promote social and moral policy that would be considered unethical by most religious standards.[21] Moreover, the existence of a CSR programme within a company is not necessarily an indicator of ethical business practices. Enron and Tyco, for example, had extensive CSR activities yet these did not prevent serious ethical violations that led to losses of millions of dollars, thousands of jobs and dried up the pension funds of most of their workers.

Ultimately, CSR's neglect of the moral value of work in its transitive and intransitive dimensions, combined with its failure to appreciate the moral and social benefits of business, actually undermines the positive role that business can play in society. Besides being costly and generally ineffective (and at times harmful), CSR can breed a cynicism toward ethics in business, which can have deleterious effects on both individuals and communities. Firms, business leaders and business schools need to recognize the moral value of their calling and strive to re-invigorate ethical approaches to business that are rooted not in visions like CSR, which view business and the market economy with suspicion, but in a proper conception of the human person and an understanding of business as a moral enterprise.

CONCLUSION

In this chapter I have attempted to show from both the perspective of the common good and the Judeo-Christian tradition a positive view of business as a moral enterprise. While there are clear warnings about the dangers of riches, we find a general affirmation of work and business in general. Like other moral endeavours, business is fraught with challenges and temptations but, in general, a life of business can and should be consistent with a deep moral life. Business indeed can be a school for virtue, which can permeate all areas of life and human relationships.

I have used an explicitly Christian framework to analyse the morality of business but this approach could also be presented in a more natural-law approach to resonate with a larger audience. However, we do well to remember that there are many Christians in the workplace who experience a deep disconnect between their faith and moral lives on the one hand and their business lives on the other. A Christian articulation can be helpful in resolving these difficulties. Beginning with a view of business as a moral enterprise can have practical applications in the areas of management, human resources, strategy, business ethics and globalization.

Business of some sort or other is the way that most people make their livelihood and fulfil their responsibilities to their families and to society at large. Business is a model of innovation and ingenuity. Business has been a force for lifting people out of poverty, creating opportunities, curing disease, promoting peace and enabling culture, leisure and a rich human life. It is not the ultimate end of life itself but it is a moral good and should be recognized as such.

8. Modern business and its moral and ethical dilemmas in a globalized world

Philip Booth

INTRODUCTION

The *Compendium of the Social Doctrine of the Catholic Church*, published in 2005, states very clearly the various roles of business. In so doing it is clearly supportive of the business economy in complete consistency with recent papal encyclicals such as *Centesimus Annus* (*CA*) (John Paul II, 1991, 42) discussed below. It is worth beginning by quoting parts of paragraphs 338 and 339 of the *Compendium* as, in general terms, these lay out the benefits of a business economy and the potential dilemmas for business owners and managers from a Christian perspective:

> *Businesses should be characterized by their capacity to serve the common good of society through the production of useful goods and services* . . . [B]usinesses create wealth for all of society, not just for the owners but also for the other subjects involved with their activity . . . *A business's objective must be met in economic terms and in accordance with economic criteria, but the authentic values that bring about the concrete development of the person and society must not be neglected. . . All those involved in a business venture must be mindful that the community in which they work represents a good for everyone and not a structure that permits the satisfaction of someone's merely personal interests* (*Compendium of the Social Doctrine of the Church*,[1] taken from paragraphs 338 and 339, italics in original).[2]

Thus the economic function of business is clearly expressed. That economic function can only be fulfilled by businesses responding to price signals to seek to make profits. However, there are clear implications also that a business has functions that are not directly economic and this point has been understood and articulated by scholars such as Novak[3] and Gregg[4] who have been at the forefront in stressing the legal, cultural and moral environment in which markets must operate.

Of course, not all Christian scholars on economic issues welcome the market economy and agree that business exerts a positive influence in society. Indeed, official Catholic Church documents significantly qualify the statements made above. These differences of opinion can exist for a variety of reasons. Some authors would argue that a free, business economy would encourage materialism as a result of its very success in providing for material needs; there has long been widespread intellectual suspicion of the worlds of international finance, banking and commerce, including among Christian authors. Some writers propose that a business economy should be heavily regulated or the fruits of the business economy taxed in order to transfer income to the poor or to protect the poor in other ways; anti-business sentiment is apparent among some Christian scholars who have clearly been influenced by Marxist ideas even if that influence is not explicit; and there has long been a strand of Catholic intellectual support for an economy based on the primacy of the local economy, worker-owned business and rigid professional associations. We do not argue in detail about the merits of the business economy in this chapter, but the reader is referred to Hayek (1988), especially Chapter 6, Novak (1982), especially Chapter XIV and Woods (2005), especially Chapter 6, for a taste of, and a rebuttal of, some of these approaches. Additionally, Himes (2005) provides a wide-ranging discussion of modern Catholic social teaching, which references a large number of authors who have a variety of different perspectives.

Despite the general welcome for the business economy in official Catholic teaching, it is difficult to point to a unified theory of business *behaviour* that clearly has the authoritative backing of the Catholic Church – or indeed any received body of Christian teaching – on the subject. The modern discourse on corporate social responsibility and business ethics is not especially helpful. It can be very woolly, often exhibiting an incomplete understanding of the economic system, entrepreneurship, corporate governance[5] and, perhaps more alarmingly, of the meaning of responsibility and ethics.[6] It is dangerous for Christians simply to absorb terms such as 'corporate social responsibility' because they are phrases with which one empathizes. Business ethicists, like businesses, like to use phrases that have a marketing impact to describe their wares.

The Catholic Church had an interesting flirtation with corporatist business models in the 1930s. The precise role that government might have played in such models is ambiguous. But, rather unusually, the Church through papal documents[7] laid out in formal terms a proposed business model. We will begin by briefly discussing that model. We will then examine further the Catholic Church's broad acceptance of the principles of the business economy while examining in more detail the challenges that the operation of a business economy poses for Christians operating in business. This chapter is grounded in Catholic teaching on social issues – not because there are not important strands of non-Catholic Christian thinking on social issues but because it is easier to identify and critique the continual stream of thinking produced by the Catholic Church. Furthermore, on such issues, Catholics and non-Catholics tend to feed off similar value systems so it is hoped that nothing substantial has been omitted by taking Catholic teaching as the basis of discussion.[8]

THE CHURCH AND CORPORATISM

For many years, a dominant strain of thinking within the Catholic Church upheld corporatist models of economic organization. Many would see elements of the proposed corporatist model, such as the emphasis on cooperation at group level and the restraints that the model would place on the market economy, as providing a framework for overcoming the dilemmas that face companies in a globalized world. Versions of the corporatist model have been pervasive in continental Europe and, for a time, in the United Kingdom. For example, the EU Commission, at times influenced by individuals such as Jacques Delor who have taken Catholic social teaching seriously, sees aspects of the corporatist model as being important in 'taming' business.

In the late-19th century, there were various developments, often admired by the Catholic Church, which championed explicit cooperation between workers and business owners.[9] Léon Harmel, a French factory owner, formed a series of clubs for workers, which had a paternalistic form of organization, with the duties of managers towards other workers being similar to those of a father towards his family. In Germany, corporatist models were proposed as an alternative to capitalism and socialism, with individuals grouped according to their professional duties and social functions. These were not just voluntary groupings within the business arena but were intended to be organized groupings within the political arena too. The late-19th-century corporatist movements believed that political institutions should be made up of representatives of different societal groupings such as agricultural interests, workers' interests, commercial interests and so on. This form of political and commercial organization would lead, it was argued, to greater cooperation and goodwill. These movements and the intellectual ideas underpinning them had significant influence on the development of the early social encyclicals of the Catholic Church (see Shannon, 2005).

Quadragesimo Anno (*QA*) (Pius XI, 1931), the most important Catholic Church document promoting the corporatist form of business organization, was written at the height of the Great Depression and during the rise of the fascist movements whose economic policies were often based on corporatism. The modern corporation with limited liability was strongly criticized, as was the principle of free competition. Pope Pius XI said that 'free competition . . . [though] certainly useful provided it is kept within certain limits, clearly cannot direct economic life' (*QA*, 88). The corporatist model proposed in *Quadragesimo Anno* involved workers being involved in the ownership of their firms – something that is not precluded by capitalism, of course.

The corporatist model is important for our discussion. Where partially adopted, it has led to explicit cooperative structures for the resolution of potential conflicts such as the setting of wage levels, policies on redundancy and so on. It is therefore a possible model for resolving ethical dilemmas in business. A version of the model was followed in Britain in the post-war period, but, by the 1970s, the economic and social outcomes were clearly very poor. Conflict and not cooperation resulted. Aspects of the model, perhaps influenced by Catholic teaching, have also been adopted in countries such as Germany, where there are two-tiered boards, with worker representatives on one level having input into management decisions. These structures are sometimes imposed from outside by law and sometimes they are developed by companies themselves. There may be benefits from such forms of organization but it is certainly not clear what the benefits are, especially when one examines economic evidence on unemployment and returns on business capital.[10] It could be argued that the corporatist model, as once proposed by the church, has never in fact been implemented. This is true, though some individual enterprises do follow such a model, in whole or in part. However, where aspects of the model have been adopted, it appears not to have the flexibility to respond to changing human needs. Furthermore, cooperative structures have not proven better than freedom of contract in resolving differences among owners, managers and workers.

THE CHURCH WELCOMES BUSINESS

In more recent years, the Catholic Church has been more explicitly welcoming of a 'business economy'. The provision of goods through a business economy accords with the principle of subsidiarity and with the belief in dignity of the human person. The church's support for the free business economy is perhaps best summed up by the following statement from *Centesimus Annus* (*CA*, 42) which answers the rhetorical question of whether the market economy is the most appropriate economic system:

> If by 'capitalism' is meant an economic system which recognizes the fundamental and positive role of business, the market, private property and the resulting

responsibility for the means of production, as well as free human creativity in the economic sector, then the answer is certainly in the affirmative, even though it would perhaps be more appropriate to speak of a 'business economy', 'market economy' or simply 'free economy'.

The market is regarded by the church as being an important means for attaining prosperity. Pontifical Council for Justice and Peace (2005, paragraph 347) sums up the arguments succinctly. It states that free and competitive markets have proven capable of ensuring that material needs are met and that they encourage conservation of resources while giving central place to a person's desires and preferences. Business is also regarded as integrating social and entrepreneurial activity as part and parcel of its function (see also *CA*, 32).

Indeed, Catholic teaching also leaves us in no doubt that it is not just for economic reasons that we should reject alternatives to the market economy. *Centesimus Annus* states:

> Socialism likewise maintains that the good of the individual can be realized without reference to his free choice, to the unique and exclusive responsibility which he exercises in the face of good or evil . . . This makes it much more difficult for him to recognize his dignity as a person, and hinders progress towards the building up of an authentic human community. (*CA*, 13)

The use of mechanisms other than business to meet economic needs fundamentally disorientates the relationships that should be at the heart of a society built upon the principle of subsidiarity. This can be seen where goods and services are produced by the state. While, for example, many – if not most – individual teachers will orientate their vocation towards meeting the needs of children, at an institutional level the incentives of schools in the state education system are such that they tend to orientate themselves towards the government's ends. This will include focusing (in the United Kingdom) on government-compiled league tables, Ofsted[11] inspections, implementing government regulations on admissions and curricula, obtaining government grants given for special purposes and so on. Sometimes such activity is compatible with meeting the aims and objectives of parents, but this is not necessarily so. Intrinsically, government institutions focus on looking upwards towards the state bureaucracies and not downwards towards the families they serve, except coincidentally. Thus, the comments made by Pope John Paul II regarding socialism in its more extreme form apply in proportionate measure to socialism when employed only in sectors of the economy.

As will be noted below, the acceptance of the market is qualified and it is held that the market economy is not an end in itself but serves other ends – such as the provision of goods and services that meet important human needs. Nevertheless, a grudging acceptance of the market economy is mistaken. A business economy brings many benefits, not simply utilitarian economic benefits.

SOME PERCEIVED PROBLEMS OF A BUSINESS ECONOMY

The Roles of Owners and Agents

Businesses, while showing a profit in an economic sense, can offend the dignity of those working for them or supplying them. While profit is recognized as a legitimate signal that resources are employed in a worthwhile manner, the pursuit of profit at all costs is not acceptable. Pontifical Council for Justice and Peace (2005) states that a business should be a community of solidarity and, by its activities, promote the common good (paragraphs 340 and 341) – these are both natural features of business in a normal environment subject to the rule of law. However, it then adds, rather out of context, though not insignificantly, that businesses must 'protect the natural environment'. We take up this theme below.

The *Compendium* also states (paragraph 348) that the profit of an enterprise, though legitimate, must not be an enterprise's sole objective: also important is the orientation of a business towards social usefulness so that the market is of service to the common good. This cautious welcome to the role of business in a free economy leaves many dilemmas both for businesses and policy-makers.

In considering this issue, it is first necessary to distinguish between the respective roles of management and shareholders. The relative roles of management and shareholders from both an economic and philosophical perspective are discussed in Sternberg (2004). Shareholders own the business property and employ management to manage the property to satisfy the shareholders' objectives.[12] The managers are employees and it is not their role to manage the assets of the business in a way that is contrary to the desires of their owners – even if Christian managers believe that they are promoting the common good by doing so.[13]

This can be illustrated by way of an analogy. If a family left the country for six months and asked a letting agency to let out their property, it would not be the job of a Christian employee of the letting agency to decide that the common good could be aided by housing homeless people at a low rent – contrary to the contractual agreements between the agency and the family. In the case of business managers, it is not their role, unless sanctioned by the board, acting within the powers given to it by shareholders to, say, install enhanced insulation in all factories at significant net cost to the business because the managers believe the net social benefits make this worthwhile. The managers may give advice to the board, express an opinion or choose to work for another company that has a different attitude, but the managers' role is to be a steward of the property of the investors in the company – who, if the investors are pensioners or widows and orphans benefiting from an insurance fund, may be in greater social need than those who might benefit from any 'social action' undertaken by managers of their own volition.

Managers and the Moral Law

Managers should, of course, refuse to do anything that is contrary to the moral law. The interpretation of that moral law may have grey areas in certain fields but it would clearly be wrong for a Christian manager in business, for example, to bribe contractors, treat workers unjustly or, to take an extreme case, force female employees to have abortions in order to raise their value to the corporation. There are other offences against the moral law mentioned in the *Catechism*, such as price manipulation to take advantage of the ignorance of others (see *Catechism*, 1994, paragraph 2409 for example) where the responsibilities of business managers might go beyond those of civil and criminal law. If managers feel pressurized to take decisions that Christian teaching would deem immoral, they should reconsider their positions.

The Profit Motive

For shareholders and boards of directors there are dilemmas about how businesses should behave when legitimate objectives appear to conflict, given economic backgrounds and legal frameworks that can be far from ideal. Some of these areas will be recognized as legitimate areas for judgment by Christians. For example, the precise relationships between the wages of different workers within a business will depend on a number of different factors, such as the contribution of the individual to the value of the business, the wage scale that the business uses to reward loyalty, the difficulties of recruiting workers with a particular skill and so on. But, while it is reasonable for Christians within business to take heed of warnings from the Catholic Church and other churches about the essential social mission of business, we should be careful before jumping to hasty conclusions when overriding decisions based on the profit motive.

For example, to Westerners it may seem obvious that multinational businesses should pay all employees a 'just wage', as judged by Western

Christianity and modern business

standards, pay a 'fair price' for primary products or refuse to employ child labour. However, overriding price signals in the hope of achieving wider social goals may actually compromise business's contribution to the common good. Obliging businesses to pay higher than the market price for primary products may draw in more supply and lead to unsold produce. Obliging them to pay higher than the market price for labour can lead to unemployment, to substitution of labour by capital, inhibit the development of competition within labour markets, and to 'insider–outsider' markets where the privileged have a job and others do not. The employment of child labour is sometimes necessary for families in less-developed countries to ensure a reasonable standard of living and to help finance part-time school fees (see Kis-Katos and Schulze, 2005).[14] If we do not follow the profit signal – which is an important signal of the social value of our economic activities – how do we know whether business is making a social contribution or not?[15]

The dilemma a business faces here is not unlike the dilemmas faced by central planners within governments – and, of course, it is because of the impossibility of resolving such dilemmas in a central planning system that a free economy is favoured. We can easily see the first-round effects of our actions (such as raising the wage of a poor employee) but the second-round effects of such action (including potential employees remaining unemployed) may be hidden. Many of these dilemmas arise as a result of governments not undertaking their functions properly. If the economic and business environment is unfavourable due to misguided government policy, opportunities for exploitation may be exacerbated. The ultimate wrong in such cases lies with poor government, though firms still have to face up to the added responsibilities that come from poor public oversight (see below).

It is difficult to lay down a precise way in which these dilemmas can be resolved. Those who own firms, and their representatives, should be sensitive to such problems and should treat their employers and suppliers humanely and sensitively. With such an outlook, it should be possible to balance concern for the persons connected with the enterprise with the intrinsic function of the enterprise in a market economy. This is not an entirely satisfactory solution because it does not propose specific ways of dealing with defined problems – it is therefore out of tune with a society where people like to be governed by codes of conduct and detailed rules. In the following sections we examine specific dilemmas faced by businesses in further detail.

'Excessive' Wages, 'Unjust' Wages and 'Unjust' Prices

Popular criticisms of capitalism often focus on excessive wages and profits of a few people in business and 'unjustly' low wages for others. The

Catholic Church has frequently expressed concern about extreme inequality, while recognizing that some inequality is part of the natural order (see *Populorum Progressio* 57 [Paul VI, 1967]; *Sollicitudo Rei Socialis 12*, [John Paul II, 1987]; Charles, 1998, pp. 18, 26 and Pontifical Council for Justice and Peace 2005, paragraph 362, for example).[16] It is perhaps helpful to focus on four different aspects of inequality. The first is the very high levels of wages that are earned by senior executives in business. The second is the very low levels of wages, at least by Western standards, received by some employees. The third is the low level of product prices received by primary product producers and the fourth is the high level of prices that Western firms can charge for goods based on intellectual property.

'Unjustly' high and 'unjustly' low wages
From an economic point of view, there are various ways of thinking about the wage hierarchy in a business, and none leads to the conclusion that any particular degree of inequality within the wage structure of the firm is immoral per se. Departing from economic principles in determining the wage structure is highly likely to produce more economic harm than good.

A well-managed company should try to ensure that its wage structure reflects the contribution of employees to the value of the firm. Consider the case where the chief executive of a firm is paid £5 million per year, whereas his value to the firm is £10 million per year. If the chief executive has a value of £6 million to another company, and that company is willing to pay £6 million to secure his or her services, the individual may change jobs, moving to a company where he or she adds less value. There is an overall welfare loss from this transaction as the employee is moving to an activity where his or her talents are worth less. Certainly, nobody at the bottom end of the wage scale gains from the decision to pay the chief executive only £5 million in the name of 'justice'.

Similarly, at the bottom end of the wage scale, if a company decides to pay an individual more than he or she is worth to the company, given his or her productivity, the company is likely to employ fewer such individuals leaving some of them unemployed. Such a company is also likely to use less labour and more capital. Ironically, a company that decides to employ fewer people at a higher wage is likely to be praised by commentators (see the chapter by Woods in Booth, 2007) because the fact that the company has employed fewer people and more capital will not be perceptible – whereas the low wages of a company that decides to take on all the labour it can at the prevailing wage will be observable.

There is a genuine dilemma here for business. Businesses may well, in fact, undermine not just the market economy but the economic prospects of the low paid if they pay salaries to employees that do not reflect value-added to the business. However, the outsider, including 'ethical investors', may look upon the moral position of a business that has a more 'equal' wage distribution more favourably. There are some companies that, as a matter of policy and established culture, do have more equal wage structures and relatively pyramidal and stable employment environments. This can be done, among other reasons, to help recruit labour that has particular (often risk-averse) characteristics. The author would argue that these are business decisions that are not necessarily less or more moral than decisions to pay wages that reflect supply and demand in the market. Investors who believe that they are taking an 'ethical' position should be careful to understand both the 'seen' and 'unseen' effects of distorting wage structures.

There are some exceptions, however, where we might not accept that the market wage is equivalent to a 'just' wage or a morally acceptable wage (see Charles, 1998, e.g., vol. II, p. 430). It has been articulated by papal encyclicals from *Rerum Novarum* onwards that an employer must not exploit a worker's weakness. Thus freedom of contract can be the basis of a just wage but is not necessarily so. Weakness can arise from various situations, such as the ignorance of an employee about the treatment of others in an organization or ignorance of alternative employment opportunities. Alternatively, a weak bargaining position might arise from the existence of monopsony[17] combined with the inability of potential employees to relocate and look for employment in other areas. In such cases, a firm should try to ensure that wages reflect the contribution of individuals to the enterprise and not exploit their circumstances. This is simply part of the requirement to manage the enterprise and relationships with employees in a just and fair manner.

This does not necessarily mean that, where there is a large pool of unemployed people, the enterprise cannot choose to pay less and employ more workers (and perhaps employ less capital) than the enterprise would in another area where employment conditions are tighter. If enterprises did not choose to vary wages in this manner, unemployment would rise and unemployment terms would lengthen. It also does not mean that two people doing the same job cannot be paid different amounts if market conditions merit this. If one employer pays the same wages in (say) India as in the United Kingdom, it would potentially damage indigenous enterprises and prevent the emergence of more companies who would provide increased employment opportunities. However, the employer should not systematically exploit the ignorance or weakness of employees.

Catholic teaching has generally regarded a wage as just only if the wage is above the level of subsistence and provides a dignified livelihood (see, for example, *Catechism*, 1994, 2434, which mentions various papal documents and biblical references). Exceptions are suggested if the livelihood of a business is in peril from paying higher wages. This approach does create a genuine dilemma for economists. There may well be situations where the market wage, even if there is neither monopoly nor monopsony, is insufficient for a dignified living.[18] But a decision to pay labour more than the market wage may have a number of detrimental effects. Less labour is likely to be employed; labour might be replaced with capital; and high-quality labour may well be drawn from other firms who are left in a position of having to employ less productive labour. Indeed, this may well lead to resentment and calls for the regulation of the 'poaching' of labour.

We do not resolve this dilemma here, except to comment that, in such situations, it is important that employers look to their wider responsibilities and are satisfied in good conscience that they are not exploiting the weakness of counterparties to their contracts. It may reasonably be asked, however, why the productivity of labour is so low that a living wage is not justified by somebody's productivity. Very often, the answer lies in dysfunctional governments that create a poor business environment. Without a good business environment, a market economy cannot generate competition in the labour market that leads to the high levels of productivity that are ultimately the basis of high wages.[19] But it should also be noted that the *Catechism* states: 'Agreement between the parties is not sufficient to justify morally the amount to be received in wages' (2434). Perhaps this precise phraseology is significant. There may be occasions when the just wage is different from the agreed wage but we cannot necessarily say what the just wage is in such circumstances. It is therefore important that Christian employers are aware of their responsibilities to treat employees appropriately and strive to meet those responsibilities. A right attitude towards God and neighbour is more important than a, perhaps fruitless, attempt to determine a figure for the 'just' wage.

Indeed, though a business must consider these dilemmas in good conscience, responsibility does not totally, or indeed mainly, lie with business. If business conditions are such that the lowest paid cannot demand sufficient compensation to help them give their families the basic necessities, the state has a role in providing social assistance to the lowest paid – the level of which should vary depending on family circumstances.[20] Most economists would accept that this approach is better than a statutory minimum wage.

'Unjustly' low Prices?
When somebody who is self-employed is selling products that are being purchased by a business, the purchaser cannot be immune from similar arguments to those surrounding the discussion of the just wage. This has been discussed widely in the context of the 'fair trade' movement, particularly

with regard to the coffee market.[21] While it cannot be said that it is unreasonable for a business to pay low prices if they are justified by supply and demand conditions, the agreed price cannot necessarily be regarded as a just price if there is monopoly or monopsony power in the market. The 'fair trade' movement has been established to try to help small-scale primary producers in such situations, though its impact is not necessarily beneficial – particularly if it artificially inflates prices and prevents outsiders entering the market. But, in this situation, while an intrinsically low price is not necessarily an indicator of injustice or immoral business practices, systematic exploitation of suppliers who have limited information about alternative opportunities would be inappropriate.[22]

Laborem Exercens (*LE*) (John Paul II, 1981, 17) outlines a role for 'indirect employers'. Though this phrase was mainly explained in terms of the role of regulators and legislators, it is also reasonable to suppose that consumers have a responsibility as indirect employers.[23] This could involve consumers choosing not to purchase from firms that act unethically in labour markets or in purchasing from suppliers. The issues here are complex too. The disastrous consequences for thousands of desperately poor children in Bangladesh who were thrown out of work after the threat of US trade sanctions over child labour have been well reported.[24] Again this dilemma cannot be resolved definitively except to say that consumers must bear some responsibility for their purchasing decisions.

'Unjustly' high prices?

A further dilemma for business concerns the protection of intellectual property. Intellectual property confers a monopoly advantage on a producer. The generally accepted Catholic understanding of private property regards private property rights not as inviolable but as essential for the common good. Thus, if it is felt that the common good is not promoted by the protection of intellectual property through patents and copyrights, there should be no presumption of absolute protection. Interestingly, the law in most developed countries tends to take such a pragmatic position – intellectual property rights are protected by law but not to an unlimited or absolute extent. Most developed countries also favour reinforcing the protection of property rights through international free trade agreements. The *Compendium* states (in relation to biotechnology):

> Entrepreneurs and directors of public agencies involved in the research, production and selling of products derived from new biotechnologies must take into account not only legitimate profit but also the common good. This principle, which holds for every type of economic activity, becomes particularly important for activities that deal with the food supply, medicine, health care and the environment. (Paragraph 478)

Moral and ethical dilemmas

It also states that: '*Equitable commercial exchange, without the burden of unjust stipulations*, is to be facilitated' (italics in original, paragraph 475) and that this requires transfer of technology to developing countries.

As has been noted, the law relating to intellectual property is developed pragmatically within developed countries and there is no unanimity, even among staunch proponents of private property, as to the legitimate position of intellectual property rights.[25] While patent protection prevents developing countries from producing medicines and technologies at minimal cost through the copying of products, contract provisions and world trade rules that allow companies to block the re-importation of medicines sold at cheaper prices in developing countries than in developed countries, facilitate greater access to medicines by people of developing countries. The economics of these complex issues is described very lucidly in Lilico (2006).

It is clear from an understanding of the economics of the issue that, in this area as in many others discussed in this chapter, clear guidance about specific forms of behaviour cannot be given. Assuming that the principle of private intellectual property is accepted, it is clear that companies cannot be expected simply to give away their intellectual property rights – otherwise research and development in new products would suffer. Even where the preferential option for the poor is accepted, and the lack of availability of patented drugs leads to suffering, the principle of private intellectual property can serve the common good. The responsibility to help the poor in such situations must lie more widely than with business producers of technological products themselves. At the same time, a Christian approach to business should not simply involve maximizing the monopoly profit potentially available from the exploitation of intellectual property when there is clear suffering. Patent law confers monopoly rights, and moral responsibilities accompany these rights. Similarly, developed countries, acting individually or as a group, should not try to negotiate trade rules in a way that simply maximizes the value of patents to industries in their own countries.[26] This is another genuine dilemma for business where only a well-informed conscience can provide the necessary guidance about how to act in specific situations.

The Treatment of Employees: Preserving Jobs

Pope Benedict XVI in a statement to the Italian Entrepreneurs' Group in May 2007 said: 'all business enterprises are to be considered primarily as groups of people, whose rights and dignity must be respected'. He urged entrepreneurs to protect the jobs of their workers and offer real prospects to younger workers.

This statement is problematical for an economist. If companies cannot use more profitable production techniques or reduce employment to increase efficiency, labour will not move from less productive to more productive sectors of the economy. This, in turn, can exacerbate unemployment by making labour less productive and less remunerative relative to available social security benefits. The young, who are likely to be the least experienced and productive, are likely to suffer most from such a policy. Preserving particular jobs can be at the expense of creating a climate in which those who are unemployed can easily obtain employment. It is not, of course, remotely possible for an employer to determine whether any particular decision to make labour redundant promotes or detracts from the overall common good, given the possible impact of an employer's action on other parts of the labour market.[27]

But the Pope's words should be taken seriously and perhaps, once again, the resolution of this dilemma lies in the employer having an attitude of solidarity with and compassion towards his or her employees. Employers should not shirk from essential business decisions but implement them in a way that recognizes the human needs of employees. When a business owner has an 'attitude of solidarity', it does not refer in the first place to a desire for political action and regulation but, rather, to: 'a firm and persevering determination to commit oneself to the common good; that is to say to the good of all and of each individual' (*Sollicitudo Rei Socialis* [SRS], 38). The virtue of solidarity requires that we respect persons for their dignity as persons, not as instruments or means (Curran, Himes and Shannon, 2005). Such an attitude of solidarity will not lead an employer to avoid difficult decisions; but neither should it lead an employer to be indifferent to the weakness and suffering of employees.

Respect for the Environment and Property Rights

Presciently, in paragraph 342, Pontifical Council for Justice and Peace (2005) points out that businesses take on greater levels of responsibility in states that are not properly governed. This statement is legitimate and also helpful in focusing on the underlying problem where businesses are in a position to exploit property rights and environmental resources, particularly in less-developed countries. If businesses are not working within a proper juridical framework that involves the protection of property rights, the enforcement of contracts and a stable economic environment, they have added responsibilities.[28] In such circumstances it would surely not be moral for a business to take property without compensation or pollute the natural environment without compensation, even if the civil law of a particular country allowed it. Christian business people should show restraint and/or ensure just compensation when they use or acquire the property of others, even if the law of the relevant country does not compel them to do so. However, there are still grey areas where businesses must make judgments about how to behave. Many activities (such as open cast mining) cause environmental harm that might well be tolerated in countries with good governance systems because the benefits are greater than the costs. It is certainly not immoral, as such, to pursue such activities in a less-developed country with a poor system of legal protection. However, the Christian business should ensure, in the absence of proper legal protection of property rights, that all those who would justly receive compensation for the loss of their property or amenity in a well-functioning, just legal system are properly compensated when these restraints are absent. Of course, businesses in countries with poor legal environments also need to be especially careful not to engage in bribery and corruption or collusion with government.[29] Indeed, business can provide a good example of the just operation of private rules in the absence of well-functioning public law.

Not all Goods are Good

While being generally welcoming of a business economy, the Catholic Church has frequently been critical of a culture of materialism and the pursuit of goods that are harmful to the development of the human person. This leads to the question of whether Christian business people should be in the business of producing 'goods' that lead to moral harm – that is, 'bads'.

Very often the definition of such 'bads' is highly subjective, especially as something that is good in one context might be bad when used in another. Most, though not all, Christians would accept that smoking, gambling, drinking and weapons all have their place in Christian societies. However, all these products can be used for bad purposes too. In other words, these products are not intrinsically bad but they may be put to bad uses.

The main responsibility for restraining the use of 'bads' in society must lie with consumers. It is only consumers themselves, restrained by a well-informed conscience, who can fully understand the context in which different goods are consumed and therefore whether their consumption is sinful in particular circumstances. However, there is also a responsibility on producers:

> Widespread drug use is a sign of a serious malfunction in the social system . . . [I]n this way the innovative capacity of a free economy is brought to a one-sided and inadequate conclusion. Drugs, as well as pornography and other forms of consumerism which exploit the frailty of the weak, tend to fill the resulting spiritual void. (*CA*, 36)

Given the reference to exploitation of the weak, it is clear that consumer choice alone is not regarded by the church as an adequate safeguard against products being used for bad purposes: business has a responsibility too. There may also be a role for government and other institutions of civil society.

So where does the responsibility of Christian business people lie? Once again, it would seem necessary to conclude that the most important source of restraint comes from a well-formed conscience that can help business people make prudent judgments about the impact of their actions. Clearly, the production of some things, including pornography and certain biotechnology products produced by unethical means (see *Compendium*, paragraphs 472–480) must always be contrary to the moral law. In other cases, businesses may have little effective control over how a product is used but, where they do, Christian business people should certainly not pursue profit at the expense of the moral weakness of their neighbour. Issues such as the way products including alcohol and tobacco are sold to young people, whether marketing methods deliberately distort the image of a product and whether a business has effective methods of control to limit access to a product by people suffering from addiction are examples that a Christian business person should consider very seriously. Exploiting a customer's ignorance by concealing the truth about a product would seem to be just as immoral as straightforward dishonesty. The more personal the services being offered by a business, the greater are the potential opportunities for exercising moral restraint. But such opportunities exist in transnational companies too. It would not be right, for example, for a business to exploit consumer ignorance about the adverse effects of a particular product in a new market if the effects of long-term use had become known from experience in other markets.

The distinction between the roles of management and owners is important. As has been noted above, it would not seem right for managers to flout the will of owners: managers do have a stewardship responsibility, even if they regard the business policies of owners as immoral. However, a Christian manager would have to question his or her position if he or she felt compelled to act in an immoral way by owners. The position for owner-managers is, of course, more straightforward, as is the position of companies that have concentrated ownership where the moral disposition of a small number of owners is similar. Where the ownership of companies is dispersed, the main responsibility lies with shareholders. It is reasonable for Christian shareholders to put pressure on a firm's directors to pursue specific moral behaviour. Alternatively, owners can sell shares in companies they believe do not behave ethically or buy shares using so-called 'ethical funds'. However, it is doubtful whether the most prominent ethical funds on offer today resolve the dilemmas discussed in this chapter. There is a danger of 'ethical' funds not distinguishing between products themselves and the ends for which products are used.[30] It is easy to rule out firms that produce a whole range of products from an investment portfolio. But this, in fact, merely avoids the difficult moral decisions that relate not to the production of particular products but to the ends to which those products are put.

CONCLUSION

Although the corporatist form of business organization once proposed by the Catholic Church might be appropriate for specific enterprises, it is not an effective model for structuring a whole economy. The corporatist model seems often to have led to stagnation and industrial conflict – thus not proving true to its cooperative ideal after all. The real world of business is based on entrepreneurship and decentralized decision-making rather than top-down planning and organization.

Christians acting within this framework should clearly strive not to break the moral law. They also need to be particularly careful when their enterprises are not circumscribed within an appropriate juridical framework or when operating in environments where property rights are not enforced and corruption is rife. With regard to economic and social relationships, it can be dangerous to set rules and regulations – or even develop codes of practice – for business operations. Such an approach can entrench established firms in the market by raising the costs of entry to new business; it can also allow managers to set business objectives at the expense of owners; and it removes the ability to take both moral and economic decisions from the very people who are in the best position to make such judgments. There is no substitute for a Christian business owner having a properly informed conscience that acts as an appropriate restraint in the thousands of day-to-day decisions that he or she takes each year. The business person should exhibit an *attitude of solidarity* in relationships with others – particularly those who are most vulnerable – whether consumers, suppliers or employees.

9. Treating 'affluenza': the moral challenge of affluence

Ian R. Harper and Eric L. Jones

We are a society oppressed not by lack but by surfeit; not by strife but by ease.
(Archbishop of Canterbury, 1999)

Acquiring more discretionary income obviously, even tautologically, releases constraints on consumption: it makes poor people rich. But in so doing it widens the range of behaviour open to individuals – for good and ill. If you become rich you can ape the rich, and the wealthy have always been ambiguous role models. Even their benign choices may create problems when imitated en masse. The spillover of undesirable behaviours may have to be subtracted from the benefits to society. What are at stake are the perverse consequences of rising wealth, most of all the negative moral effects.

LET THERE BE LIGHT!

In rich countries today it is certainly easy to underestimate the benefits that growth has brought, or to put this the other way round, it takes a conscious effort to visualize the privations from which we have been rescued. We should establish this at the outset; we are not opposed to economic growth. As an example of the gains, most people now living cannot recall the spartan reality that preceded the marvels displayed on the shelves of supermarkets. The number of items on offer has increased literally a hundredfold since the end of World War II. We do mean literally; yet apparently it is easy to take this for granted and feel disgruntled, even sated, amidst the profusion.

Hence, few people seem to appreciate the extent of the advance, in either sense of the term 'appreciate'. Those who can do so best are the ones who have experience of goods-scarce economies and societies beset by high infant mortality, afflicted by adult diseases that can now be cured and condemned to an unceasing round of toil, not least for the housewife. Nevertheless, even in developed countries, life was accompanied by numerous inconveniences as recently as a generation or two ago. Young people may perhaps be forgiven for finding it hard to credit, for instance, that when CS First Boston established its Australian office in 1972, each week's business was accumulated until Friday, when a single operator-assisted call was placed back to head office in the United States On the contrary, it is no surprise that the young think international phone calls are a free good, when various schemes provide them over the Internet at zero marginal cost.

As another example, artificial lighting has come to be taken as a virtually free good. Yet the history of lighting was the slowest, most arduous advance. Transparent materials for glazing windows were long hard to come by; technical change was sluggish. The first improvement had to take the form of letting natural light indoors. At the start of the Middle Ages, church windows were scarcely bigger than arrow slits and were only gradually enlarged over the passing centuries. Happily, large windows became possible at the end of medieval times. When a nouveau riche wool merchant called John Tame endowed St Mary, Fairford, Gloucestershire, in the 1490s, he gave it the best medieval stained glass in Britain, with windows reaching towards the ceiling. The central tower was made airy, and the church became known as Tame's Lantern. The luxury of natural light came flooding in.

Private homes remained less fortunate. Blown glass was still expensive and the windows of town houses, boxed in their frames, remained so valuable they were not necessarily fixed in place but could be moveable property. The Lunar Society, a predecessor of scientific thought led by Darwin's grandfather, met only at full moon. On dark nights in Jane Austen's time, gentlemen led the way to dances by hanging out their white shirt tails for the ladies to follow: Dursley lanterns they were called. Ordinary country folk, unable to afford many candles for their homes, so hungered for light they would walk miles to gawp at fairground illuminations. Good lighting, like so many amenities, was scarce until the day before yesterday: one of us watched the moon shot with Sir Kenneth Swan, son of the man who actually invented the incandescent bulb (the patent in the United Kingdom is Swan-Edison). That was as recently as 1969.

The craving for something as elementary as lighting, long unsatisfied, makes modern complaints of satiation appear petulant. Nor can all our gains be dismissed as undesirable, materially or morally – it is hard to think that worse things must happen under bright lights than in dark corners. In any case the same saga reflects the opposite side: the very fact that the misery of perpetual gloom has been quickly forgotten exemplifies the so-called 'hedonic treadmill', whereby we adapt to whatever we have acquired, soon obtain little further psychic gain, take abundance for granted and let the most affluent societies appear to be sinking into 'sloughs of despond'.[1]

THE DARKER SIDE OF AFFLUENCE

The negative effects of greater wealth and wider choice have attracted much attention. Here, too, instances are easy to find and the greedy, personally damaging trend of over-eating and becoming obese has drawn particular scorn. Equally, being able to afford plenty of injurious, habit-forming tobacco and alcohol is no automatic advance in human welfare. A survey of 10 000 school children in North-west England shows that those with surplus pocket money are the ones who buy alcohol at the youngest ages and grow up to be binge drinkers – though we shall come back to the point that poverty failed to halt Hogarth's Gin Age.[2] At any rate, modern expectations that the problems of excessive consumption would fade have not been realized. Dental students, told in the 1970s that tooth decay would vanish and, before their careers were over, they would need a second job, have been horrified (or delighted) to find that the mass ingestion of fizzy drinks has caused an epidemic of caries.

In reality some unfortunate by-products of affluence are crowding effects. They are genuinely inadvertent results of the way more people have been enabled to share in pastimes once confined to the few. In small countries this especially affects land- and water-using activities, whose facilities cannot be readily expanded or, if they are, produce only inferior substitutes like jam-packed marinas or fish farms instead of trout streams. Some envied activities have become disappointments, as if every person must kill the thing he or she loves. Mass tourism has had to be restricted in historic houses because the tramp of endless feet damages the staircases, while visitors to the countryside disturb and drive off the very animals they have come to see. Yet, although individual satisfaction may be below former levels, the sum of the gains must be presumed to have risen, or people would have given up flocking to these activities.

Is there a pattern to what happens when incomes rise? When the German economic miracle abolished post-war poverty, journalists witnessed three distinct waves of expenditure. The offerings of each successive wave became part of everyday expectations and demand moved along to the next wave. Taking their tip from Engel's Law, in which a smaller proportion of income is spent on food as wages rise, the journalists discerned, first, a *Fresswelle* ('gobbling wave') based on higher absolute spending on food, second, a *Kleidungswelle* ('clothing wave') as money was lavished on buying adornments, and third, a *Reisewelle* ('travel wave'), which surged into indiscriminate spending.[3]

Businesses, with advertising agencies in their employ, did their very successful best to encourage all this consumption. They do so in every developed economy. That is their job and it is forlorn to deride it, as Jill Ker Conway did when she said that, 'if one looked at the subculture of designers and dressmakers as an anthropologist would, they assumed their place in the long continuum going back to painting the body and putting bones through one's nose'.[4] Fashion serves a sufficiently basic biological function – sexual display – to protect it from such slick moralizing.

Once prosperity is assured and routine physical goods are secured, competition for status and status goods becomes more noticeable. These are what Fred Hirsch called 'positional goods', items in finite supply: not everyone can eat caviar, fish the River Test, go to Harvard, or dance with the rich and famous.[5] Yet in itself, status competition is not called into being by affluence. It may even be more acute when the scope for expressing superiority is compressed. Social critics and rich women bemoaned for centuries that maids could no longer be told apart from their mistresses, because they insisted on dressing above their station. The theme was recurrent. Each fashion trickled down from the salon to the kitchen, from the hall to the cottage. Tellingly, Jung Chang recounts in *Wild Swans* how, during the adamantine uniformity of Mao's Cultural Revolution, people resorted to distinguishing themselves by the tiniest modifications of dress.[6] Nevertheless, affluence does widen the range of goods and services for which people can strive. It broadens the sections of the population who can enter the competition. It may spark a frenzy and increase the sum total of discontent.[7]

Indeed, while advertising remains able to combat flagging demand by persuading people to 'trade up' to luxuries and convert them into 'necessities', there is no overall problem about unloading ever more commodities onto the market. The want-creation industry is still doing a good job, encouraging by every possible means what Silverstein and Fiske call the 'new luxury'.[8] For example, otherwise sober newspapers come replete with fat supplements about automobiles, clothes, gadgets and houses; one such supplement is called 'How to Spend It' and seems to be aimed at people who are clever at making money but breathtakingly unimaginative about getting rid of it.

From the economic perspective the most threatening feature of affluence lies on the side of supply rather than demand. Affluence is held to reduce effort and undermine the work ethic. John Wesley and Joseph Schumpeter both famously warned of this possibility, which in more recent times has been translated into the catchy neologism of affluence-plus-influenza, hence 'affluenza'.[9] Wesley worried that the worldly success of the Methodists would cause them to slacken off; as more and more of their worldly needs were met, they would cease to strive. Quickly, too. Schumpeter generalized this anxiety to the entire capitalist world. He thought too successful an economy would erode the moral imperative – labour for the night is nigh – that had produced so much industrial wealth in the first place.

Riches may certainly have this impact. A descendant of the biscuit-making dynasty, the Palmers, turned away from the Quakers to the Church of England with the phrase, 'you can't take a carriage and pair to the meeting house'.[10] Families like this one, rich from profits made by the sweat of their forebears, have repeatedly abandoned industry, turned landowners or rentiers, rested on their laurels and left the management of the family firm to hired managers. They may also have set the seal on their social arrival by switching to a church of higher status, as the Palmers did. For the moment the point is that affluence led them away from striving. They adopted, as it were, the sterile upper class motto, attributed to Tallyrand, '*surtout pas trop de zele*' ['above all, no excessive enthusiasm'].

The time is not ripe for this nirvana. It is not ready for Marx's utopia where one works in the morning to produce enough for one's wants and spends the remainder of the day in fishing and philosophical discourse. Fears of reduced entrepreneurship may be overblown because fresh entrants will come forward to replace those who retreat to their villas or estates. But the world cannot afford indolence among a significant proportion of the workforce. There is too much genuine privation, too much unrequited demand for basic necessities, for hard work to be given up.

Anxieties about affluenza understandably surface from time to time. In the early 1990s they arose among the ever-alert politicians of Singapore, who shifted abruptly from boasting about the values underlying their country's success to announcing the fear that prosperity might turn self-defeating. They worried that the ethic that had driven the first generation in independent Singapore was waning, as young people took for granted a live-in maid and a Mercedes to chauffeur them to school. They thought the very state might be imperilled.

Undoubtedly affluenza can be real. Those who have spoken about it, from Wesley onwards, mostly conceive it in terms of rich kids 'dropping out' – Thomas Mann's 'Buddenbrooks effect' or from shirtsleeves to shirtsleeves in three generations. There is some evidence of effort slackening in the advanced welfare states and the fact that this is a bleat of right-wing politicians does not make it false. People respond to incentives and numbers of the young now find they can have what seems to them an adequate life by living on a mixture of handouts from their parents, welfare benefits and odd jobs, among which casual work tending bar figures prominently. They are under little pressure to seek full-time employment. In spite of a booming economy where 80 per cent of graduate vacancies are open to applicants from any discipline, a survey of over 17 000 British students finds that almost half of arts and humanities graduates have no definite plans for life after university and are not vigorously seeking work.[11]

The effects of this casual attitude are masked by the rise in productivity among those who actually are in work and who command more capital per head and better technology than in previous generations. It is still a waste. The lost productivity may just possibly be borne, at least if one is not among the world's poorest. But cohorts of aimless individuals are socially unrewarding.

Yet just how serious and lasting the outbreak of affluenza may be is uncertain. Wesley, Schumpeter, the Palmers and the Singaporeans were separated by long stretches of time. The disease may have waned in the intervals or it may strike only sections of the community. Although a slackening of effort is by no means rare, it does not predominate. The ship is kept afloat by the capital invested in social training on the one hand, and what Thorstein Veblen stigmatized as conspicuous consumption on the other, with the worst excesses dampened down and the capitalist economy still well able to function.[12]

SOMETHING NEW UNDER THE SUN

The colligation problem – where to start – can be solved with respect to the history of affluence by starting wherever the argument can be made to stick. This emphasizes the relative nature of the concept. Growth has been taking place for centuries and each upturn in prosperity has sowed its crop of social criticism. To the fury of preachers, Puritan restraint was early assaulted and the dams began to break with the abandonment or repeal of sumptuary legislation. Laws enacted between the 14th and 17th centuries had prescribed the clothing and adornments proper to each social rank. But fortunes made in trade and industry stepped round the prohibitions, while mass production simply swamped efforts to restrict what the common folk might buy.

Has the upward trend of consumption since the Industrial Revolution ever been reversed? Yes, times of depression have brought checks. In general, however, the juggernaut kept rolling right into the mass affluence of the years after World War II and keeps rolling still. Affluence ignites social change and this has always mesmerized critics and moralists, who come in two types. Conservative moralists prefer refinement over the crassness of the working class. The sociologist, Daniel Bell, even takes the heterodox view that a return to religion will be necessary to avert social breakdown.[13] Left-wingers take a different tack: they wish consumers would scorn material goods (and not coincidentally the capitalist machine) in favour of spontaneous, passionate, non-commercial forms of self-expression.[14] In their various ways, post-war critics like Galbraith,

Riesman, Marcuse and Hirschman point to materialism, meaning material abundance, as the root of all evil.

Have the critics anything fresh to complain about? Are they not, as it were, still worrying compulsively about maids dressing like their mistresses? The sheer scale of contemporary affluence, the ready attainability of cheap goods (or cheap credit) by all except the very poorest members of society, suggests there really is something new under the sun. Relative the concept of affluence may be, its benchmarks continually ascending with economic growth, but there has been a step-change. Forty years ago higher real incomes began to promise people all over the developed world liberation-through-materialism. The wordsmith, Clive James, who arrived in Britain from Australia at the start of the 1960s, noted that Harold Macmillan made 'a bid to touch the common pulse' by referring to 'a way of life based on the glossy magazine', but at that date 'his very words told you how remote the idea was from everyday experience'.[15] Shortly afterwards it was remote no longer.

The sternest parental authority and other ascetic role models – burned as self-control into the psyches of the Depression and war generations – fell into abeyance after about 1968. Actually they were pushed. Advertisers and an increasingly non-religious media (American television executives in particular are far less likely to attend church than their audiences) spotted their chance. They eagerly portrayed the world as a fairy tale of liberation from constraint. The fairy tale in question was compulsive viewing but became highly unedifying and may as well have been scripted by the Brothers Grimm.

The strain all this consumerist propaganda has placed on familiar institutions and existing ways of inducing discrimination has been without precedent. For centuries, settled communities had permitted the neighbours – and pastors – to make moral judgments good for a lifetime. Families always sat in the pew in church that was tied to their house or farm. No doubt the judgments made in face-to-face societies were sometimes unforgiving but it is difficult to believe they did not reinforce more formal deterrents to unjust behaviour. Character mattered. Modern society is far more mobile and seldom typified by lifetimes spent in the same place. Character is easier to fudge.

Old-style moral oversight is scarcely possible in an internationally mobile society where there are innumerable encounters with strangers every day; where place of work is separated from place of residence; and where, once one has made one's pile, local reputation ceases to matter. The loss of self-restraint, and of external restraints that were *morally based*, may ultimately be more responsible for unethical behaviour than the mere fact of affluence: consider again that Hogarth's Gin Age portrays destructive, uncontrolled behaviour in a society that was infinitely poorer than ours. Affluence, we may say, magnifies temptation but does not uniquely cause it. The temptation to engage in destructive and self-destructive behaviour overwhelms some individuals in any age. The violence of the Roman arenas may have ceased but such behaviour, for which tasteless would be too kind a term, has continued or (worse) reappeared. A loss of dignity and common sense too readily dizzies those in whom weak moral compasses co-exist with great resources and prominent positions. If they do not go literally whoring after false gods, they are certainly tempted into louche behaviour; witness the way so many leading sportsmen and their womenfolk are destablized by sudden riches and lured to fill the vacuum of their lives with crazed shopping sprees. Or they are tempted into irrationality, resorting like one American President's wife to an astrologer and a British Prime Minister's wife to the murmurings of a guru.

People like this have transferred their faith in conventional authority to what Frank Furedi calls 'an uncritical acceptance of the banal, morally illiterate pronouncements of lifestyle gurus, psychics and astrologers'.[16] Nor is any amount of secular education proof against this: the President's and Prime Minister's wives both attended elite tertiary institutions. With 'anything goes' examples like these at society's heights, it is not surprising we are witnessing mass phenomena like the wildfire spread of casinos or the ludicrous spectacle of Big Brother television programmes. Fish rot from the head.

The waterfall of cash in modern business has clearly revved up competition of an 'everyone for themselves' type. This is at its most persistent in the financial sector, the morality of which can scarcely be mentioned without contempt, but occurs barely checked throughout the business world – we have only to murmur 'Enron'. Even in the richest societies criminality and corruption occur at all levels, from stealing the boss's stationery to widespread insider trading, accompanied by an abject failure of external controls, indeed with a banging of the stable doors by public regulators after the horses have bolted.

The boards of public companies are inclined to look after their own. Consider the CEO of BP, who one year was punished (sic) for safety failures and deaths on his watch by having his pay docked to £4.57 million and the shares awarded to him reduced to a trivial £2 million worth. Despite his failures, though before he was caught lying in court, 103 business leaders for the seventh time voted this man the most impressive business leader in Britain.[17] Super-affluence tends to throw checks and balances out of the window.

WILL AFFLUENZA SELF-CORRECT?

What is unusual, many observers think, is the sheer speed with which white-collar crime recurs and effort threatens to slacken among age groups that have only recently become prosperous, or among their children. Affluenza itself is not new. As we have noted, richer, though smaller, elites have regularly withdrawn from business and retreated from openness, or at any rate from open-mindedness. This was Veblen's insight in *The Theory of the Leisure Class* of 1899.

Individuals announced their joining of the leisured few, said Veblen, and took to implying that their families had long been members of the elite, by imposing on their hapless offspring a near-purposeless education in the dead languages – a 'futile classicism'. There was little comfort in the fact that this tendency was much worse in the Far East. Arrivistes displayed their arrival by niggling insistence on correct spelling and by familiarity with syntax and prosody. They participated in sports that were marked, as they are today, by a belated uptake of new techniques and equipment: fly-fishing and horse-racing are examples. These activities do evolve, but only slowly. Elites concerned themselves with fancy-bred animals like dogs and horses, and went in for the breeding of these poor animals for abnormally specialized purposes, in the case of some breeds of dog to the point of cruelly incapacitating them for any purpose except show.

Veblen's point was that these interests and avocations demonstrated one's time was not passed in industrial employment. The origin of many a family fortune had been industry: the aim was to disguise the fact. The cultural lag involved survives because the persistence of fundamentally Victorian modes of education, sport, address and manners denotes 'an unproductive expenditure'. Therefore, of course, it marks out those who have arrived from those still obliged to earn their living and not yet possessed of resources to burn.

Veblen also introduced the concepts of conspicuous consumption and conspicuous waste, though he hedged his bets by admitting that the objects purchased may have some faint, residual utility. Moreover, he observed that part of the knowledge required by the elite was a grasp of the latest 'pro-prieties' of dress, furniture and equipage – the last of which we may translate into modern idiom as cars with speed, power and size beyond any real need or consideration for other road users. This, then, was the two-fold requirement: consumption sufficient to keep the wheels of industry humming (affluence), coupled with enough leisure to stultify the work ethic (affluenza). Consume but do not produce.

Are matters this simple, even allowing for the high level of abstraction with which social behaviour has to be discussed? Is affluenza truly so virulent and lasting a disease? May it not prove self-correcting? Perhaps affluence creates little more than a one-generation shock among many in each freshly-prosperous cohort. Most people are surely not quite so rudderless. After all, whole groups have continued in a self-denying state for generations. Low-key lifestyles have been espoused by prosperous groups throughout history, starting perhaps with the Humiliati around 12th-century Milan; while medieval monks and nuns clearly 'had the Protestant ethic without Protestantism'. To understand the quality of affluence, and particularly affluenza, we need to examine the dynamics of changing attitudes under the stimulus of rising wealth.

The self-consciously stodgy consumption pattern of Veblen's leisure class sounds more like exclusiveness founded on disdain than an urgent hunger for new goods. Contrary to the strongly-held view that 'new money' is more conservative than 'old money', a thoughtful study of the politics of the Forbes 400 richest Americans in the 1990s, compared with samples of rich people drawn from earlier decades, found the opposite to be true.[18] Old money is the more uniformly conservative. The new rich are more likely to have been raised in Democratic households, and although ultimately some become conservative Republicans, others do not. As a class, their political orientations 'tend to fall somewhere between the norm for their class of origin and that of their class of destination'.[19]

The old rich, whose families have by definition occupied the same social and economic position for generations, are less subject to these cross-pressures. Just as it is said to take three generations to make a 'proper gentleman', so it may require three generations to make a rock-ribbed Republican. Affluence, or at any rate super-affluence, does induce changes in opinions: no doubt the mechanism is cognitive dissonance, whereby values adjust to accommodate the new behaviour made possible, even probable, by a surge in purchasing power. Yet even if wealth is sufficient to support a change in social rank, rather than merely the acquisition of a lot of baubles, the accompanying shift in values is not likely to be instantaneous. An apprenticeship is needed before the new behaviour beds down. The initial grab for social status will be followed by a more sedate waltz towards the norms of old money snobbery and old money politics.

A recent account of the Australian situation divides the country's upper middle class into materialists and culturists.[20] The materialists are depicted as competitive where not downright greedy; eager for instant solutions (furnishing their McMansions en bloc from IKEA); and generally demanding the shiniest, biggest and newest of commodities. Their requirement of education is that it be utilitarian – at college they study information technology or engineering. The culturists differ in that they are keener on self-improvement for its own sake; they take their degrees in the humanities and social sciences; they are active travellers. They may take 10 or 20 years to furnish their houses, often using items obtained on overseas journeys.

In essence these are new money and old money groups. The latter includes families from the former landed elite who may have lost part of their fortunes and certainly fear being overtaken by the materialist 'aspirationists'. The implicit competition between the two groups unconsciously introduces ambiguity into the vignette, because the culturists are noted as spending, however reluctantly, just to keep ahead. Otherwise the dichotomy is a typical presentist, cultural fixity thesis, which freezes the membership of the groups at a given moment and does not allow for affluence to produce a different effect over time.

Such change as the account does recognize actually runs the 'wrong' way. Culturists are portrayed as feeling obliged by the competition from the visible display by materialists to spend more than they otherwise would. Maybe this is what does happen in fast-moving, goods-rich, suburban societies that lack a clear reference group like Veblen's elite, when society was more influenced by ancient landed values. But the analysis is static and does not admit the tendency for new money to norm on the less showy, more 'cultural' behaviour of old money.

Status will trump goods, at least above some threshold of wealth. We suspect that this really will happen and probably is happening, although minute examination of the budgets of families hovering on the frontier between aspiration and established status will be needed to detect the transition while it is under way. Speaking more broadly, freshly-minted business fortunes are being poured into the art market today, signifying that cultural prestige does continue to be attractive to new money.

The exponents of 'happiness economics', or rather unhappiness economics, seem to envisage people as gluttonous automata sinking into sullenness when the novelty of a new good wears off, but goaded into a further frenzy by the next offering of the wants-creation industry. Despite the likelihood that newly-affluent groups will splurge at first, an inverted U-shaped curve of response is possible: initial and swelling excess followed by a settling to more modest consumption. Affluence is not a one-off state, as the waves of consumption in post-war Germany suggest. If affluence can systematically self-transform in one direction, presumably it can alter in the other. The weariness of satiation need not mean appetites so jaded they can be prodded into life only by fresh material stimuli. Revulsion at excess can bring its own shift away from the pursuit of Mammon.

Admittedly there is plenty of evidence of affluent excess, but then we live in an age when more and more new social tiers are being made better off. The conspicuous element is the ability of the working classes in developed countries to rise up to middle-class levels, despite complaints that this particular ladder is harder to climb than before. It is hardly astonishing that rising real incomes can catch so many off-guard, given a barrage of advertising beyond any precedent – a feature that amounts to a steep fall in the price of information and itself represents an additional increment of affluence.

For all this, hedonic adaptation has a self-cancelling component. Consider the presence in any newsagency of magazines with covers depicting vulgarly naked young women, which would have been inconceivable a generation or so ago. Presumably someone does buy these magazines, and no doubt the eyes of young boys bulge at the titillation, but the more interesting fact is that few adults seem even to register their presence on the shelves. Response is dulled beyond outrage or even concern; satiation cuts two ways. The whole of society has not been seduced into the stews of lust, despite the fact that people may now, if they wish, afford to buy armfuls of the material every week.

A more compelling example of the muffled impact of materialism is the shift in attention towards non-material goods. Rather than rushing to lay out their marginal dollar on the latest product, a sizeable fraction of the population engages in cultural and political activities that do not necessarily cost much and do not involve accumulating commodities. The prevalence of hobbies like painting, photography, music-making, amateur theatricals, museum-visiting and so forth is a feature of the age. Affluence has freed large numbers of people whose parents, let alone earlier forebears, had too little time, too few resources and too poor an education to engage in these pastimes.

The tendency is better seen in the growing economies of East Asia than in established Western countries, because everything is happening faster in Asia. The Chinese are said to be the new Japanese, an allusion to their predilection for luxury goods and the fact that they are currently the highest spenders among tourists in Paris. But this makes it too easy to overlook the emergence of contrary attributes among the ranks of the new rich, such as massive spending on Asian art by the truly wealthy and a widespread return to traditional activities like calligraphy or composing *haiku*, even by business people.

More evident still is the start of a wave of political activism in societies typically written off as too cowed to engage in such things. This movement starts with environmental NGOs, because once people have filled their bellies with food and their dwellings with gadgets, the next thing they realize is that they do not want to live, or have their children live, amidst pollution. Demands for direct political representation and independent law show signs of following quickly.

There is nothing abnormal about this, though it is worth noting that it is happening in societies that, while awash with new consumer goods, are already moving beyond them. The same cycle occurred in the West, a generation or so earlier. For example, the 1960s generation in the United States felt secure in employment. It felt well enough off to pass from the bread-and-butter politics of the Democratic party machine that had dominated in its parents' day to begin agitating for environmental clean-up and pollution control.[21] Affluence releases energies and sustains tastes quite unlike the grosser forms of indulgence.

EXTERNAL RESTRAINTS ON GREED

Undoubtedly, the flood of information today does inspire acquisitiveness even without the help of the advertisers. There are always product innovations to catch the attention. Someone else is always objectively better off and the ability via modern communications to keep half-an-eye on so many individuals rubs the fact home. Nevertheless the most interesting aspect remains that greed is not entirely unconstrained. If it were, we would be choked by extreme competition and overrun by even larger hordes of discontented people. The appearance of a chronically dissatisfied population is created by observing someone around us who at any given moment really is dissatisfied, goading us into believing that *everyone* is.

What is it, then, that reins in greed? The mechanisms may be divided into external and internal restraints, that is, imposed solutions versus self-denial. External restraints, which we will deal with in this section, may be further separated into secular institutions and proposed authoritarian solutions. Society's institutions are mostly non-market ones, like the family, the law and local communities. Granted these bodies may not always work well and we have already mentioned that mobile societies permit some people to evade disapproving neighbours. Nevertheless, society's institutions have been voted into existence or assented to voluntarily, at least in principle.

The great secular ideologies lay claim to being ethical systems. Pope Benedict inveighs against the pretensions of both capitalism and Marxism to be substitutes for Christianity. While Marxism's record is too murderous to be taken seriously, even capitalism's record of self-policing is mediocre. Corruption and white-collar crime are endlessly exposed in the business world and the exposures are presumably only the tip of the iceberg. The checks and balances of auditing have been shown to be unreliable, even meaningless, at the summit levels of business. The legal system offers some remedy post hoc, but although law is essential for dispute resolution it is a weak reed, a moral maze that lawyers negotiate for cash. Lawyers scarcely find it in their interest to halt disputes in the first place, something more likely to happen through self-censorship on the part of those who believe God sees every sparrow fall.

Beyond society's ordinary institutions lies an illiberal layer of response that seems affronted by economic success and so hostile to individual rights that it seeks to suppress rather than persuade. This is the authoritarian approach, a new Puritanism that recognizes little merit in material well-being and would love to undermine capitalist society. The approach is quite different from older attempts to steer people away from misusing their incomes, such as the voluntarism of the 19th-century temperance movement.

Thus, (un)happiness economists are seizing on the finding that happiness does not increase proportionately above some rather arbitrary threshold of income, or more accurately that people will not declare they are positively happy when quizzed by interviewers. Armed with surveys apparently supporting their view that affluence is ipso facto self-defeating, advocates of the New Puritanism are proposing extreme interventions in the market.

Book reviews sometimes highlight the implications of texts more starkly than the books themselves and this is certainly true of works about affluence. According to a review by Andrew Oswald (2007), the author Oliver James urges in *Affluenza* (2007) that foreigners should be banned from owning the mass media in Britain; insists that the use of attractive young men and women in advertisements should also be banned; and makes a number of similar pronouncements, ending by insisting that education should be less focused on exam results and divorced from the needs of industry.[22] Despite his own sympathy with parts of the analysis, Oswald understandably concludes that *Affluenza* is 'ranting, sensationalist and journalistic'.

Before asking whether any notice should be taken of illiberal demands like James's, consider another book review, this time of the magisterial treatment, *The Challenge of Affluence*, by Avner Offer (2006). The review in question is by an American psychologist, Barry Schwartz, who concludes by saying he is not sure that Offer would endorse his proposals, 'but it seems to me that if he takes his own analysis seriously, he should. And so should the rest of us.'[23]

In Schwartz's version, *The Challenge of Affluence* amounts to a frontal assault on the view that choice is good and that raising GDP multiplies the options for more and more people. On the contrary, choice may have made us worse off, at least in the United States and United Kingdom. There are two reasons. First, we may be paralysed or reduced to exhaustion by too wide a choice and left unsatisfied by the feeling that something we did not choose is still on the table. Second, we are incapable of exerting self-control and as a result we indulge our short-term interests rather than long-term ones – Offer's book contains an entire chapter on the obesity epidemic to bolster this point. More broadly we acquire new possessions, says Schwartz, only to feel short-changed and thus continue trudging on the 'hedonic treadmill'. Beyond material possessions we seek status and jostle for positional goods. All this uses up our time, which is finite and should not be wasted.

Time is taken away from nurturing friends and family, including marriage partners (Offer shows an inverse relationship between marital stability and GDP). Inequality increases, which subjects us to psychological and physical harm. Insecurity is heightened. Poor us! So far these accusations are well known, though the evidence is more comprehensively researched in Offer's book than ever before. The question is, what is to be done? Here Schwartz steps in on his own account. Rather than raising GDP in order to expand resources for all, including the poorest, he wants to tackle poverty by 'a significant redistribution of wealth'. He argues that the logic of Offer's analysis is that the rich will benefit too: stripped of some of their wealth, they will be less plagued by choice and less tempted to lose self-control. 'This is a true Pareto optimal policy.'

Moreover, instead of policies to raise GDP, we should provide better schools, better health care, greener parks and more comfortable community centres. The working week should be reduced. A new system of national accounts should be introduced to measure 'what really matters to well-being'. Schwartz does not so much as hint at what would be involved, nor does he say explicitly how his programme is to be decided upon and carried out. One can guess straightaway that the decisions are to be lifted out of the hands of the fallible individual – but with the costs landed squarely on his or her back.

Distressed as he is by humanity's failure to make what he thinks are the right choices, and the failure of the economics profession to grasp what those choices should be, Schwartz wants to substitute politics, meaning power relations. His solution to the sins of fallible consumers, to be imposed by presumably infallible politicians and bureaucrats, chimes with that other fashionable consumption-reducing programme, the one playing on fears of global warming. 'Don't be an Exxon', says James Russell of the Clinton Global Initiative, 'work out what you can do to drive down energy consumption. Travel agents should push hotels for carbon disclosure'.[24] Like this anti-global warming campaign, the anti-affluence drive may become politically powerful. Both propose regimes run by people who, like the Puritans of old, are convinced they are right to think society needs to be prevented from consuming. At least the ostensible aim of the climate lobby is to reduce the negative externalities of carbon emissions; the anti-affluence lobby wishes to oblige us to reduce consumption as an end in itself.

The New Puritans will need coercive measures to get their way, because of the deadweight of human fallibility of which they complain so loudly and because there is a counter-movement among the young – surprisingly, not a drop-out or Voluntary Simplicity movement like the 1970s but a new aggressively consumerist trend. This is 'bling bling', a hip-hop craze that promotes free spending on flashy jewellery and a lifestyle of ostentation. The dominant urban youth culture now celebrates materialism, reports the *Financial Times* of Britain when describing 'bling bling'; in the United States it celebrates hyper-consumerism.[25] One way or another, the excesses of affluence are always with us.

THE MORAL ANTIDOTE TO AFFLUENZA

If external restraints on the ills of affluence are unsatisfactory for one reason or another, whence cometh our help? The answer may be summed up in two words: our consciences. All the world religions contain scepticism about aspects of earthly life, virtually by definition, but it is Confucianism (strictly a philosophical system) that seems to come closest to Christianity in providing a means for curbing opportunism on the part of the individual. Yet Confucianism does this by external means: the threat of public shaming. We would argue that this is less likely to be effective than the internalized restraint implied in the Christian conscience, the 'policeman in the mind'. One feature alone would seem to guarantee this, the fact of portability. Those brought up in the Christian tradition carry their moral code always with them. It cannot be abrogated by a change in context or abode. The words on a tee-shirt seen in Australia can never apply: 'It's only illegal if you get caught'.

For a Christian, wealth and material possessions are not of themselves the problem. As St Paul reminded his protégé, Timothy, it is not money but rather the 'love of money' that is 'a root of all kinds of evil' (1 Timothy 6:10).[26] Affluence tends to affluenza when the accumulation of material wealth becomes an end in itself and especially when people begin to measure their own worth and that of others in purely material terms.

In recent years, social scientists have warmed to this Christian theme. In a comprehensive analysis of *The Loss of Happiness in Market Democracies*, Robert Lane (2000) sums up his argument as follows:

(a) When income is plentiful compared to companionship, people who (b) believe that income and wealth are the primary sources of well-being, (c) see themselves and others primarily in terms of income and wealth, (d) engage disproportionately in activities they think will bring material success (rather than activities that are intrinsically enjoyable), and (e) derive their life satisfaction from their success or failure in materialist pursuits – will (f) enjoy relatively lower well-being than others.[27]

In other words, materialism may very well make you sick. Intrinsic goals, on the other hand, have been found to promote well-being and ward off symptoms of psychological distress.[28] Intrinsic goals are characterized by less reliance on the approval of others: 'by self-acceptance, good relations with others, a desire to help the community, and physical fitness and good health'.[29]

Christians are unsurprised that secular social science should turn up such convincing evidence against materialism as a source of meaning and purpose, let alone happiness, in this life. Christians believe that life's meaning and purpose – and the ultimate source of joy, if not happiness – is to be found in the biblical injunction to love God and love one's neighbour as oneself. Christianity also recognizes the inherent difficulty of doing just these things and Christians are therefore unsurprised to witness a world in which misery and lack of meaning are the markers of so many people's lives.

Stripped of a framework of morality, the market economy will call forth perversions of justice and humanity in the name of material progress. The upside of increasing affluence is that people come to recognize and welcome the need for moral restraint of untrammelled market forces, whether it be to protect weak and defenceless human beings or to promote environmental amenity. The superior record of developed market economies in upholding human rights and battling environmental degradation compared with non-market economies, both developed and less developed, speaks volumes in this regard.[30]

Without a moral compass, participants in the market economy can find that increasing affluence leaves them cold, or worse, clinically depressed and anxious. The downside of affluence is the subtle substitution of extrinsic materialist aspirations – which are life-diminishing – for intrinsic motivations – which are life-enhancing. Affluence can breed affluenza. Unlike the natural tendency for growing prosperity to increase the value placed on goods like universal human rights and environmental amenity, it is not clear that the value of intrinsic goals in personal motivation is similarly enhanced. Indeed, by strengthening the links between extrinsic goals and material abundance, growing affluence may undermine the very qualities that might otherwise lend affluence some lasting value.

Fortunately, as with Dick Whittington, the bells may yet sound the call to 'turn again'. People may learn to accommodate higher material living standards in ways that do not undermine their well-being. This may take the form of a religious awakening or a more secular adjustment in outlook and values.[31] We should not discount the power of scarcity – in this case of well-being – to call forth a supply response.

Christians will welcome a renewed focus on non-material values and motivations, especially service to one's fellow human beings, but also contentment which, combined with godliness, St Paul reminds Timothy, is 'great gain' (1 Timothy 6:6). Equally, Christians will look doubtfully on any response that urges a search for meaning beyond the love of God and neighbour.

Affluenza is a disease but the antidote is at hand. Heavy-handed intervention to curb the excesses of advertising agencies and other stimulants of materialism are neither warranted nor likely to succeed. But new mechanisms to cope with growing affluence are required – bulwarks against materialism and the 'senseless and harmful desires that plunge people into ruin and destruction' (1 Timothy 6:9). This is an opportunity and a challenge to Christians, as well as all those who see ultimate value and purpose beyond what we can taste, touch and see.

10. The role of business in the fight against poverty

Peter S. Heslam

Business has become one of the most significant and influential institutions of society for three key reasons. First, business is the means by which most people experience the impact of scientific and technological innovation, which has rapidly increased in recent years and has dramatically affected the way people live. Second, business is becoming a global form of culture in which millions of people across the world interact with each other on a daily basis. There has never been a time when so many people across the world have belonged to the same community of work. Third, global business enterprise demonstrates an ability to help lift people out of poverty by virtue of their own honest endeavour. These three factors alone are sufficient to indicate that business is vested with unprecedented opportunities to be an agent of positive social, material and spiritual transformation in the contemporary world. No account of contemporary culture, theological or otherwise, is adequate, therefore, if it fails to understand the purpose, potential and constraints of the commercial sphere.

Reasons abound why theology, in particular, should engage with business. The most important of these are clustered around the third of the factors above – the role of business in poverty alleviation. This issue provides the best starting point for theologians and religious believers to reflect on the significance of business, not least because of the conviction, held widely across the faiths, that poverty is not part of the divine plan for human beings. In terms of the biblical traditions, human beings are made in the image of God and as such are destined for *shalom*, a form of well-being that is as much physical as spiritual. Because poverty scars that image, it must be overcome. God has, therefore, a 'bias to the poor', which for Christians is embodied in the life, death and resurrection of Jesus Christ, whose message to the poor is one of good news. For this reason, material poverty is a theological as well as a socioeconomic scandal.

Business is the primary means by which, in the redemptive purposes of God, this scandal is addressed. This is because material wealth is the only solution to material poverty, and the only sphere that generates such wealth is business. This ought to mean that being pro-poor, as all people of faith must surely be, is tantamount to being pro-business – that to be concerned about poverty is to be enthusiastic about wealth. In reality, however, this is far from the way things are, at least in rich societies. Contrary to popular perception, it is people in poor countries who are generally most alive to the benefits of wealth.

One reason why the vocation of business to alleviate and safeguard against poverty is so often overlooked is the focus of the development community on definitions and causes of poverty. Even if a decisive definition of poverty could be found, and the causes of poverty properly understood, it is questionable how useful this knowledge would be compared with rigorous answers to the question: 'What causes wealth?'[1] While attention is often drawn to the fact that nearly half the world's population lives on less than US$2 dollars per day, the question of what happened to the other half is rarely asked, even though the answer to that question is vital to addressing poverty. To address poverty effectively, a solutions-oriented approach is necessary – that is, an approach in which the question of wealth is placed at the centre of engagements with the problem of poverty.

Without a focus on the drivers of wealth, and the conditions needed to maintain it, development thinking remains tied to a belief in the effectiveness of aid, despite all evidence to the contrary. This is reflected in the Millennium Development Goals (MDGs), on which much of the development community is focused. These goals, and the non-governmental organizations (NGOs) that so vigorously promote them, appear to underestimate how much enterprise development is needed to achieve them. To provide clean drinking water, for instance, in support of these goals will mean that approximately 270 000 households per day need to be connected to clean water supplies over the next 15 years. This will require thousands of engineers, builders and plumbers to lay the necessary supply infrastructure, the vast majority of whom will come from the private sector.

Business, in other words, is indispensable to the very goals it is so often assumed are achievable merely through public and charitable initiatives. To promote the MDGs without the promotion of private enterprise and economic growth is to implement a model that has long been tried but has almost always ended in failure. Charitable donations and government aid may bring short-term improvements, particularly in situations of economic crisis. But over the long term they tend to create dependency and victimize the poor. A more sophisticated approach to development is needed that recognizes the vast numbers of poor people who are dignified, resilient and creative entrepreneurs and value-conscious consumers.

Development agencies need to take a fresh approach to aid that focuses on catalysing, creating and facilitating enterprise development in poor countries. The recent experience of low-income countries such as India and China ought to be sufficient to indicate that there is no more effective way to alleviate poverty than through the vigorous growth of enterprise. This has been true for every rich country, and it is now true for every poor one.

Business alone is not enough to achieve prosperity, of course. This requires two particularly important factors that are frequently overlooked: first, the social institutions that characterize all free societies, such as property rights, the rule of law, an independent judiciary and a free press; and second, the cultivation and exercise of virtue beyond the requirements of the law. These elements have strong biblical foundations, and provide the context in which business can flourish.

Basic conditions such as these aside, there is simply no other way to banish poverty in the long term than through the vigorous growth of enterprise. Why then is this so often ignored or denied, not only by the development community but also in the media, academia and civil society in general? One reason is the negative attitude towards business that is so prevalent in the churches, which have played a key role in highlighting the plight of the poor and have had a profound impact on Western culture over the past 2000 years. Though the traffic in attitudes flows, of course, in both directions – there is good evidence that the church's attitude grew out of its wider cultural context during the early centuries of its history.[2] However, insofar as the contemporary blind spot towards the potential of business is attributable to Christian teaching, this chapter seeks to make the case that at least part of the remedy is the development of a theology of business, and that such a theology has greater prospects, both in theory and in practice, if it is based on the theological paradigm of *transformation* rather than the one on which it has been based ever since the advent of liberation theology in the 1960s, which is *liberation*.

CHRISTIAN ATTITUDES TO BUSINESS

To set this task in a theological framework, we use Niebuhr's characterization, or 'typology', of Christian perspectives on contemporary culture in his book *Christ and Culture*.[3] Although this typology involves inevitable simplification, it remains a useful analytical tool. For this reason, the Church of England Bishop of Lincoln, John Saxbee, has referred to Niebuhr's book as 'the key text for studies in religion and culture during the second half of 20th century'.[4] Similarly, the US theologian Stanley Hauerwas writes:

Reinhold Niebuhr may remain better known than H. Richard Niebuhr, but it is arguable that H. Richard Niebuhr's work has had a more lasting impact on contemporary theology. . . . H. Richard Niebuhr published 'only' six books, but his influence on American theology was immense. He became the teacher of teachers who would determine the main directions in theology and ethics in the second half of the twentieth century. (Hauerwas, 2005, pp. 194–5)[5]

When Niebuhr's typology is applied to attitudes towards business, the following types emerge:

Type I – Christ against business
Type II – Christ subsumed by business
Type III – Christ subsumes business
Type IV – Christ and business in paradox
Type V – Christ transforms business

While there is merit and deficiency in all five of these types, space allows discussion only of the first and last.[6]

Christ Against Business

With this type, the impact of the Fall on business is stressed to such an extent that Christ is seen in opposition to business. The only option for Christians, therefore, is to dissociate themselves as much as possible from the corruption of the business world and to focus instead on the new order established by Christ. As already indicated, this attitude has a venerable history that goes back to some of the early Church Fathers and their cultural context. Tertullian (c. 160–225), for instance, argued that trade can hardly be considered a servant of God, and that the acquisition of goods is motivated by covetousness, which is a form of idolatry. In the same vein, Jerome (c. 345–420) wrote: 'Avoid, as you would the plague, the clergyman who is also a man of business'. Today this sentiment pervades academic theology, though its origins probably owe less to aristocratic leanings of the Church Fathers than to the socialist leanings of the liberation theologians.[7] It is not necessary, however, to be familiar with academic theology to find examples of this type. Its influence can be found in many forms of popular spirituality, from the contemplative to the charismatic. Indeed, I have met business people from a great variety of spiritual traditions who have related to me encounters they have had with fellow believers who assume that business is so compromised a profession that they cannot imagine why anyone would choose to remain in it except for its material rewards.

Christ the Transformer of Business

With this final type, business is affirmed as an arena of Christ's transforming work. Culture, it maintains, is under divine rule and represents corrupted good, rather than evil. While all human achievements are vulnerable
to error, perversion and evil, human beings have the capacity to embody
within their work God's ordering and creativity. Culture needs constant
conversion, therefore, rather than outright rejection and replacement. The
process is one of transformation, involving both personal and social
change. Given the possibility of such change, those belonging to this type
tend to focus more on the strengthening and promotion of good practice
than on negative campaigning against the failures of business, their
concern being to work *with* business, rather than to antagonize it. They
endeavour to take a holistic approach, paying attention to the material as
well as the spiritual, the individual as well as the communal. While they
often express concern for economic distortions, they maintain hope in the
possibility of real change and improvements that are beneficial for all
concerned.

As already indicated, Type I is the most pervasive attitude in the church,
at least amongst its pastoral and theological leaders. It coincides with a
general antipathy towards business, which pervades both intellectual and
popular culture, stimulated in part by sensation-seeking media portrayals,
factual or fictional, of reprehensible behaviour amongst the business elite.
Against this background, it is particularly important that the weaknesses
of Type I are exposed. I shall pay attention to two of these before turning
to two features that commend Type V.

WHY TYPE I WILL NOT DO

Focus on Distribution

In recent years most mainline denominations have produced official statements on the economy. These documents generally express an admirable
solidarity with those in poverty and a commitment to letting their voice be
heard. They help raise awareness about poverty, encourage debate and
shape opinion amongst church leaders. In general, however, they fail to give
adequate recognition to the fact that, as business is the means of wealth creation, the market has a key role in poverty alleviation.

Three documents stand out as exceptions to this trend. The first is one
that, though without official ecclesiastical status, involved crucial input
from economists and business leaders as well as theologians and ethicists:

the *Oxford Declaration on Christian Faith and Economics*. One of its passages reads:

> We recognize that poverty results from and is sustained by both constraints on the production of wealth and on the inequitable distribution of wealth and income. We acknowledge the tendency we have had to reduce the causes of poverty to one at the expense of the other. We affirm the need to analyse and explain the conditions that promote the creation of wealth, as well as those that determine the distribution of wealth.[8]

A second notable exception is the papal encyclical *Centesimus Annus*, issued in 1991. Here Pope John Paul II is forthright in advocating 'a society of free work, of enterprise and of participation', and insists on 'the positive value of the market and enterprise'.[9] He is even prepared to highlight the advantages of the free market and provides a qualified endorsement of capitalism, if by that term is meant 'an economic system which recognizes the fundamental and positive role of business, the market, private property and the resulting responsibility for the means of production, as well as free human creativity in the economic sector'.[10] In John Paul II's estimation, it is when poor countries are able to produce goods and services for the global market that they have the best chance of escaping poverty:

> Even in recent years it was thought that the poorest countries would develop by isolating themselves from the world market and by depending only on their own resources. Recent experience has shown that countries which did this have suffered stagnation and recession, while the countries which experienced development were those which succeeded in taking part in the general interrelated economic activities at the international level. . . . It would appear that, on the level of individual nations and of international relations, the *free market* is the most efficient instrument for utilizing resources and effectively responding to needs.[11]

A third exception is the ecumenical document *Prosperity with a Purpose*, published by Churches Together in Britain and Ireland (CTBI).[12] As with the two documents just mentioned, there are plenty of qualifications; its endorsement of the market is by no means absolute. It is remarkable, however, that any endorsement at all should exist in an official church publication. The church representatives responsible for producing it clearly wish to distance themselves and their churches from the censorious attitudes that such statements have tended to convey:

> A purely negative appraisal of economic activity is unacceptable and an injustice to those engaged in it. Economic activity is instead something to celebrate. When it raises the standard of living of the population while relieving the lot of the poor, it is part of God's will for humanity. There is a need to redress a

perceived imbalance in the way Christians have regarded the creation of wealth by economic activity. They should recognize that it is one of the chief engines of progress and greater well-being in the modern age, both directly and indirectly; and thank God for it.[13]

Exceptions aside, most official church statements assume that the creation of wealth and the mechanisms of production are of little moral importance compared with the ethical imperative to address the inequities of distribution.

Productive justice is, however, no less important than distributive justice. Indeed, the ethical demands of distribution cannot be considered in isolation from the ethical demands of production, not least because without wealth production there cannot be any wealth distribution. For this reason, contemporary theologies and spiritualities that focus on identifying with the poor and reading the Gospel through their eyes need to be careful not to misrepresent the attitudes of many people trapped in poverty and not to misunderstand what is in their best interests. These interests have to include the ability to take part in the wealth-creating processes of production – they cannot be reduced to benefiting from more equitable distribution. It is perhaps significant in this regard that a major survey of attitudes to globalization across the world found that support for free markets is higher in many African countries than in the developed world as a whole.[14]

It is remarkable, therefore, how little has changed since the fall of communism; theological opinion within most mainstream churches still tends to regard capitalism as a system built on greed, acquisitiveness, materialism, consumerism, economic 'rationality' and individualism. Within this critique, there is little constructive discussion of the role and function of business and how theology might apply to it. Developed as it is in isolation from business, most contemporary theology is deemed irrelevant by the vast numbers of people who spend most of their lives working in the commercial sector or being closely associated with it.

Business Theology Stifled

Second, the mistrust that inevitably accompanies the notion of Christ against business serves to stifle a full-orbed theology of business. Some have sought to justify such mistrust by appealing not only to the teachings of the Church Fathers but to the New Testament, citing such passages as James 5:26–28 and the teachings of Jesus. In many cases, however, the origins of this attitude are far more recent, lying in the period between the two World Wars of the 20th century.[15]

To British intellectuals and other members of the higher social classes at this time, a career in business was a dull and contemptible way of life.

'Successful business is devastatingly uninteresting' is the way one of C.P. Snow's characters puts it (Snow, 1951, p. 93).[16] C.S. Lewis expressed utter distain for the car manufacturer, William Morris (Viscount Nuffield), Oxford's biggest employer at the time and one of the university's most generous benefactors. Comparing Cambridge – to where he moved in 1954 to take up a professorial chair – to Oxford, where he spent most of his career, he wrote to an American penfriend, Mrs Allen:

> Cambridge is charming. No Lord Nuffield (drat that man!) has come to turn it into a huge industrial city, and one can still feel the country-town under the academic surface. In that way it is more like what Oxford was in my young days.[17]

And he once wrote with disdain about the current 'Managerial Age':

> The greatest evil is not now done in those sordid 'dens of crime' that Dickens loved to paint . . . But it is conceived and ordered (moved, seconded, carried, and minuted) in clean, carpeted, warmed, and well-lighted offices, by quiet men with white collars and cut fingernails and smooth-shaven cheeks who do not need to raise their voice. (Lewis, 1961, p. x)[18]

In a similar vein, J.B. Priestley reproached, 'the shoddy, greedy, profit grabbing, joint-stock company industrial system we'd allowed to dominate us' as the real villain in English society (Priestley [1934] 1977, p. 66). H.G. Wells, likewise, dismissed entrepreneurs as belonging to:

> the urban variation of the peasant type, for whom urban property, money, and visible triumph over one's neighbour are the criteria for success. The first exploitation of the gifts of invention and science was very largely instinctive, unintelligent exploitation. And to this day the typical face of the big industrialist and the big financier has a boorish quality. (Wells, 1932, p. 318)

Even children's literature was influenced by this phenomenon. See, for instance, the attitudes expressed by George Banks, the London banker, in P.L. Travers's *Mary Poppins*.[19]

This situation appears not to have pertained to the United States, or at least not to the same degree. Abraham Flexner, an American observer of British university education, noted in 1930:

> Practical courses in salesmanship are conspicuous by their absence. The teaching staff are not unfamiliar with American developments, but they are out of sympathy with them. They do not pretend to be practical men capable of advising business concerns; no member of the business or commerce faculty at Manchester has any remunerative connection with industry . . . they have also found that successful businessmen have nothing to tell their students. (Micklethwait and Wooldridge, 2003, p. 87)[20]

The contrast between the British attitude to William Morris (1877–1963) and the American attitude to his older contemporary and fellow car manufacturer, Henry Ford (1863–1947), is particularly striking. Whereas Ford became something of a folk hero, attracting both fame and controversy, Morris was generally ignored or given only unenthusiastic recognition (McKendrick, 1976, p. vii).

It was commonplace during this period for industry to be accused of polluting the countryside, debasing culture and eliminating peace and quiet. Not surprisingly, therefore, pre-World War II Britain produced no more than a handful of university departments of business and accounting, and those that did appear took pains to resist contact with the business world itself. Inevitably, British companies were thereby denied both able recruits and up-to-date expertise. Some rebelled, of course, against the prejudices of their parents. Ian MacLaurin (Baron MacLaurin of Knebworth), formerly chairman of Tesco and Vodafone, who was born in 1937, writes in his autobiography about the snobbish, anti-trade sentiments of his mother (MacLaurin, 1999). But amongst those graduating from Cambridge University in 1937–38, fewer sons followed their fathers into business than into any other vocation.[21] In general, business was left to recruit people who had failed to make it into university or the traditional professions (Wiener, 1981).

Negative attitudes to business that were shaped in the interbellum have manifested a diehard quality. The obituary columns of newspapers have shown a relative uninterest in lives spent in business.[22] When historians refer to William Morris, it is generally to the Victorian writer, designer and socialist activist, who targeted his products to the rich, rather than his namesake and fellow resident of Oxford who sought to make cars for all (McKendrick, 1976, p. xxxix). Likewise, entries for business people in the monumental 61-volume *Oxford Dictionary of National Biography* (2004) are disproportionately fewer than for other major professions.

More recently, anti-business sentiment has been focused largely on multinationals (MNCs). National elites have seen them as threats to their rightful authority; conservative populists have condemned them as agents of cosmopolitanism; socialists have anathematized them as symbols of the highest stage of capitalism; extremes on both left and right have blamed them for the loss of Western jobs to workers in the East. The political power of MNCs, real or imagined, is often seen as particularly objectionable, responsible for the loss of democratic freedoms.[23] Such opprobrium appears to be intensifying, most likely reflecting the recent surge in the number of MNCs, facilitated through the revolution in communication and information technology, the lowering of trade barriers and the spread of deregulation.

This 'globalizing agenda' has provoked a rigorous response from a relatively new protest movement of so-called anti-globalization demonstrators. They burst onto the global media stage around the turn of the millennium, when some of their more anarchistic elements resorted to violence at major demonstrations in Seattle, Washington, Geneva and London. Challenging what they regarded as the awesome power of multinationals, they cast a number of well-known and successful companies in a sharply negative light. Multinationals, they claimed, represent a new form of imperialism. Their sheer size and strength allow them to penetrate traditional societies and thus to contaminate them with their perverted values. The effects include increasing inequality, social fragmentation and environmental degradation.

In response, big corporations and business journalists have sought to show how multinationals adapt their products to local taste and how their chief thrust on world markets is for ideas rather than cheap labour. MNCs combine, they insist, global scale with local knowledge. They also point out that multinationals are considerably less powerful and more socially and environmentally responsible than their critics claim and that they have helped to increase productivity, thereby raising living standards for ordinary people. Because of this, they maintain, they should be regarded as a force for good in the world.[24]

It is within this debate, which is often highly polarized, that a theology of business has so much to offer. It can provide a basis from which what is good about contemporary global business enterprise can be affirmed and what is bad can be challenged – on the grounds, for instance, of the basic goodness, fallenness and redemption of the created order, as we shall see below.

But the legacy of such a negative attitude towards business, which in church circles was significantly strengthened in the 1960s and 1970s through the impact of liberation theology, is that contemporary business is more frequently regarded as the problem that needs to be confronted, rather than a possible means by which problems of poverty can be addressed. The upshot is that the moral vocation of business, as distinct from those of family, education or public service, is simply ignored. This is a significant failure for the church, as it is the church's task to help the institutions of contemporary life, including business, to find and fulfil their various callings and charisms. As long as it maintains an attitude of contempt or suspicion, the church will be unable to articulate what it expects of these institutions. It will be left with a mode of theological and ethical discourse that has little contemporary relevance.

The theological resources available to us for a substantive Christian engagement with the ethics and purpose of business are perilously thin at a time when the business sphere has become so pervasive and influential in contemporary culture. This is a lamentable situation for the church to find itself in, not only because, as the economist Michael Hudson puts it, 'Civilization's economic institutions are the product of religious organization', but also because so much of the church's teaching could be made relevant to business, if only its considerable intellectual energy could be released in this sphere. As it is, the current situation, in terms of developing a theology of business, resembles that of the Church of England in the early-17th century in Richard Tawney's famous quip: 'The social teaching of the Church had ceased to count, because the Church itself had ceased to think' (Tawney, 1937, p. 188). Left in this state of affairs, the church is more likely to help make poverty permanent than to help make it history.

WHY TYPE V WILL DO

Whereas Type I will not do, Type V will do. The choice of words is deliberate. It is not that Type I has to be dismissed entirely; there will be times and contexts in which this type will be valid, such as in the case of corruption in business. In such situations, Christ's 'No!' can and should be heard. Likewise, in the case of Type V, 'transformation' is not so all-encompassing that it is the only paradigm with which business can adequately be addressed. It is, rather, one that is badly needed in developing a theology of business that resonates both with those in poverty and with those in business. There are two key reasons why this is so.

It Takes Account of the Impact of Business

In thinking about the contribution business can make to the positive transformation of society, it is helpful to go back to the Latin roots of some of the key words used in contemporary business. The word 'company' derives from *cum* and *panis*, which when compounded mean 'breaking bread together'; the word 'corporation' comes from *corpus*, meaning 'body'; the word 'credit' comes from *credo*, 'I believe (I will be repaid)'; and the word 'commerce' comes from *commercium*, meaning exchange, not only of goods and services but of opinions and attitudes. The intimacy in communication and relationship implied by the word *commercium* is reflected in its use to denote both a traditional feast at universities in Central and Northern European countries and sexual intercourse (the latter in Shakespeare, for instance). These meanings are deeply suggestive of the way in which contemporary business can be a transforming agent in society, helping to build credible, meaningful and inclusive patterns of community based on trust.

They even suggest that in doing so they manifest a form of sacramentality. This certainly corresponds with the experience of many Christian business people, who find that their workplaces provide a relational context for exercising their gifts that is deeper and more effective than those provided by their churches.

A single example from history is sufficient to highlight the transformative potential of an inclusive approach to business. Liberation theology assumes that the task of social revolution is the preserve of those excluded or oppressed by the wealth-creating processes of contemporary economies. The history of Marks & Spencer suggests, however, that business itself can be a vehicle of such revolution, by way of its inclusivity. By the mid-1920s, the four brothers-in-law who ran the company, which had begun penny bazaars in Manchester in 1884 and variety stores in 1915, had turned the company into a major chain of variety stores. At this point, they could have decided to sit back and enjoy their considerable wealth. Instead, after visits made by Simon Marks to US retailers in 1924, they decided to re-think the overall objective and mission of their business. The purpose of Marks & Spencer, they decided, was not retailing but 'social revolution'. It would seek to subvert the class structure of Victorian England by making goods of upper-class quality available to the working and lower-middle classes, at prices they could easily afford. This vision influenced the company's decision to concentrate on clothing, as, in the England of the time, what people wore was the most visible of class distinctions.

Therefore, instead of seeing business as the power from which we must be liberated, it may be more fruitful if we were to hold business organizations in similar regard to the way we hold our churches, neighbourhoods, voluntary organizations, schools and hospitals. We may even grow to love business, though to do so we would need to make concerted efforts to understand it and become more familiar with its constraints and opportunities because, as in the words attributed to St Augustine, 'you cannot love what you do not know'. This need for understanding is well expressed by two Roman Catholic writers, who call for 'intellectual caution by religious thinkers when speaking about anything as complex as modern business. The theologizing is bound to be better if there is a comprehensive understanding of what it is businessmen and women do' (Williams and Houck 1982, p. 23).

If theologians and church leaders were to do this, they would still find plenty wrong with business. But the attitude of trust that would spring from such love would mean that any judgments and moral demands they make are far more likely to be heeded and acted on by those within the business sphere. The prophetic, in other words, needs to be balanced with the pastoral. To fail in this would be to allow the role of the church to be banished yet further from the mainstream of society. As Ronald Cole-Turner writes: 'It is altogether too likely that the church will marginalize itself in the role of chaplain, picking up the pieces, caring for the bruised, mopping up the damage, but never engaging the engines of transformation themselves, steering, persuading and transforming the transformers' (Cole-Turner, 2001, p. 143). Change will come only when this work of engagement and transformation comes to be seen as a sacred task. Though sharply critical of the market for substituting God's economy of gift with an economy of exchange, Peter Selby writes: 'Those who engage with the business of economic transformation, which is the opening of the world to justice and the freeing of the world to a future of hope, are in my view doing work that is not just good but sacred' (Selby, 1997, p. 168).

Without developing a transformative theology of business, it is doubtful, indeed, whether the church will be able to construct a viable vision for the strengthening and renewal of civil society, as business has become the chief agent of social transformation. It is also the social form distinctive of an increasing amount of cooperative activity outside the family, government and personal friendships. As such, it is a cornerstone of society. Estimations as to which sector of society is most fundamental have often been exaggerated, of course, with damaging effects. For Hegel it was the state; for Marx, the commune; for Lenin and Hitler, the political party. Earlier estimations have included the church, the feudal lords and the monarchy. Each of these suggestions reflects the historical context in which they were forged. Today, however, there can be little doubt that business has become a pre-eminent social sphere in most of the Western world.

Within this world, nation-states are generally on the defensive, churches are in numerical decline, trade unions have lost their vitality and muscle, families are disintegrating and education (particularly higher education) and health care are under intense financial pressure. In the meantime, however, business has been going from strength to strength. Most employed people in the West now work in business and business supplies most of the world's products and services.[25] In the space of just a couple of decades, the role of business in Western society has changed out of all recognition. Areas of social life that were once assumed to be 'public' are increasingly regarded as the preserve of business – schools and hospitals included. Given such a seismic change in circumstances, it could be argued that anyone intent on maximizing their social impact would be better pursuing a career in business, rather than running for political office, climbing the academic ladder, joining the armed forces or becoming a cleric (Micklethwait and Woodridge, 2003, p. 10). As an article in *Fortune* magazine had it in February 1993:

Business and society are in the midst of a revolution comparable in scale and consequence to the industrial revolution. Years from now people will want to know what it was like in the great business revolution of the late 20th Century. They will look back in awe at enormous changes – globalization, the rise of networked information technology, radical new ways of organizing work, the emergence of a knowledge-based economy – and how these converged in that historic period. They will wonder how you got through it!

Whatever the pros and cons of this situation, it does seem generally to hold true that where opportunities to form businesses are constricted or the skills needed to sustain them are deficient, societies stagnate and remain materially deprived. The converse is also true – many countries in Asia, most notably India and China – are undergoing vigorous development in circumstances in which the amount of red tape surrounding the formation of businesses has been considerably reduced.[26] The United States and Canada now have more inter-corporate trade with Asia than with Europe, reflecting the fact that the focus of global commerce is shifting from the Atlantic community to an emerging Asia-Pacific community of nations. And despite the ongoing vigour of liberation theology in Latin America, the larger nations of that region are turning to a renewal of democratic patterns of governance, with an increased role for business.

Business is clearly a social institution to which more and more of the world is becoming committed. The biblical message needs, therefore, to be dynamically reconceived in social and economic environments far removed from those of biblical times. This task is at least as important to the future of humanity as today's theologies of sexuality and biomedical ethics. The biblical, doctrinal, ethical and interpretive resources of the churches have more to offer contemporary culture by means of a focus on business than has yet been seen to be the case. A rediscovery of these resources is the first requirement of all Christians and church communities that wish to speak with social and ethical relevance in today's rapidly changing culture (Stackhouse and McCann, 1991). The second requirement is to listen carefully and humbly to people in business, who are immersed in that culture and often face ethical dilemmas from which theological ethicists are generally protected. Otherwise there is a danger that the church's teachers will become like the lecturer in liberation theology that Harvard Business School's Laura Nash encountered who, when asked whether he had ever engaged in a discussion with managers of multinational corporations with responsibilities in developing countries, answered with surprise: 'Why should I do *that?*' He was quite certain that he understood the psychology of business people, which was bound by selfishness and greed and lacked theological grounding (Nash, 2007).[27]

It Takes Account of The Biblical Story

A second key advantage of the transformative paradigm is that it takes account of the biblical story of Creation, Fall, Redemption and Consummation. It is thereby able to avoid extreme positions that either denounce business as irretrievably corrupt or embrace it as synonymous with God's Kingdom. Unlike a liberational perspective, a transformational one advocates the reform, rather than replacement, of the means of production. The market economy, existing as it does under the sovereignty of God, is an arena in which Christians can confidently participate, affirming and strengthening what is good, mitigating the effects of the Fall, furthering the effects of Redemption and anticipating the coming new order.

Therefore, a transformational perspective allows business to be seen as one of the foundational spheres of human life that provide the moral framework for human flourishing. This sphere is constituted and shaped, at least in the current era, by market-oriented institutions and practices – in a similar way to which, in the political sphere, at least in high-income countries, democratically-oriented institutions and practices are predominant. Just as democracy has proven, in theory and practice, to offer the best prospects for human flourishing over other systems of government, the same is true of the market economy. Both 'systems' should, therefore, be accorded the kind of qualified ethical affirmation given in the papal encyclical *Centesimus Annus*, noted earlier in this chapter.

This is not to suggest that the market principle, any more than the democratic principle, should be read back into the pages of Scripture in an effort to gain blanket biblical endorsement. It is to suggest, however, that in developing a Christian ethical view of the role of business, the positive as well as the normative is important (the way things are, not just the way things should be). It follows from this that, if democratic and economic freedom can be shown to contribute to human well-being, this is of moral significance; the empirical is not necessarily antithetical to the ethical. Business can and should be seen as a key moral agent, towards which Christians ought to be committed, striving to provide moral guidance, inspiration, challenge, support and friendship for those who work within it.

The positive impact of such action would be felt on many levels, contributing to the reform not only of business but of society at large. As two leading proponents of 'relationism' argue: 'Reform seeks to create an environment in which it is easier to live righteously. It is both reasonable and right to mould society so as to minimize the conflict between Christ and culture. . . . Transforming society is about getting relationships right' (Schluter and Ashcroft, 2005, pp. 26–8). Moreover, it would help to maximize the potential of business to help extend the Kingdom of God. This kingdom is breaking into the created and fallen world through the redeeming work of Christ, even in instances in which Christ is not named. In words from the Second Vatican Council, to which Pope John Paul II appealed in his encyclical on work: 'Earthly progress must be carefully distinguished from the growth of Christ's kingdom. Nevertheless, to the extent that the former can contribute to the better ordering of human society, it is of vital concern to the Kingdom of God'.[28] Whether the extension of God's Kingdom through business occurs in explicit or implicit ways, Christian mission and development agencies are gradually waking up to this potential. Some are beginning to encourage business professionals to use their commercial skills to bring both spiritual and material uplift to needy countries. This new model of mission reflects the fact that business is becoming a transcendent global culture. Through their involvement in it, business people are finding that otherwise impenetrable societies are opening up to Christian witness *and* experiencing increasing economic well-being.

Again, this global business culture has great potential for ill as well as for good. It can be used to dominate, exploit and demean, as neo-Marxist post-colonial intellectuals are often swift to point out (see, for instance, Hardt and Negri, 2000).[29] The principle of reciprocity must always be maintained, therefore, as a safeguard against abuse. In other words, the transformers need the consent of those whose lives they propose to transform. It is arguable, however, that markets based on free exchange provide a rudimentary form of reciprocity. Many people in poor countries are finding that business, though having the potential to exploit, can be a vehicle of social justice, dignity and freedom from oppression. Indeed, a recent GlobeScan survey commission by the Commission for Africa found that most Africans lay the primary responsibility for the problems in their countries at the door not of global business, nor of the former colonial powers, but of their own national governments.[30] The critical question is not, therefore, whether globalization is good or bad but what *kind* of globalization is good? Whether it turns out in practice to be largely good or largely bad depends, at least to some extent, on how radically and creatively people with the appropriate skills follow Christ into the global marketplace, seeking to pervade every area of business with his truth, liberty and justice. As Richard Harries writes:

> We need a new vision of capitalism existing for all God's children. Such a vision and the determination to bring it about is the work of Christian discipleship in the social, economic and political spheres. The risen Lord, whom Christians seek to serve, calls us to follow him not only in our personal lives but by denying ourselves, taking up our cross and following him into the companies, markets, exchanges and parliaments of the world. If we do this we are bound to come up against vested interests, and deeply ingrained forces of institutional self-interest

as well as personal selfishness. But in suffering with Christ on behalf of the poor we will enter more fully into the joy of the resurrected life. (Harries, 1992, pp. 175–6)

For the call to seek first the Kingdom of God (Matthew 6:33) is not just for ministers and professional missionaries, leaving business people merely to support them financially. Rather, in the 21st century, business holds a vital key to unlock societies to the freedoms and joys of the Kingdom of God. Countries that have closed the door to traditional missionaries are competing with each other to attract professional entrepreneurs who can help grow their economies. Taking the opportunities for Christian witness that are naturally available in commerce is a vital and strategic means of cooperating in God's mission to the world.

This mission involves bringing salvation, healing and *shalom* to every sphere of society. The impact of the Fall is waiting to be undone. Because of the Cross and Resurrection, evil can be overturned and the scourge of poverty can be addressed. History is replete with examples of how Christians have picked up this challenge – through the political and economic framework of the Roman Empire, the trade relations of the Age of Exploration, the invention of the printing press, even through the colonial apparatus, and most recently, through global business enterprise.

Christian business people working in the global economy are uniquely placed to bring transformation to the circumstances of the world's poor. As they do so, they are ensuring that globalization works as a blessing, rather than as a curse. They are helping to realize globalization's potential to bring social uplift, serve the common good and help protect the environment. While the emphasis in liberation theology on seeing the world from the perspective of the poor is to be cherished, its economic dogmatisms, and those of other Type I attitudes, have to be set aside in favour of a rigorous and theologically balanced engagement with the transformative role of business in today's world. Without this, it is not obvious that the church will have a sufficiently compelling vision to allow it to 'make a difference' in contemporary culture. For a reconstruction of its theology will require a major shift in orientation and tone. But such a reconstruction is an important first step in making poverty history.

Notes

CHAPTER 1

1. Some authors have interpreted chrematistics as a technique that serves both *oikonomike* and *politike* (see Barker, 1959, p. 357 and Arendt, 1959, p. 28). Given that the former deals with the house and the latter with the *polis*, they consider that 'political economy' would be a contradiction in terms for Aristotle. In my opinion, however, they are stressing something that could be left aside because, independently of the terms adopted, the criteria proposed by Aristotle for using properties in the house and in the *polis* are the same. Thus, in this chapter I subsume in the term *oikonomike* the use of wealth both in the arena of the house and that of the civil community.
2. For this argument, see also Bochenski (1969, p. 187) and Sanguineti (1991, p. 46).

CHAPTER 2

1. This chapter draws (with permission) on work previously published by the author in Grabill (2007, pp. xiii–xxxv).
2. In criticizing the trade of the petty usurer (i.e., money-changer), Aristotle penned these immortal words, words that have shaped the development of Western commercial, legal, religious and ethical institutions since their inception: 'The natural form, therefore, of the art of acquisition is always, and in all cases, acquisition from fruits and animals. That art, as we have said, has two forms: one which is connected with retail trade, and another which is connected with the management of the household. Of these two forms, the latter is necessary and laudable; the former is a method of exchange which is justly censured, because the gain in which it results is not naturally made [from plants and animals], but is made at the expense of other men. The trade of the petty usurer [the extreme example of that form of the art of acquisition which is connected with retail trade] is hated most, and with most reason: it makes a profit from currency itself, instead of making it from the process [e.g., of exchange] which currency was meant to serve. Currency came into existence merely as a means of exchange; usury tries to make it increase [as though it were an end in itself]. This is the reason why usury is called by the word we commonly use [the word *tokos*, which in Greek also means 'breed' or 'offspring']; for as the offspring resembles its parent, so the interest bred by money is like the principal which breeds it, and [as a son is styled by his father's name, so] it may be called "currency the son of currency". Hence we can understand why, of all modes of acquisition, usury is the most unnatural' (I, x, 4–5). For Aristotle's fuller treatment of exchange and the origin, nature and purpose of currency (money), see I, ix–xi.
3. Aristotle's account of money (complementary to that found in the *Politics*), wherein he examines the proportion of reciprocity that must obtain in exchanges for them to be just, can be found in Aristotle (1962, V, 5).
4. Roger Backhouse provides an explanation of how the sterility idea informed the discussion of usury: 'The fundamental idea underlying all discussions of usury was that money is sterile. Making money from money is unnatural. Thus, if a borrower makes a profit using money he or she has borrowed, this is because of his or her efforts, not because the money itself is productive. This idea of the sterility of money was reinforced by the legal concept

181

of a loan. In law, most loans took the form of a *mutuum*, in which ownership of the thing lent passes to the borrower, who subsequently repays in kind. The original goods are not returned to the lender. This can apply only to fungible goods, such as gold, silver, wine, oil or grain that are interchangeable with each other and can be measured or counted. Because ownership passed to the borrower, it followed that any profit made using the goods belonged to the borrower, and that the lender was not entitled to a share' (2002, p. 46).

5. For more on this point and Albertanus in general, see Felice (2004, p. 606) and Nuccio (2005).

6. 'Along that subterranean and long-forgotten fault, periodic bursts of seismic activity are inevitably to be expected: the bumping, the grinding, the subduction, if you will, of those great tectonic plates of disparate Greek and biblical origin which long ago collided to form the unstable continent of our *mentalité*. And the later Middle Ages, I would suggest, can be helpfully understood as a period distinguished, intellectually speaking, by a recrudesence of precisely such seismic activity leading to, among other things, a reconceptualization of the metaphysical grounding of the law of nature in both the moral/juridical order and the order of physical nature' (Oakley, 2005, pp. 26–7).

7. 'From an analytical and terminological point of view', writes Langholm, 'there is much of Scholastic teaching that can be seen to have survived into modern economics. This is not surprising, since (at least if this observation is limited to our Western civilization) it was in the high Middle Ages that the foundations were laid for the kind of systematic reasoning about social relationships that has run on continually to the present day. Sometimes, as in the case of the fairness of the market price, it was deemed pertinent to point out a subtle shift in the moral basis which supported an apparently unaltered doctrine. Elsewhere, where doctrines have changed as radically as in the case of lending at interest, the Scholastics can still be credited with posing the terms of an ongoing argument. So it would seem that much of the old vessel remained to receive new content. The question is how completely it was ever emptied of the ferment prepared for it in the medieval schools. This is a subject which requires a book rather than a few lines. In fact, it has been the subject of many books, some of them provoked or inspired by Max Weber's ideas about religion and capitalism. For simplicity, let us recall that Scholastic economics rested on three intellectual traditions. The first support was the tradition of the Bible and the Church Fathers with its emphasis on individual duty. The second was the tradition of the recently rediscovered Roman law with its emphasis on individual rights. The two traditions were made to balance briefly and precariously in the Thomist synthesis by means of a third support in Aristotelian social philosophy' (Langholm, 1987, pp. 132–3).

8. Blaug states: 'One may doubt, therefore, whether recent work on Scholastic economics required a revision of the history of economic thought prior to Adam Smith. The Schoolmen may have contributed ideas that passed through Grotius, Locke, and Pufendorf to Francis Hutcheson and Adam Smith, but we are hardly justified for that reason in following Schumpeter's reduction of mercantilism to a mere by-current in the forward march of economic analysis' (1997, p. 31).

9. For more on *recta ratio*, see Bredvold (1959) and Grabill (2006, p. 217).

10. I accept the broad outline of Grice-Hutchinson's thesis regarding the School of Salamanca, but I prefer a more generic designation such as 'late-Spanish scholastics' precisely because its elasticity can better distinguish and still unify the later writers such as Luis de Molina, Leonardus Lessius and Juan de Mariana who are farther removed from Vitoria. Karl Pribram has noted some important differences between Molina and the Jesuits and the rest of the largely Dominican Salamancan group. He opted to segregate Molina, in particular, from the rest of the Salamancans, while still affirming a large degree of consensus on economic ideas between them (Pribram, 1983, pp. 27–30). This makes sense, as Laurence Moss and Christopher Ryan point out, 'because Molina, like his eminent contemporary Francisco Suarez, had comparatively weaker ties with Salamanca and the teachings of Vitoria. Their studies at Salamanca occurred well after the death of Vitoria and both had their longest tenures at the Universities of Coimbra and Evora' (Moss and Ryan, 1993, p. xi).

11. This text was published by the Clarendon Press of Oxford University. Those same translations have been reprinted as the Appendix: 'Translations by Marjorie Grice-Hutchinson of Texts by Spanish Authors', in Moss and Ryan (1993, pp. 143–68).

CHAPTER 4

1. Contributions to the economics and theology dialogue are collected in Oslington (2003).

CHAPTER 5

1. It will be understood that all our references to theology are to Christian theology – not because we want to deny that there can be theological reflection from other religious traditions but because we address ourselves to the tradition we identify as our own, and because it is simply tedious to add adjectives in any context where the meaning will be obvious.

CHAPTER 6

1. I take 'market economics' to mean the same thing as 'free market liberalism' (or 'economic rationalism').
2. During my doctoral studies at Oxford, I asked an Oxford Union leader about the narrow focus of debating within the Union. He acknowledged the problem, and put it down to the widespread and uncritical acceptance of free market liberalism, democracy and sexual freedom.
3. An actual Pareto improvement in the economic welfare of a society is one where at least one person is made better off without anyone else being made worse off. In reality, such improvements rarely occur, since they depend upon politically difficult compensation schemes. A potential Pareto improvement is one where the winners could, in principle, compensate the losers, even if this does not in fact occur.
4. Despite this tendency, economists are not typically behaviourists, as will be explained later.
5. A debate ensued, which is summarized by Frank, Gilovich and Regan (1996).
6. For more on this debate, see also Yezer, Goldfarb and Popper (1996).
7. The meaning of 'representative' diverges widely. The economic representative is an approximation or generalization, while 1 Corinthians 15 makes a stronger claim that every human person is literally (though mysteriously) a part of their Head – Adam or Christ.
8. As Stott helpfully argues (Edwards and Stott, 1988), Scripture and nature are divine revelation but theology and science are fallible human enterprises. I have called my construction 'theological man' rather than 'Scriptural man' to emphasize this point. The theology used is based on an evangelical understanding of Scripture. The admittedly non-inclusive 'theological *man*' is used to pair stylistically with 'economic man' but I will attempt to redress the gender imbalance presently.
9. Volf is commenting on Genesis 1:28.
10. Mill is quoted in Blaug (1993, pp. 60–61). On some accounts, the Enlightenment ended prior to Mill. I am using the term loosely to embrace the period of optimism about science and progress, which is generally thought to have ended in the early-20th century.
11. Quoted in Robbins (1932) p. 2.
12. The abstract reads, in part, 'This paper seeks to explain the initial successes and failures of Protestantism on economic grounds. It argues that the medieval Roman Catholic

Church, through doctrinal manipulation, the exclusion of rivals and various forms of price discrimination, ultimately placed members seeking the Z good "spiritual services" on the margin of defection. These monopolistic practices encouraged entry by rival firms, some of which were aligned with civil governments. The paper hypothesizes that Protestant entry was facilitated in emergent entrepreneurial societies characterized by the decline of feudalism and relatively unstable distributions of wealth and repressed in more homogeneous, rent-seeking societies that were mostly dissipating rather than creating wealth.'

13. The striking example of the Israeli crêche is even acknowledged in *Freakonomics* (Levitt and Dubner, 2006), who otherwise claim a very wide application for economic methodology.

14. However, it is not completely tautological. Inconsistent rankings do falsify this model.

15. The Hebrew for man (*adam*) sounds like and may be related to the Hebrew for ground (*adamah*) and it is also the name Adam (see Genesis 2:20).

16. Gunton draws his ideas from the theory of the Trinity. Reflecting the waning influence of the Enlightenment in theology, recent decades have seen the Trinity used as a source of theories for the relational aspects of creation. Prior to that, it tended to be seen as a logical puzzle to be wrestled with.

17. The command to fill the earth and 'subdue' it has engendered much controversy, with White (1967) famously blaming Western Christianity for environmental degradation. It is true that the description of man's dominion over nature is in terms of subduing it and controlling it. But the act of naming animals and caring for a garden speaks of respect for nature. Prior to the Fall, there is no mention of eating meat.

18. The adversarial language of Genesis 3:17–19 sounds as though Adam does battle with the ground, only to be swallowed up by it when he returns to the dust.

19. The biblical doctrine of original sin is complex, with some claiming that Adam had more freedom than his progeny. Regarding Adam's descendants, no one starts with a 'clean slate', but no one can claim that they are not responsible for their own addition to the stock of evil in the world. The Bible also states that sin is universal (Romans 3:23). Evans writes, 'although it is important not to view sin as essential to man's being (in that case it becomes a metaphysical necessity, not a moral choice), it is equally important to understand actual concrete man as sinful, in rebellion against God' (Evans, 1979).

20. In 1 Corinthians 12:12 Paul uses the image of a body with many parts to describe the single entity of the church, which is the body of Christ. 1 Corinthians 15 describes how fallen humanity is 'in Adam' and redeemed humanity is 'in Christ'. The use of the body in 1 Corinthians 12 could just be a literary device but this seems unlikely given the later usage in 1 Corinthians 15.

21. This is not true of Mill, who wrote that the pursuit of wealth has to be the *acknowledged* end to legitimize economic methodology. He thus took speech seriously, something that behaviourists are reluctant to do.

22. In reading the Bible, the 'heart' should not necessarily be given the modern association with emotion. In the Old Testament, it has a cognitive emphasis, even though it is a holistic term. In the New Testament, translators have wrestled with the appropriate translations of *nous* (literally 'mind') and *kardia* (literally 'heart'), sometimes rendering each 'heart' or 'mind'. In a personal communication with Dr William Andersen, he put it to me that these translation difficulties imply that it might be most accurate to translate them as 'heart and mind'. This combined concept might be a rough biblical equivalent to the more modern notion of 'identity', which is traditionally thought to include the affective, cognitive and conative (feeling, mind and will).

23. The Luddites were a social movement of British textile artisans in the early-19th century who protested against the Industrial Revolution by destroying machinery.

24. Stott's definition comes from G.K. Chesterton, who is quoted in Blamires (1980).

25. I am using 'Enlightenment' loosely to cover the whole scientific revolution up to the early-20th century – the latter being the high water mark for the prestige of science. Some of the following comments in the text about unbounded admiration of science may sound strange to post-modern ears, but Alexander Pope's epitaph (1727) of Newton

reminds us of another age: 'Nature and Nature's Laws lay hid in Night, God said, Let Newton be, and all was Light'. Interestingly, Newton had a more reflective assessment of his contribution than some of his popularizers: 'I do not know what I may appear to the world; but to myself I seem to have been only like a boy playing on the seashore, and diverting myself in now and then finding a smoother pebble or a prettier shell than ordinary, whilst the great ocean of truth lay all undiscovered before me' (Brewster, 1855). Mary may find it easier to live in the post-modern world than in the modern world.

26. Mary is conflating personal income with national income, and not worrying too much about any stock/flow issues. None of these are important to her point.
27. Mark 2:27, 'The Sabbath was made for man, not man for the Sabbath'.
28. Indifference curves are an analytic device for the modelling of optimal economic behaviour.
29. Harriet Taylor was a long-time friend to, and finally the wife of, John Stuart Mill.
30. Matthew 10:16.

CHAPTER 7

1. Here Drucker is presupposing a market economy since, in a socialist economy with no competition and regulated prices, human needs and wants are made subordinate to large-scale economic and industrial plans and the price mechanism is not allowed to function.
2. He writes: 'In a way, work is a condition for making it possible to form a family, since the family requires the means of subsistence which man normally gains through work'.
3. 'People of the same trade seldom meet together, even for merriment and diversion, but the conversation ends in a conspiracy against the public, or in some contrivance to raise prices.'
4. For an in-depth discussion of the importance of trust in business and market economies, see Fukuyama (1995).
5. God says to man, 'Be fruitful and multiply, fill the earth and subdue it, rule the fish of the sea, the birds of the sky, the animals, and every creature that crawls on the earth' (Genesis 1:28).
6. John Paul II writes in *Centesimus Annus* (1991): 'Indeed besides the earth, man's greatest resource is man himself'.
7. Proverbs 6:6–11: 'Go to the ant you sluggard/Observe its ways and become wise. Without a leader, administrator or rule it prepares its provisions in the summer; it gathers its food during the harvest./How long will you stay in bed you sluggard? When will you get up from your sleep? A little sleep, a little slumber, a little folding of the arms to rest/and your poverty will come like a robber/your need, like a bandit'. Proverbs 14:23 'All hard work brings a profit, but mere talk leads only to poverty'. Proverbs 31 praises the industrious and entrepreneurial woman.
8. See Sirico (2001).
9. See Noel (2007) for an analysis of market conditions in 1st-century Palestine. He posits that Jesus's teachings on wealth need to be understood in the context of the market arrangements in 1st-century Palestine.
10. See, for example, *Fortune* magazine's '100 Best Companies to Work For'. Many of these same companies also top lists in productivity and customer satisfaction.
11. For an overview of the contributions of the late-scholastics to modern economic thought, see de Roover (1974) and Chafuen (2003).
12. See previous section.
13. An involuntary action is, for example, swinging one's arm when startled in which there is no moral culpability. Non-voluntary is slightly more complicated. An example of a non-voluntary action is one in which a person is performing a voluntary action, say, for example, driving a car, and he or she runs over someone crossing the street. He or she is

driving the car so the act is not involuntary but he or she had no intention to hit the person so the act is not completely voluntary either. St Thomas would label this a non-voluntary action. Unlike involuntary actions, however, a person could have some moral culpability for his or her actions depending on the state of this will and intellect. With the example of the car accident, if the driver discovered that he or she had run over his or her enemy by accident and rejoiced in it, he or she would have moral culpability for taking pleasure in the evil that was done. The area of non-voluntary action and moral culpability can be quite complicated.

14. See especially, *Laborem Exercens* (1981), *Centesimus Annus* (1991) and *Person and Community* (1993).
15. For a helpful analysis on the difference between ontological and economic value and its relation to market price, see Chafuen (2003).
16. One sometimes sees this tendency among intellectuals and academics, who either may not themselves be interested in business and hence tend to absolutize their predilection, or worse, want to adopt a sort of aristocratic disdain for common work. The latter is more insidious since it often manifests itself in political policy action to restrain business. It is also quite ironic, since many academics are from common backgrounds and are able to engage in their profession precisely because of the wealth and economic stability created by business in a market economy.
17. For a general critique of CSR see Henderson (2004).
18. See Porter and Kramer (2006). They suggest that firms should engage in CSR activities related to their core business and strategy. While this is clearly an improvement and an understandable pragmatic approach, it still fails to critique the foundational misconceptions underlying the entire movement.
19. For example, Time Warner gives money to the Atlanta Gay Men's Chorus and the NYC Gay Hockey Association, both of which are most likely not comprised of economically disadvantaged members.
20. This disturbing trend turns corporate donations into almost a type of 'protection money' whereby firms 'buy off' potential critics whose protests or criticism could result in a loss of revenue for the firm.
21. For example, Planned Parenthood, which supports abortion advocacy worldwide, is a major recipient of corporate donations from places such as Banc One, Microsoft and Enron.

CHAPTER 8

1. Hereafter referred to as Pontifical Council for Justice and Peace (2005) or as 'the *Compendium*', depending on the context.
2. Throughout this chapter, there are many references to papal encyclicals and other Catholic Church documents. The author is not assuming that readers necessarily accept the authority of those texts but, rather, the documents are used to represent one consistent stream of specifically Christian analysis of economic issues that is intended to be global in application (see also the comment at the end of this introduction).
3. See Novak (1982).
4. See Gregg (2007).
5. See Sternberg (2004) for a very clear explanation of the meaning of corporate governance and of the dangers of undermining corporate governance by the pursuit of poorly understood notions of 'social responsibility'.
6. These points are well illustrated in the UK government's report: *Corporate Social Responsibility: a Government Update* (available from www.csr.gov.uk, undated, accessed 31 August 2007). The report has senior industry figures highlighting the importance of CSR for 'engaging business in regenerating our communities', 'contributing to sustainable development' but above all it states: '[the government] has linked corporate social

responsibility with competitiveness and . . . a trading advantage in global markets'. These goals may well conflict. Moreover, the first goal raises the question of whether the objective of business should not be to regenerate communities through wealth creation (there are other institutions that play more direct roles); the second goal raises the question of why the government has not set up a juridical framework with property rights and environmental amenities being appropriately protected so that business activity is naturally sustainable; the third goal has no ethical content whatsoever: if firms feel that certain forms of behaviour lead to raised profits, this is simply a restatement of the shareholder value approach to managing business. What is notable about the corporate social responsibility agenda is how it gives a wider role for governments, bureaucrats and business managers in a firm, thus blurring lines of accountability and responsibility.

7. Most notably, though not exclusively, through *Quadragesimo Anno* (Pius XI, 1931).
8. It is also worth noting that it is not unusual for non-Catholics to use Catholic social teaching to assist them in thinking through the implications of the Christian Gospel for the moral dilemmas one encounters in life: for one of many examples of this approach, see Griffiths (2007).
9. I use the phrase 'explicit cooperation' because a system of capitalism based on voluntary contracting always involves cooperation. How else could business flourish on the basis of freely agreed contracts without the cooperation of the parties involved?
10. It should not be thought that returns on capital are not important to general welfare because business owners are a small minority. If returns on capital are low, every man and woman saving for a pension – rich and poor alike – has to save more to achieve a given income in retirement.
11. The government school inspection agency in the United Kingdom.
12. There are many corporations that are not value-maximizing bodies – and these bodies are complementary in a market economy to those corporate bodies that are businesses whose aim is to maximize their business value. We do not concern ourselves with non-value-maximizing corporations here.
13. There is a huge literature on what is known as the 'principal–agent problem'. Though corporations may be an efficient form of business organization, it is difficult to ensure that the agents (managers) follow the objectives of principals (shareholders) because of the divorce between ownership and control. Many of the proposals of the corporate social responsibility lobby exacerbate this problem.
14. Indeed the Catholic Church does take a very pragmatic line on child labour (see *Compendium*, paragraph 245).
15. There are times when profit does not measure the full social contribution of business, because of the existence of monopolies, externalities and so on. These specific economic problems are normally best alleviated by the promotion of competition and the wider application of property rights (although externalities can sometimes better be dealt with by regulation and taxes or user charges). Nevertheless, notwithstanding the comments below about the operation of business in countries with poor legal systems, profit is normally the best indicator of a business's economic contribution.
16. However, the empirical evidence advanced in the *Compendium*, *PP* and *SRS* is questioned in Booth (2007, p. 65).
17. For example, a single employer in a particular locality.
18. Leaving aside for the moment the definition of a dignified living.
19. This has become a generally accepted point in economics. There are good discussions of this in de Soto (2000), Gwartney and Lawson (2004) and Wolf (2004).
20. See *Quadragesimo Anno* (Pius XI, 1931) and *Laborem Exercens* (John Paul II, 1981).
21. See Booth and Whetstone (2007) for an analysis of 'fair trade' and the references contained therein.
22. For example, if one farmer were paid (say) £200 per tonne for a particular raw material and the buyer then visits another farm whose owner is illiterate, ignorant of alternative opportunities and desperate for food, it could be regarded as unjust to pay that farmer £100 per tonne, even if that were the agreed price.
23. See also the excellent discussion in Lamoureux (2005).

24. See Kis-Katos and Schulze (2005).
25. For example, Prof. Terrence Keeley, Vice-Chancellor of the University of Buckingham, is a prominent advocate of abolishing all patent protection.
26. This is not to say that trade rules should not be compatible with maintaining patent protection but that countries should not act as a cartel to exploit their advantage.
27. There is a wide body of evidence comparing unemployment durations in countries with more liberal labour laws with circumstances in countries that have less liberal labour laws. See also Table 2 in Siebert (2005), which shows that, in France, the proportion of workers employed with less than one year of prior experience can be less than 10 per cent of the proportion in the United Kingdom. Youth unemployment in France is twice the level in the United Kingdom. It is also worth noting that, as the United Kingdom has tightened labour market regulation in the last ten years, youth unemployment as a proportion of total unemployment has increased.
28. In fact, the precise statement is ambiguous. '[I]n which national States show limits in their capacity to govern the rapid processes of change that effect [sic] international economic and financial responsibilities'. This could refer to a situation in which all governments are increasingly finding it difficult, for good or ill, to control economic activity that has a global context or a situation where particular governments are generally inadequate.
29. There may be some difficult situations in practice here. For example, if a lorry load of perishable goods is crossing the border of a poor country, is it morally correct to bribe a customs officer to allow the goods to cross? There may be an element of 'choosing the lesser of two evils' but one should be careful not to 'pursue evil so that good might come from it'. More discussion of such issues among Christians would be extremely helpful.
30. There is an enormous range of 'ethical' funds and investors should make their own judgments. However, the Friends Provident Stewardship fund (one of the oldest 'ethical' funds) gives companies a negative rating if they are involved with the manufacture or sale of weapons, nuclear power, significant involvement in tobacco or alcohol production (though there is some discretion in the case of alcohol) or gambling.

CHAPTER 9

1. Brickman and Campbell (1971).
2. BBC Radio 4, 11 May 2007.
3. Behrend (2006, p. 246).
4. Ker Conway (1992, p. 209).
5. Hirsch (1978).
6. Chang (1993).
7. See Offer (2006). For the benefit of his readers, whom he evidently presumes to be affluent and hence impatient, Offer sums up the theme of his book in one line: 'Affluence breeds impatience, and impatience undermines well-being' (p. 1).
8. Silverstein and Fiske (2003).
9. Use of the term 'affluenza' has evolved over time. In the current context, the term refers to the mooted effect of affluence on the work ethic. In recent times, the term has come to refer more to the effect on people's psychological condition or moral outlook, and may be marked (among other things) by a morbidly increased rather than diminished devotion to work (so-called 'workaholism'). Our use of the term should be clear from the context.
10. The late Miss Felicity Palmer, pers. comm.
11. *Financial Times*, 8 May 2007.
12. Veblen (1918).
13. Bell (1976, p. 29). If secular meanings prove an illusion, what holds one to reality [he writes] is, 'the return in Western society of some conception of religion'. For a similar sentiment, see Goff and Fleisher (1999, p. 209ff.)

14. Horowitz (1985).
15. James (1986, p. 176).
16. See Furedi (2005).
17. *Financial Times*, 15 January 2007 and 7 March 2007.
18. Burris (2000, pp. 360–78).
19. Ibid., p. 374.
20. West (2006).
21. Crenson (1971).
22. Oswald (2007); James (2007).
23. See Offer (2006) and Schwartz (2007).
24. *Financial Times*, 14 May 2007.
25. *Financial Times*, 12 May 2007.
26. Quotations from *The Holy Bible* are according to the *New International Version* (1984), Grand Rapids, Michigan: Zondervan Bible Publishers.
27. Lane (2000, p. 146).
28. Kasser and Ryan (1996, pp. 280–87).
29. Lane, op cit.
30. For development of this point, see Friedman (2005).
31. Fogel (2000).

CHAPTER 10

1. In a forthcoming article, Peter Heslam argues that it was mainly Pope John Paul II's willingness to ask this question that makes his encyclical *Centesimus Annus* of 1991 distinctive in Catholic social teaching. An earlier version of this article is 'Entering the circle of exchange: Catholic social teaching and the role of business in the eradication of poverty', a conference paper presented with Ben Andradi and available at www.stthomas.edu/CathStudies/cst/conferences/thegoodcompany.
2. For an exposition and evaluation of the key teachings on wealth and poverty of the patristic period, see Heslam's forthcoming article 'Can Christianity give a positive value to wealth? An engagement with the Church Fathers'. An earlier version of this article is available at www.transforming business.net.
3. Niebuhr ([1951] 2002).
4. *Church Times*, 28 May 2004.
5. For a more detailed account of Niebuhr's impact, see Werpehowski (2003). Notable critiques of Niebuhr's scheme include Yoder (1996), Marsden (1999), Gathje (2002) and Gorringe (2004a, pp. 12–16).
6. For fuller applications of Niebuhr's scheme to economic institutions, see Preston (1979, pp. 7–9); van Wensveen Siker (1989) and Krueger (1997, pp. 30–34).
7. See, for example, Gorringe (2004b). Many theologians influenced by feminist and Radical Orthodox theology conform to this type. See, for instance, Moe-Lobeda (2004). John Milbank, one of the foremost representatives of Radical Orthodoxy, is sharply critical of market economics (Milbank, 1990). For a robust critique of Radical Orthodoxy, see Insole (2004).
8. The declaration was first published in *Transformation* (April/June 1990), pp. 1–8. It was later published, with analysis and comment, in Schlossberg, Samuel and Sider (eds) (1994) and in Stackhouse et al. (eds) (1995), pp. 472–82. The citation is from section 36.
9. *Centesimus Annus* (John Paul II, 1991), sections 35 and 43.
10. *Centesimus Annus* (John Paul II, 1991), sections 40 and 42.
11. *Centesimus Annus* (John Paul II, 1991), sections 33 and 34. It is important to re-emphasize that Pope John Paul II's endorsement of the free market is not unqualified and he reserves a strong role for the state in regulating the economy.
12. Churches Together in Britain and Ireland (2005).

13. Ibid., pp. 15–16.
14. Taking all the countries surveyed, support for free-market economic systems is greater in high-income rather than low-income countries, but only marginally so (66 per cent compared with 63 per cent). Nigeria (80 per cent) and the Ivory Coast (79 per cent) were the developing countries showing the greatest support in Africa. Vietnam (90 per cent) showed the greatest support overall. See The Pew Global Attitudes Project (2003, pp. 103–5).
15. Precedents can, however, be found in the Victorian novel. See, for instance, the prejudice expressed towards those involved in trade in Gaskell (1855). The heroine, Margaret Hale, attempts to defend John Thornton, a wealthy manufacturer, against the snobbery of her mother but unwittingly her words are full of irony: 'And as for Mr Thornton being in trade, why he can't help that now, poor fellow. I don't suppose his education would fit him for much else' (vol I, p. 114). Later Margaret exclaims: 'I don't like shoppy people. . . . I like all people whose occupations have to do with land; I like soldiers and sailors, and the learned professions, as they call them. I'm sure you don't want me to admire butchers and bakers, and candlestick-makers, do you mamma?' Eventually, however, Margaret becomes conscious of her own snobbery. Another example of Victorian anti-business sentiment is Mr Bulstrode, the 'evangelical' though hypocritical banker in Eliot (1871–73).
16. This novel is part of Snow's *Strangers and Brothers* series, which was published between 1940 and 1974 but depicts English life between 1930 and 1960.
17. The letter is dated 26 November 1955. Cited in Green and Hooper (1974), p. 286.
18. From the Preface. Further reflections by Lewis on commerce and industry can be found in Lewis (1960).
19. First published in London by Peter Davies in 1934.
20. No source given.
21. *University Education and Business: A Report by a Committee Appointed by the Cambridge University Appointments Board*, published in 1946. Cited in Sanderson (1972), p. 283.
22. Roy Lewis and Rosemary Stewart studied the obituaries in *The Times* for three months in 1957 and noted that out of 203 obituaries only 12 featured business people (whereas 34 featured military professionals) and that these 12 were comparatively short. See Lewis and Stewart (1961), p. 29.
23. The irrelevance of traditional categories of 'right' and 'left' within this debate is noted in Heslam (2002), pp. 4–5.
24. See de Grauwe and Camerman (2003). The defensive tone of the argument is reflected in the titles of Norberg's *In Defence of Global Capitalism* (2001) and Bhagwati's *In Defence of Globalization* (2004). See also Lloyd (2001); Hilton and Gibbons (2002); Mosbacher (2002) and Wolf (2004).
25. According to the National Audit Office, there are around 4 million companies in the UK, 99 per cent of them being relatively small (employing fewer than 50 people).
26. Registering property in Norway requires one step, but 16 in Algeria. To incorporate a business takes two days in Canada, but 153 in Mozambique. In Haiti it takes 203 days longer than in Australia. In Sierra Leone it costs 1268 per cent of average income, compared with nothing in Denmark. To register in Ethiopia, a would-be entrepreneur must deposit the equivalent of 18 years' average income in a bank account, which is then frozen. In Lagos, Nigeria's commercial capital, recording a property sale involves 21 procedures and takes 274 days. These and other regulatory and bureaucratic obstacles to prosperity can be found in the World Bank's *Doing Business* reports available at www.doingbusiness.org.
27. Nash and her colleague Scotty McLennan came across many examples of this attitude in the extensive surveys and interviews they carried out in preparation for their co-authored book, Nash and McLennan (2001).
28. *Gaudium et Spes* (1965), section 39; *Laborem Exercens* (John Paul II, 1981), section 27.
29. See especially sections 3.4 and 3.6.
30. The results showed that 49 per cent blamed their own politicians; 16 per cent blamed former colonial powers; and 11 per cent blamed other rich countries. In other words, three times more Africans blamed their own countries than former colonial powers. See the Commission for Africa (2005), p. 41.

Bibliography

Abellán, José Luís (1979), *Historia Crítica Del Pensamiento Español*, 5 vols, Madrid: Espasa-Calpe.

Akerlof, George. A. and R.E. Kranton (2000), 'Economics and identity', *Quarterly Journal of Economics*, **140** (3), 715–53.

Albertanus of Brescia (1243), '*Genovese Sermon*', translated by Patrick T. Brannan, S.J., *Journal of Markets & Morality*, **7** (2), 623–38.

Alvey, James E. (1999), 'A short history of economics as a moral science', *Journal of Markets & Morality*, **2** (1), 53–73.

Alvey, James E. (2004), 'The secret, natural theological foundation of Adam Smith's work', *Journal of Markets & Morality*, **7** (2), 335–61.

Anderson, Digby (1984), *The Kindness That Kills: The Churches' Simplistic Response to Complex Social Issues*, London: SPCK.

Aquinas, Thomas ([b. 1225–d. 1274] 1948), *Summa Theologica*, reprinted in Anton C. Pegin (ed.), New York: Random House.

Aquinas, Thomas (1949), 'De Veritae', in *Quaestiones Disputatae I*, Torino and Rome: Marietti.

Arendt, Hannah (1959), *The Human Condition*, New York: Doubleday.

Aristotle (1958), *The Politics of Aristotle*, edited and translated by E. Barker, Oxford: Oxford University Press.

Aristotle (1962), *Nicomachean Ethics*, translated by Martin Ostwald, Indianapolis and New York: Bobbs-Merrill.

Aspinwall, Bernard (1999), 'William Robertson and America', in T.M. Devine and J.R. Young (eds), *Eighteenth-century Scotland: New Perspectives*, East Lothian: Tuckwell Press, pp. 152–75.

Augustine of Hippo (1958), *De Doctrina Christiana*, reprinted in D.W. Robertson's translation, *On Christian Doctrine*, New York: Liberal Arts Press.

Ayres, Clarence E. (1955), *The Theory of Economic Progress: A Study of the Fundamentals of Economic Development and Cultural Change*, Chapel Hill, NC: North Carolina University Press.

Backhouse, Roger E. (2002), *The Ordinary Business of Life: A History of Economics from the Ancient World to the Twenty-first Century*, Princeton, NJ and Oxford: Princeton University Press.

Barker, Ernest (1959), *The Political Thought of Plato and Aristotle*, New York: Dover Publications.

Barnes, Jonathan (1980), 'Aristotle and the methods of ethics', *Revue Internationale de Philosophie*, **133** (4), 490–511.

Barnes, Jonathan (1993), *Aristóteles*, Madrid: Cátedra, translated by Marta Sansigre Vidal from (1982), *Aristotle*, Oxford: Oxford University Press.

Barnes, Jonathan (1995), *The Complete Works of Aristotle: The Revised Oxford Translation*, 6th printing with corrections, Princeton, NJ: Princeton University Press.

Barrera, Albino (2001), *Modern Catholic Social Documents and Political Economy*, Washington, DC: Georgetown University Press.

Barrera, Albino (2005), *God and the Evil of Scarcity: Moral Foundations of Economic Agency*, Notre Dame, IN: University of Notre Dame Press.

Bastiat, Frederic (1850), *Harmonies Economiques*, Paris: Guillaumin.

Bateman, Bradley W. (forthcoming), 'Reflections on the secularization of American economics', *Journal of the History of Economic Thought*.

Bateman, Bradley W. and Ethan B. Kapstein (1999), 'Between God and the market: the religious roots of the American Economic Association', *Journal of Economic Perspectives*, **13** (4), 249–58.

Bauer, Peter T. (1984), 'Ecclesiastical economics: envy legitimized', in *Reality and Rhetoric*, Harvard: Harvard University Press.

Bavinck, Herman (2003), *Reformed Dogmatics*, vol. 1, in John Bolt (ed.), *Prolegomena*, translated by John Vriend, Grand Rapids, MI: Baker Academic.

Baxter, Richard ([b. 1615–d. 1691] 2005), *Directions About Our Labour and Callings*, reprinted in William C. Plancher (ed.), *Callings: Twenty Centuries of Christian Wisdom on Vocation*, Grand Rapids, MI: Wm B. Eerdmans.

Becker Gary S. (1976), *The Economic Approach to Human Behaviour*, Chicago, IL: University of Chicago Press.

Becker Gary S. (1981), *A Treatise on the Family*, Cambridge, MA: Harvard University Press.

Behrend, Ivan T. (2006), *An Economic History of Twentieth-century Europe*, Cambridge: Cambridge University Press.

Bell, Daniel (1976), *The Cultural Contradictions of Capitalism*, New York: Basic Books.

Berti, Enrico (1992), 'La razionalità pratica nella concezione aristotelica', in Sergio Galvan (ed.), *Forme di razionalità pratica*, Milan: Angeli, pp. 55–76.

Bettenson, Henry (ed.) (1956), *The Early Christian Fathers: A Selection from the Writings of the Fathers from St. Clement of Rome to St. Athanasius*, London and New York: Oxford University Press.

Bhagwati, Jagdish (2004), *In Defence of Globalization*, Oxford: Oxford University Press.

Black, Robert A. (2006), 'What did Adam Smith say about self-love?', *Journal of Markets & Morality*, **9** (1), 7–34.

Blair, H. ([1777] 1819), *Sermons*, reprinted in W. Creech (ed.), *Sermons*, 3 vols, London: T. Cadell and W. Davies.

Blamires, Harry (1980), *Where Do We Stand?*, London: SPCK.

Blaug, Mark (1985), *Great Economists Since Keynes*, Aldershot, UK and Brookfield, US: Edward Elgar, p. 256.

Blaug, Mark (1993), *The Methodology of Economics or How Economists Explain*, 2nd edn, London: University of London.

Blaug, Mark (1997), *Economic Theory in Retrospect*, 5th edn, Cambridge: Cambridge University Press.

Bochenski, Joseph Maria (1969), *Los métodos actuales del pensamiento*, Madrid: Rialp, also published as *Die zeitgenössischen Denkmethoden*, translated by Raimundo Drudis Baldrich, Bern: A. Francke Verlag and Munich: Leo Lehnen Verlag.

Boettke, Peter J. (1998), 'Is economics a moral science? A response to Ricardo F. Crespo', *Journal of Markets & Morality*, **1** (2), 212–19.

Bonar, James (1966), *A Catalogue of the Library of Adam Smith, Author of the 'Moral Sentiments' and 'The Wealth of Nations'*, 2nd edn, New York: A.M. Kelly.

Booth, Philip M. (ed.) (2007), *Catholic Social Teaching and the Market Economy*, London: Institute of Economic Affairs.

Booth, Philip M. and L. Whetstone (2007), 'Half a cheer for fair trade', *Economic Affairs*, **27** (2), 29–38.

Bredvold, Louis I. (1959), 'The meaning of the concept of right reason in the natural-law tradition', *University of Detroit Law Journal*, **36** (December), 120–29.

Brewster, Sir David (1855), *Memoirs of the Life, Writings and Discoveries of Sir Isaac Newton*, 2 vols, Edinburgh: Thomas Constable & Co.

Brickman, Philip and Donald T. Campbell (1971), 'Hedonic Relativism and Planning the Good Society', in M.H. Appley (ed.), *Adaptation-level Theory: A Symposium*, New York: Academic Press.

Brooke, John H. (1991), *Science and Religion: Some Historical Perspectives*, Cambridge: Cambridge University Press.

Broome, John (1999), *Ethics Out of Economics*, Oxford: Oxford University Press.

Buber, Martin ([1923] 1970), *I and Thou*, reprinted with translation by Walter Kaufman, New York: Touchstone.

Burnet, John (1900), *The Ethics of Aristotle*, London: Methuen.

Burris, Val (2000), 'The myth of old money liberalism: the politics of the *Forbes* 400 richest Americans', *Social Problems*, **47** (3), 360–78.

Burtt, Edwin A. (1954), *The Metaphysical Foundations of Modern Science*, Garden City, NY: Doubleday Anchor Books.

Camacho, Francisco Gómez (1985), 'Luis de Molína y la metodología de la ley natural', *Miscelánea Comillas*, **43** (82), 155–94.

Camacho, Francisco Gómez (1990), 'El triángulo Glasgow, París, Salamanca y los orígenes de la ciencia económica', *Miscelánea Comillas*, **48** (92), 231–55.

Camacho, Francisco Gómez (1998a), *Economía y filosofía moral: la formación del pensameinto económico europeo en la Escolástica Española*, Madrid: Síntesis.

Camacho, Francisco Gómez (1998b), 'Later scholastics: Spanish economic thought in the XVIth and XVIIth centuries', in S. Todd Lowry and Barry Gordon (eds), *Ancient and Medieval Economic Ideas and Concepts of Social Justice*, Leiden, Netherlands and New York: Brill, pp. 503–61.

Cameron, Samuel (2003), *The Economics of Sin: Rational Choice or No Choice at All*, Cheltenham, UK and Northampton, MA, USA: Elgar.

Carey, George (1999), comments by the Archbishop of Canterbury to the Anglican Conference on Evangelism, 9–12 March, accessed at www.cofe.anglican.org/news/news_item.2004-10-19.9724640881.

Carey, Henry C. (1837), *Principles of Political Economy*, 3 vols, Philadelphia, PA: Carey, Lea & Blanchard.

Carmichael, Gershom ([1724] 2002), *Natural Rights on the Threshold of the Scottish Enlightenment: The Writings of Gershom Carmichael*, reprinted in James Moore and Michael Silverthorne (eds), *Natural Rights on the Threshold of the Scottish Enlightenment: The Writings of Gershom Carmichael*, Indianapolis, IN: Liberty Fund.

Catechism (1994), *Catechism of the Catholic Church*, London: Geoffrey Chapman.

Chafuen, Alejandro A. (2003), *Faith and Liberty: The Economic Thought of the Late Scholastics*, Lanham, MD and New York: Lexington Books.

Chalmers, Thomas (1833), *On the Power, Wisdom and Goodness of God Manifested in the Adaption of External Nature to the Moral and Intellectual Constitution of Man*, London: Henry Bohn.

Chang, Jung (1993), *Wild Swans: Three Daughters of China*, London: Flamingo.

Charles, Roger (1998), *Christian Social Witness and Teaching: the Catholic Tradition from Genesis to Centesimus Annus*, 2 vols, Leominster: Gracewing.

Chrysostom, St John (2007), *Homily Four on Ephesians*, chapters 1–3, accessed at www.newadvent.org/fathers/23014.html.

Churches Together in Britain and Ireland (CTBI) (2005), *Prosperity with a Purpose: Christians and the Ethics of Affluence*, London: CTBI.

Clark, John B. (1886), *The Philosophy of Wealth*, New York: Augustus Kelly Reprint.

Clark, John B. (1899), *The Distribution of Wealth*, New York: Augustus Kelly Reprint.

Clark, Jonathan C.D. (2000), *English Society, 1660–1832: Religion, Ideology, and Politics During the Ancién Regime*, Cambridge, New York: Cambridge University Press.

Coats, Alfred W. (1985), 'The American Economic Association and the economics profession', *Journal of Economic Literature*, **23** (4), 1697–727.

Coleman, William D. (2002), *Economics and its Enemies: Two Centuries of Anti-Economics*, Basingstoke: Palgrave.

Cole-Turner, Ronald (2001), 'Science, technology, and the mission of theology in a new century', in Max L. Stackhouse with Don S. Browning (eds), *The Spirit and the Modern Authorities*, Harrisburg, PA: Trinity Press International, pp. 139–65.

Commission for Africa (2005), *Our Common Interest: Report of the Commission for Africa*, London: Commission for Africa, accessed at www.commissionforafrica.org.

Copleston, Frederick (1985), *A History of Philosophy, Volume V, Hobbes to Hume*, London: Image Books.

Courtenay, William J. (1984), *Covenant and Causality in Medieval Thought: Studies in Philosophy, Theology and Economic Practice*, London: Variorum Reprints.

Covey, Stephen (1989), *Seven Habits of Highly Effective People*, New York: Simon & Schuster Inc.

Cramp, A.B. (1975), *Notes Towards a Critique of Secular Economic Theory*, Toronto: Institute for Christian Studies.

Crenson, Matthew A. (1971), *The Unpolitics of Air Pollution*, Baltimore, MD: The Johns Hopkins University Press.

Crespo, Ricardo F. (1998a), 'Is economics a moral science?', *Journal of Markets & Morality*, **1** (2), 201–11.

Crespo, Ricardo F. (1998b), 'Is economics a moral science? A response to Peter J. Boettke', *Journal of Markets & Morality*, **1** (2), 220–25.

Crespo, Ricardo F. (2006), 'The ontology of "the economic": an Aristotelian perspective', *Cambridge Journal of Economics*, **30** (5), 767–81.

Curran, Charles E., K. Himes and T. Shannon (2005), 'Commentary on Sollicitudo Rei Socialis [On Social Concern]', in Kenneth R. Himes (ed.), *Modern Catholic Social Teaching: Commentaries and Interpretations*, Washington, DC: Georgetown University Press.

Davenport, Stewart (forthcoming), *Friends of the Unrighteous Mammon, Northern Christians and Market Capitalism 1815–1860*, Chicago, IL: Chicago University Press.

de Grauwe, Paul and Filip Camerman (2003), 'Are multinationals really bigger than nations?', *World Economics*, **4** (2), 23–37.

Dempsey, Bernard W. (1958), *The Functional Economy*, Upper Saddle River, NJ: Prentice Hall.

de Roover, Raymond A. (1948), *Money, Banking and Credit in Medieval Bruges; Italian Merchant Bankers, Lombards and Money-Changers: A Study in the Origins of Banking*, Cambridge, MA: Medieval Academy of America.

de Roover, Raymond A. (1949), *Gresham on Foreign Exchange: An Essay on Early English Mercantilism with the Text of Sir Thomas Gresham's Memorandum: For the Understanding of the Exchange*, Cambridge, MA: Harvard University Press.

de Roover, Raymond A. (1955), 'Scholastic economics: survival and lasting influence from the sixteenth century to Adam Smith', *Quarterly Journal of Economics*, **69** (2), 161–90.

de Roover, Raymond A. (1963), *The Rise and Decline of the Medici Bank 1397–1494*, Cambridge, MA: Harvard University Press.

de Roover, Raymond A. (1967), *San Bernardino of Siena and Sant' Antonino of Florence: The Two Great Economic Thinkers of the Middle Ages*, Boston, MA: Baker Library/Harvard Graduate School of Business Administration.

de Roover, Raymond A. (1969), *Leonardus Lessius als economist: De economische leerstellingen van de latere scholastiek in de Zuidelijke Nederlanden*, Brussels: Paleis de Academiën.

de Roover, Raymond A. (1971), *La pensée économique des scholastiques: doctrines et méthodes*, Montreal, QC: Institute for Medieval Studies.

de Roover, Raymond A. (1974), *Business, Banking and Economic Thought in Late Medieval and Early Modern Europe and Selected Studies of Raymond de Roover*, Julius Kirshner (ed.), Chicago, IL: University of Chicago Press.

de Soto, Hernando (2000), *The Mystery of Capital: Why Capitalism Triumphs in the West and Fails Everywhere Else*, London: Black Swan.

de Soto, Jesús Huerta (1996), 'New light on the prehistory of the theory of banking and the School of Salamanca', *The Review of Austrian Economics*, **9** (2), 59–81.

de Tocqueville, Alexis ([1835] 2003), *Democracy in America*, New York: Penguin Classics.

Dorr, Donald (1992), *Option for the Poor: A Hundred Years of Vatican Social Teaching*, revised edn, New York: Orbis.

Dow, Alexander, Sheila Dow and Alan Hutton (1997), 'The Scottish political economy tradition and msodern economics', *Scottish Journal of Political Economy*, **44** (4), 368–83.

Drakopoulos, S. and G.N. Gotsis (2004), 'A meta-theoretical assessment of the decline of scholastic economics', *History of Economics Review*, **40** (Summer), 19–45.

Drucker, Peter (1973), *Management: Tasks, Responsibilities, Practices*, New York: Harper Colophon Books.

Edwards, David L. and John Stott (1988), *Essentials: A Liberal-Evangelical Dialogue*, Downers Grove, IL: Intervarsity Press.

Ekelund, Robert B. and Robert F. Hebert (1975), *A History of Economic Theory and Method*, New York: McGraw-Hill.

Ekelund, Robert. B., R.F. Hebert and R.D. Tollison (2002), 'An economic analysis of the Protestant Reformation', *American Economic Review*, **3** (June), 646–71.

Eliot, George (1871–73), *Middlemarch: A Study of a Provincial Life*, 4 vols, London: William Blackwood.

Ely, Richard T. (1886), *Report of the Organization of the American Economic Association*, Baltimore, MD: American Economic Association.

Emmett, Ross (1994), 'Frank Knight: economics versus religion', in H. Geoffrey Brennan and Anthony M.C. Waterman (eds), *Economics and Religion: Are They Distinct?*, Recent Economic Thought series, Boston, MA, and Dordrecht, Netherlands: Kluwer Academic, pp. 103–20.

Escriva, Jose Maria (1975), *Friends of God*, New York: Scepter Publishers.

Evans, C. Stephen (1979), *Preserving the Person*, Downers Grove, IL: Intervarsity Press.

Evans, C. Stephen (2004), *Kierkegaard's Ethic of Love: Divine Commands and Moral Obligations*, Oxford: Oxford University Press.

Everett, John R. (1946), *Religion in Economics: A Study of John Bates Clark, Richard T. Ely and Simon N. Patten*, New York: King's Crown Press.

Faccarello, Gilb (1999), *The Foundations of Laissez-Faire. The Economics of Pierre de Boisguilbert*, London: Routledge.

Felice, Flavio (2004), 'Introduction to Albertanus of Brescia's Genovese Sermon (1243)', *Journal of Markets and Morality*, **7** (2), 603–22.

Ferguson, Adam ([1767] 1978), 'An Essay on the History of Civil Society', reprinted in Duncan Forbes (ed.), *An Essay on the History of Civil Society*, Edinburgh: Edinburgh University Press.

Ferrater, Mora J. (1953), 'Suarez and modern philosophy', *Journal of the History of Ideas*, **14** (4), 528–77.

Fleischacker, Samuel (2004), *On Adam Smith's Wealth of Nations: A Philosophical Companion*, Princeton, NJ: Princeton University Press.

Fogel, Robert W. (2000), *The Fourth Great Awakening and the Future of Egalitarianism*, Chicago, IL: University of Chicago Press.

Frank, R.H., T. Gilovich and D.T. Regan (1993), 'Does studying economics inhibit cooperation?', *Journal of Economic Perspectives*, **7** (2),
159–71.

Frank, R.H., T. Gilovich and D.T. Regan (1996), 'Do economists make bad
citizens', *Journal of Economic Perspectives*, **10** (1), 187–92.

Freedman, Joseph S. (1985), 'Philosophy instruction within the institutional framework of Central European schools and universities during
the Reformation era', *History of Universities*, **5**, 117–66.

Freedman, Joseph S. (1993), 'Aristotle and the content of philosophy
instruction at Central European schools and universities during the
Reformation era (1500–1650)', *Proceedings of the American
Philosophical Society*, **137** (2), 213–53.

Frey, B. and F. Oberholzer-Gee (1997), 'The cost of price incentives: an
empirical analysis of motivation crowding out', *American Economic
Review*, **87** (4), 746–55.

Friedman, Benjamin M. (2005), *The Moral Consequences of Economic
Growth*, New York: Alfred A. Knopf.

Friedman, Milton (1953), 'The methodology of positive economics', in
Essays in Positive Economics, Chicago, IL: University of Chicago Press.

Friedman, Milton (1970), 'The social responsibility of business is to
increase its profits', *The New York Times Magazine*, 13 September.

Fry, Michael (1999), 'A commercial empire: Scotland and British expansion
in the eighteenth century', in T.M. Devine and J.R. Young (eds),
Eighteenth-century Scotland: New Perspectives, East Lothian: Tuckwell
Press, pp. 53–70.

Fukuyama, Francis (1995), *Trust: The Social Virtues and the Creation of
Prosperity*, New York: Free Press.

Furedi, Frank (2005), 'The age of unreason', *Spectator*, 19 November,
40–42.

Gaertner, Wulf (2005), '*De jure naturae et gentium*: Samuel von Pufendorf's
contribution to social choice theory and economics', *Social Choice and
Welfare*, **25** (2), 231–41.

Gascoigne, John (2002), *The Enlightenment and the Origins of European
Australia*, Cambridge and New York: Cambridge University Press.

Gaskell, Elizabeth (1855), *North and South*, 2 vols, London: Chapman &
Hall.

Gathje, Peter R. (2002), 'A contested classic: critics ask: whose Christ? Which
culture? – Christ and culture', *Christian Century*, 19 June, accessed at
www.religion-online.org/showarticle.asp?title=2641.

Gaudium et Spes (1965), Pastoral Constitution on the Church in the Modern
World, Vatican.

Gauthier, David (1986), *Morals by Agreement*, Oxford: Clarendon Press.

Gauthier, René Antoine and Jean Yves Jolif (1970), *Aristote L'Éthique a Nicomaque: Introduction, traduction et commentaire*, Louvain, Belgium: Publications Universitaires, and Paris: Béatrice-Nauwelaerts.

Gneezy, U. and A. Rustichini (2000), 'A fine is a price', *Journal of Legal Studies*, **39** (1), 1–18.

Goff, Brian and Arthur A. Fleisher III (1999), *Spoiled Rotten*, Boulder, CO: Westview Press.

Goodwin, Craufurd D.W. (1966), *Economic Enquiry in Australia*, Durham, NC: Duke University Press.

Gordon, Barry (1975), *Economic Analysis before Adam Smith: Hesiod to Lessius*, New York: Macmillan.

Gorringe, T.J. (2004a), *Furthering Humanity: A Theology of Culture*, Aldershot: Ashgate.

Gorringe, T.J. (2004b), 'The principalities and powers: a framework for thinking about globalization', in Peter S. Heslam (ed.), *Globalization and the Good*, London: SPCK, pp. 79–91.

Goudzwaard, Bob (1979), *Capitalism and Progress: A Diagnosis of Western Society*, Grand Rapids, MI: Wm. B. Eerdmans.

Grabill, Stephen J. (2006), *Rediscovering the Natural Law in Reformed Theological Ethics*, Grand Rapids, MI: Wm. B. Eerdmans.

Grabill, Stephen J. (ed.) (2007), *Sourcebook in Late-Scholastic Monetary Theory: The Contributions of Martin de Azpilcueta, Luis de Molina, S.J. and Juan de Mariana, S.J.*, Lanham, MD and New York: Lexington Books.

Granger, Gilles-Gaston (1992), 'Les trois aspects de la rationalité économique', in Sergio Galvan (ed.), *Forme di razionalità pratica*, Milan: Angeli, pp. 63–80.

Green, Lancelyn and Walter Hooper (1974), *C.S. Lewis: A Biography*, Glasgow: Collins.

Gregg, Samuel (2003), 'End of a myth: Max Weber, capitalism, and the medieval order', *Journal des Economistes et des Etudes Humaines*, **13** (2/3).

Gregg, Samuel (2007), *The Commercial Society: Foundations and Challenges in a Global Age*, Lanham, MD and New York: Lexington Books.

Grice-Hutchinson, Marjorie (1952), *The School of Salamanca: Readings in Spanish Monetary Theory 1544–1605*, Oxford: Clarendon Press.

Grice-Hutchinson, Marjorie (1978), *Early Economic Thought in Spain 1177–1740*, London: G. Allen & Unwin.

Grice-Hutchinson, Marjorie (1990), *Aproximación al pensamiento económico en Andalucía: de Séneca a finales del siglo XVIII*, Malaga, Spain: Editorial Librería Agora.

Grice-Hutchinson, Marjorie (1993), 'The concept of the School of Salamanca: its origins and development', in Laurence S. Moss and

Christopher K. Ryan (eds), *Economic Thought in Spain: Selected Essays of Marjorie Grice-Hutchinson*, Aldershot, UK and Brookfield, USA: Edward Elgar, pp. 23–9.

Griffiths, Brian (2007), *Globalization, Poverty, and International Development: Insights from Centesimus Annus*, Grand Rapids, MI: Acton Institute.

Grisez, Germain (1993), *The Way of the Lord Jesus*, Steubenville, OH: Franciscan Press.

Groenewegen, Peter D. and Bruce J. McFarlane (1990), *The History of Australian Economic Thought*, London: Routledge.

Grotius, Hugo ([1609] 2004), *Mare Liberum*, edited by D. Armitage, Indianapolis, IN: Liberty Fund.

Grotius, Hugo ([1625] 2005), *The Rights of War and Peace*, 3 vols, edited by R. Tuck, Indianapolis, IN: Liberty Fund.

Gunton, Colin E. (1992), *The One, the Three and the Many: God, Creation and the Culture of Modernity*, Cambridge: Cambridge University Press.

Gwartney, James and Robert Lawson (2004), 'What have we learned from the measurement of economic freedom', in Mark A. Wynne, H. Rosenblume and R. Formaini (eds), *The Legacy of Milton and Rose Friedman's 'Free to Choose'*, Dallas, TX: Federal Reserve Bank of Dallas.

Hankinson, R.J. (1995), 'Philosophy of science', in Jonathan Barnes (ed.), *The Cambridge Companion to Aristotle*, Cambridge: Cambridge University Press, pp. 109–39.

Hardt, Michael and Antonio Negri (2000), *Empire*, Cambridge, MA: Harvard University Press.

Harries, Richard (1992), *Is there a Gospel for the Rich? The Christian in a Capitalist World*, London: Mowbray.

Hart, David B. (2003), *The Beauty of the Infinite: The Aesthetics of Christian Truth*, Grand Rapids, MI: Wm. B. Eerdmans.

Hauerwas, Stanley (2005), 'H. Richard Niebuhr', in David F. Ford and Rachel Muers (eds), *The Modern Theologians: An Introduction to Christian Theology Since 1918*, 3rd edn, Oxford: Blackwell, pp. 194–203.

Hawtrey, Kim (1986), 'Evangelicals and economics', *Interchange*, **38** (2), 25–40.

Hay, Donald A. (1989), *Economics Today: A Christian Critique*, Leicester: Apollos.

Hayek, Friedrich A. (1979), *The Counter-revolution of Science: Studies on the Abuse of Reason*, Indianapolis, IN: Liberty Fund.

Hayek, Friedrich A. (1988), *The Fatal Conceit: The Errors of Socialism*, Chicago, IL: University of Chicago Press.

Henderson, David (2004), *The Role of Business in the Modern World*, London: Institute for Economics Affairs.

Hennis, Wilhelm (1963), *Politik und praktische Philosophie. Eine Studie zur Rekonstruktion der politischen Wissenschaft*, Neuwied am Rhein and Berlin: Hermann Luchterhand Verlag.

Henry, John F. (1982), 'The transformation of John Bates Clark: an essay in interpretation', *History of Political Economy*, **14** (2), 166–77.

Herman, Arthur (2001), *How the Scots Invented the Modern World*, New York: Crown Publishers.

Heslam, Peter S. (2002), *Globalization: Unravelling the New Capitalism*, Cambridge: Grove Books.

Heslam, Peter S. (2004), *Globalization and the Good*, London: SPCK.

Heyne, Paul (1991), *The Economic Way of Thinking*, New York: Macmillan.

Heyne, Paul (1994), 'Passing judgements', *Bulletin of the Association of Christian Economists USA*, **23**, 9–15.

Hill, Lisa (2001), 'The hidden theology of Adam Smith', *European Journal of the History of Economic Thought*, **8** (1), 1–29.

Hilton, Boyd (1988), *The Age of Atonement: The Influence of Evangelicalism on Social and Economic Thought 1795–1865*, Oxford: Clarendon Press.

Hilton, Steve and Giles Gibbons (2002), *Good Business: Your World Needs You*, London: Texere.

Himes K.R. (ed.) (2005), *Modern Catholic Social Teaching: Commentaries and Interpretations*, Washington, DC: Georgetown University Press.

Hinze Christine, F. (2005), 'Commentary on *Quagragesimo Anno* [After Forty Years]', in Kenneth R. Himes (ed.), *Modern Catholic Social Teaching: Commentaries and Interpretations*, Washington, DC: Georgetown University Press.

Hirsch, Fred (1978), *Social Limits to Growth*, London: Routledge & Kegan Paul.

Hittinger, F. Russell (2003), *First Grace: Rediscovering the Natural Law in a Post-Christian World*, Wilmington, DE: ISI Books.

Holmes, Arthur F. (1977), *All Truth is God's Truth*, Grand Rapids, MI: Wm. B. Eerdmans.

Horowitz, Daniel (1985), *The Morality of Spending: Attitudes Toward the Consumer Society in America 1875–1940*, Baltimore, MD: The Johns Hopkins University Press.

Hume, D. ([1739–40] 1951), *A Treatise on Human Nature: Being an Attempt to Introduce the Experimental Method of Reasoning into Moral Subjects*, 2 vols, reprinted in L. Selby-Bigge (ed.), *A Treatise on Human Nature: Being an Attempt to Introduce the Experimental Method of Reasoning into Moral Subjects*, Oxford: Oxford University Press.

Hutcheson, Francis ([1725] 2002), *An Inquiry into the Origin of our Ideas of Beauty and Virtue*, 2nd edn, Chestnuthill, MA: Elibron.

Hutcheson, Francis ([1755] 2000), *A System of Moral Philosophy*, 2 vols, reprinted in D. Carey (ed.), *A System of Moral Philosophy*, 2 vols, Bristol: Thoemmes Press.

Hutcheson, Francis ([1758] 1989), 'Thoughts on Laughter and Observations on "The Fable of the Bees" in Six Letters', reprinted in John Price (ed.), *Thoughts on Laughter and Observations on 'The Fable of the Bees' in Six Letters*, Bristol: Thoemmes Press.

Hutcheson, Francis ([1747] 2007), *Philosophiae Moralis Institutio Compendiaria with A Short Introduction to Moral Philosophy*, edited by Luigi Turco, Indianapolis, IN: Liberty Fund.

Hutchinson, Terence (1988), *Before Adam Smith: The Emergence of Political Economy 1662–1776*, Oxford: Basil Blackwell.

Iannaccone, Laurence R. (1998), 'Introduction to the economics of religion', *Journal of Economic Literature*, **36** (3), 1465–95.

Iannaccone, Laurence R. (2002), 'A marriage made in heaven? Economic theory and religious studies', in Shoshana Grossbard-Shechtman and Christopher Clague (eds), *The Expansion of Economics: Toward a More Inclusive Social Science*, London: M.E. Sharpe, pp. 203–23.

Insole, Christopher J. (2004), *The Politics of Human Frailty: A Theological Defence of Political Liberalism*, London: SCM.

James, Clive (1986), *Falling Towards England*, London: Picador.

James, Oliver (2007), *Affluenza*, London: Vermilion.

John Paul II (1979), 'Biblical account of creation analysed', in *General Audiences: John Paul II's Theology of the Body*, 12 September, Vatican City.

John Paul II (1981), encyclical letter *Laborem Exercens*.

John Paul II (1987), encyclical letter *Sollicitudo Rei Socialis*.

John Paul II (1991), encyclical letter *Centesimus Annus*.

John Paul II (1993), *Person and Community*, T. Sandok (trans.), New York/Berlin/Bern/Frankfurt/Paris/Wien: Peter Lang.

Johnson, Herbert L. (1959), 'Some Mediaeval Doctrines on Extrinsic Titles to Interest', in C.J. O'Neil (ed.), *An Etienne Gilson Tribute*, Milwaukee, WI: Marquette University Press.

Kasser, Tim and Richard M. Ryan (1996), 'Further examining the American dream: differential correlates of intrinsic and extrinsic goals', *Personality and Social Psychology Bulletin*, **22** (5).

Ker Conway, Jill (1992), *The Road From Coorain*, London: Minerva.

Keynes, John M. (1933), *Essays in Biography*, London: Macmillan.

Kirshner, Julius (ed.) (1974), *Business, Banking and Economic Thought in Late Medieval and Early Modern Europe: Selected Studies of Raymond de Roover*, Chicago, IL and London: University of Chicago Press.

Kis-Katos, Krisztina and Gunther G. Schulze (2005), 'The regulation of child labour', *Economic Affairs*, **25** (3), 24–30.

Knight, Frank H. (1955), 'Schumpeter's *History of Economics*', *Southern Economic Journal*, **21** (3), 261–72.

Kolakowski, Leszek (1982), *Religion*, Oxford: Oxford University Press.

Kraut, Richard (2006), 'How to justify ethical propositions: Aristotle's method', in Richard Kraut (ed.), *The Blackwell Guide to Aristotle's Nicomachean Ethics*, Oxford: Blackwell Publishing, pp. 76–95.

Kristeller, Paul Oskar (1965), 'Renaissance Aristotelianism', *Greek, Roman, and Byzantine Studies*, **6** (2), 157–74.

Krueger, David (1997), *The Business Corporation and Productive Justice*, Nashville, TN: Abingdon Press, pp. 30–34.

Lamoureux Patricia A. (2005), 'Commentary on *Laborem Exercens* (On Human Work)', in Kenneth R. Himes (ed.), *Modern Catholic Social Teaching: Commentaries and Interpretations*, Washington, DC: Georgetown University Press.

Lane, Robert (2000), *The Loss of Happiness in Market Democracies*, New Haven, CT and London: Yale University Press.

Langholm, Odd (1979), *Price and Value in the Aristotelian Tradition: A Study in Scholastic Economic Sources*, Bergen, Norway: Universitets-forlaget.

Langholm, Odd (1983), *Wealth and Money in the Aristotelian Tradition: A Study in Scholastic Economic Sources*, Bergen, Norway: Universitets-forlaget.

Langholm, Odd (1984), *The Aristotelian Analysis of Usury*, Bergen, Norway: Universitetsforlaget.

Langholm, Odd (1987), 'Scholastic economics', in S. Todd Lowry (ed.), *Pre-Classical Economic Thought: From the Greeks to the Scottish Enlightenment*, Boston, MA/Dordrecht, Netherlands/Lancaster: Kluwer Academic Publishers, pp. 115–35.

Langholm, Odd (1992), *Economics in the Medieval Schools: Wealth, Exchange, Value, Money, and Usury According to the Paris Theological Tradition 1200–1350*, Leiden, Netherlands and New York: Brill.

Langholm, Odd (1998), *The Legacy of Scholasticism in Economic Thought: Antecedents of Choice and Power*, Cambridge and New York: Cambridge University Press.

Langholm, Odd (2003), *The Merchant in the Confessional: Trade and Price in the Pre-Reformation Penitential Handbooks*, Leiden, Netherlands and New York: Brill.

Lapin, Daniel (2002), *Thou Shalt Prosper: Ten Commandments for Making Money*, Hoboken, NJ: John Wiley & Sons.

Lea, Henry Charles (1894), 'The ecclesiastical treatment of usury', *Yale Review*, **2**, 375–85.

Le Blond, J.M. (1939), *Logique et méthode chez Aristote*, Paris: Vrin.

Bibliography

Lecky, William Edward Hartpole (1887–90), *History of the Rise and Influence of the Spirit of Rationalism in Europe*, revised edn, 2 vols, London: Longmans, Green & Co.
Leo XIII (1891), encyclical letter *Rerum Novarum*.
Levitt, S.D. and S.J. Dubner (2006), *Freakonomics: A Rogue Economist Explores the Hidden Side of Everything*, revised and expanded edn, New York: Penguin.
Levy, David and Sandra Peart (2005), *The 'Vanity of the Philosopher': From Equality to Hierarchy in Postclassical Economics*, Ann Arbor, MI: University of Michigan Press.
Lewis, C.S. (1942), *The Weight of Glory*, London: Theology.
Lewis, C.S. (1960), 'Good work and good works', in *The World's Last Night and Other Essays*, New York: Harcourt, pp. 71–81.
Lewis, C.S. (1961), *The Screwtape Letters*, revised edn, New York: Macmillan.
Lewis, Roy and Rosemary Stewart (1961), *The Boss: The Life and Times of the British Business Man*, 2nd edn, London: Phoenix.
Lilico, A. (2006), 'Six issues in pharmaceuticals', *Economic Affairs*, **26** (3), 33–8.
Lloyd, John (2001), *The Protest Ethic: How the Anti-globalization Movement Challenges Social Democracy*, London: Demos.
Locke, John (1690), *An Essay Concerning Human Understanding*, London: Awnsham, John Churchill and Samuel Mansbip.
Lonergan, Bernard (1999), 'Macroeconomic dynamics: an essay in circulation analysis', in *Collected Works of Bernard Lonergan*, Toronto: University of Toronto Press.
Lonergan, Bernard (2002), 'For a new political economy', in *Collected Works of Bernard Lonergan*, Toronto, ON: University of Toronto Press.
Long, Brendan (2006), 'Adam Smith's natural theology of society', *Adam Smith Review*, **2**, pp. 124–48.
Lovejoy, Arthur O. (1941), 'The meaning of Romanticism in the history of ideas', *Journal of the History of Ideas*, **2** (2), 257–78.
Lowry, S. Todd (1969), 'Aristotle's mathematical analysis of exchange', *History of Political Economy*, **1** (1), 44–66.
Lowry, S. Todd (1987a), *The Archeology of Economic Ideas: The Classical Greek Tradition*, Durham, NC: Duke University Press.
Lowry, S. Todd (ed.) (1987b), *Pre-Classical Economic Thought: From the Greeks to the Scottish Enlightenment*, Boston, MA/Dordrecht, Netherlands/Lancaster: Kluwer Academic Publishers.
Lowry, S. Todd and Barry Gordon (eds) (1998), *Ancient and Medieval Economic Ideas and Concepts of Social Justice*, Leiden, Netherlands and New York: Brill.

MacIntyre, Alasdair (1984), *After Virtue*, 2nd edn, Notre Dame, IN: University of Notre Dame Press.

MacLaurin, Ian (1999), *Tiger by the Tail: A Life in Business from Tesco to Test Cricket*, London: Macmillan.

Malthus, Thomas R. (1798), *An Essay on the Principle of Population*, 1st edn, London: Johnson.

Malthus, Thomas R. (1803), *An Essay on the Principle of Population*, 2nd edn, London: Johnson.

Malthus, Thomas R. (1815), *An Inquiry into the Nature and Progress of Rent*, London: John Murray.

Mandeville, Bernard ([1714] 1970), *The Fable of the Bees*, edited by Phillip Harth, Harmondsworth: Penguin.

Manent, Pierre (1998), *Modern Liberty and its Discontents*, Lanham, MD: Rowman & Littlefield.

Marsden, George M. (1973), 'The gospel of wealth, the social gospel, and the salvation of souls in nineteenth-century America', *Fides et Historia*, **5** (1), 10–21.

Marsden, George M. (1989), 'Evangelicals and the scientific culture', in M.J. Lacey (ed.), *Religion and Twentieth-century American Intellectual Life*, Cambridge: Cambridge University Press.

Marsden, George M. (1999), 'Christianity and cultures: transforming Niebuhr's categories', *Insights: The Faculty Journal of Austin Seminary*, (Fall).

Marty, Martin E. (1969), *The Modern Schism: Three Paths to the Secular*, New York: Harper & Row.

Matthew, H.C.G. and Brian Harrison (eds) (2004), *Oxford Dictionary of National Biography*, Oxford: Oxford University Press.

May, Henry F. (1976), *The Enlightenment in America*, New York: Oxford University Press.

McKendrick, Neil (1976), 'General Introduction', in R.J. Overy, *William Morris, Viscount Nuffield*, London: Europa Publications.

McKenzie, Richard B. and Gordon Tullock (1975), *The New World of Economics*, Homewood, IL: Irwin.

Menzies, Gordon and Donald A. Hay (forthcoming), 'Economics and the marriage wars', *Faith and Economics*.

Merikoski, I.A. (2001), 'A different kind of Enlightenment', *Religion and Liberty*, **11** (6), 10–12.

Micklethwait, John and Adrian Wooldridge (2003), *The Company: A Short History of a Revolutionary Idea*, London: Weidenfeld & Nicolson.

Milbank, John (1990), *Theology and Social Theory: Beyond Secular Reason*, Oxford: Basil Blackwell.

Mill, John Stuart (1844), 'Essay V: on the definition of political economy; and on the method of investigation proper to it', in J.S Mill, *Essays on Some Unsettled Questions of Policital Economy*, London: John W. Parker.

Miller, Jr., Fred D. (1995), *Nature, Justice and Rights in Aristotle's Politics*, Oxford: Oxford University Press.

Milton, J.R. (1981), 'John Locke and the nominalist tradition', in Reinhard Brandt (ed.), *John Locke: Symposium Wolfenbüttel 1979*, Berlin and New York: Walter de Gruyter, pp. 128–45.

Mizuta, Hiroshi and James Bonar (1967), *Adam Smith's Library: A Supplement to Bonar's Catalogue with a Checklist of the Whole Library*, London: Cambridge University Press for the Royal Economic Society.

Mochrie, Robert I. (2006), 'Justice in exchange: the economic philosophy of John Duns Scotus', *Journal of Markets & Morality*, **9** (1), 35–56.

Moe-Lobeda, Cynthia (2004), 'Offering resistance to globalization: insights from Luther', in Peter S. Heslam (ed.), *Globalization and the Good*, London: SPCK, pp. 95–104.

Moore, James (1979), *The Post-Darwinian Controversies: A Study of the Protestant Struggle to Come to Terms with Darwin in Great Britain and America 1870–1900*, Cambridge: Cambridge University Press.

Mosbacher, Michael (2002), *Marketing the Revolution: The New Anti-Capitalism and the Attack upon Corporate Brands*, London: The Social Affairs Unit.

Moss, Laurence S. and Christopher K. Ryan (eds) (1993), *Economic Thought in Spain: Selected Essays of Marjorie Grice-Hutchinson*, Aldershot, UK and Brookfield, US: Edward Elgar.

Muller, Richard A. (2000), *The Unaccommodated Calvin: Studies in the Foundation of a Theological Tradition*, New York: Oxford University Press.

Muller, Richard A. (2001), 'The problem of Protestant scholasticism – a review and definition', in Willem J. van Asselt and Eef Dekker (eds), *Reformation and Scholasticism: An Ecumenical Enterprise*, Grand Rapids, MI: Baker Book House, pp. 45–64.

Muller, Richard A. (2003a), *Post-Reformation Reformed Dogmatics: The Rise and Development of Reformed Orthodoxy, ca. 1520 to ca. 1725*, 4 vols, Grand Rapids, MI: Baker Academic.

Muller, Richard A. (2003b), *After Calvin: Studies in the Development of a Theological Tradition*, New York: Oxford University Press.

Muñoz de Juana, Rodrigo (1998), *Moral y Economía en la Obra de Martín de Azpilcueta*, Pamplona, Spain: Eunsa.

Muñoz de Juana, Rodrigo (2001), 'Scholastic morality and the birth of economics: the thought of Martín de Azpilcueta', *Journal of Markets & Morality*, **4** (1), 14–42.

Nash, Laura (2007), 'How the church has failed business', *The Conference Board Review*, accessed at www.conference-board.org.

Nash, Laura and Scotty McLennan (2001), *Church on Sunday, Work on Monday: The Challenge of Fusing Christian Values with Business Life*, San Francisco, CA: Jossey-Bass.

Natali, Carlo (1980), 'Aristotele e l'origine della filosofia pratica', in Claudio Pacchiani *(a cura di) Filosofia pratica e scienza politica*, Padua (Abano Tevere), Italy: Francisci.

Nelson, Robert H. (1991), *Reaching for Heaven on Earth – the Theological Meaning of Economics*, Savage, MD: Rowan and Littlefield.

Nelson, Robert H. (2001), *Economics as Religion: From Samuelson to Chicago and Beyond*, University Park, PA: Pennsylvania State University Press.

New Catholic Encyclopedia (2002), entry on 'Scholasticism' edited by J.E. Gurr, vol. 12, Farmington Hills, MI: Gale, p. 1153.

Newman, W.L. (1950), *The Politics of Aristotle*, Oxford: Clarendon Press.

Niebuhr, Richard ([1951] 2002), *Christ and Culture*, New York: HarperCollins.

Noel, Edd S. (2007), 'A "marketless" world?: An examination of wealth and exchange in the gospels and first-century Palestine', *Journal of Markets & Morality*, **10** (1).

Noll, Mark (2002), *God and Mammon: Protestants, Money, and the Market 1790–1860*, New York: Oxford University Press.

Noonan, John T. (1957), *The Scholastic Analysis of Usury*, Cambridge, MA: Harvard University Press.

Norberg, Johan (2001), *In Defence of Global Capitalism*, Stockholm: Timbro.

Norman, Edward R. (1987), *The Victorian Christian Socialists*, Cambridge: Cambridge University Press.

Novak, Michael (1981), *Toward a Theology of the Corporation*, Washington, DC: American Enterprise Institute.

Novak, Michael (1982), *The Spirit of Democratic Capitalism*, New York: Simon & Schuster.

Novak, Michael (1993), *The Catholic Ethic and the Spirit of Capitalism*, New York: Free Press.

Novak, Michael (1996), *Business as a Calling: Work and the Examined Life*, New York: The Free Press.

Nuccio, Oscar (1965), *Scrittori classici italiani di economia politica*, Rome: Bizzari.

Nuccio, Oscar (1974), *Economisti italiani del XVII secolo: Ferdinando Galiani, Antonio Genovesi, Pietro Verri, Francesco Mengotti*, Rome: Mengotti.

Nuccio, Oscar (1984–91), *Il pensiero economico italiano*, 5 vols, Sassari, Italy: Gallizzi.

Nuccio, Oscar (2005), *Epistemologia della 'azione umana' e razionalismo economico nel Duecento italiano: Il caso Albertano da Brescia*, Turin, Italy: Effatà Editrice.

Oakley, Francis (1984), *Omnipotence, Covenant, and Order: An Excursion in the History of Ideas from Abelard to Leibniz*, Ithaca, NY: Cornell University Press.

Oakley, Francis (1999), 'Locke, natural law, and God: again', in *Politics and Eternity: Studies in the History of Medieval and Early-modern Political Thought*, Leiden, Netherlands: Brill, pp. 217–48.

Oakley, Francis (2005), *Natural Law, Laws of Nature, Natural Rights: Continuity and Discontinuity in the History of Ideas*, New York and London: Continuum International.

Oakley, Francis (2006), *Kingship: The Politics of Enchantment*, Oxford: Blackwell Publishing.

O'Brien, David J. and Thomas A. Shannon (1992), *Catholic Social Thought: The Documentary Heritage*, Maryknoll, NY: Orbis Books.

Offer, Avner (2006), *The Challenge of Affluence*, Oxford: Oxford University Press.

Oslington, Paul (ed.) (2003), 'Economics and religion', in *International Library of Critical Writings in Economics*, 2 vols, Cheltenham, UK and Northampton, MA, USA: Edward Elgar.

Oslington, Paul (2005), 'Natural theology as an integrative framework for economics and theology', *St Mark's Review*, **199** (December), 56–65.

Oslington, Paul (forthcoming), *Economics and Theology: Smith, Malthus and Their Followers*, London: Routledge.

Oswald, Andrew (2007), 'Review: *Affluenza*, by Oliver James', *New Scientist*, **193** (2588) 27 January.

Paley, William (1785), *Principles of Moral and Political Philosophy*, London: SPCK.

Paul VI (1967), encyclical letter *Populorum Progressio*.

Piedra, Alberto M. (2004), *Natural Law: The Foundation of an Orderly Economic System*, Lanham, MD and New York: Lexington Books.

Pieper, Josef ([1948] 1998), *Leisure, the Basis of Culture*, reprinted in *Leisure, the Basis of Culture*, translated by Gerald Malsbary, Ft Collins, CO: Ignatius Press.

Pieper, Josef ([1966] 1990), *The Four Cardinal Virtues*, reprinted in R. Winston, C. Winston, L. Lynch and D. Coogan (trans.), Notre Dame, IN: University of Notre Dame Press.

Pius XI (1931), *Quadragesimo Anno: On Reconstructing the Social Order and Perfecting It Conformably to the Precepts of the Gospel*, Oxford: Catholic Truth Society.

Plancher, William C. (ed.) (2005), *Callings, Twenty Centuries of Christian Wisdom on Vocation*, Grand Rapids, MI: Wm. B. Eerdmans.

Pontifical Council for Justice and Peace (2005), *Compendium of the Social Doctrine of the Church*, London: Burns & Oates.

Pope, Alexander (1727), epitaph for Isaac Newton, accessed at www.nature.com/nature/journal/v413/n6852/full/41310860.html.

Porter, Michael and Mark Kramer (2006), 'Strategy and society: the link between competitive advantage and corporate social responsibility', *Harvard Business Review*, December.

Preston, Ronald H. (1979), *Religion and the Persistence of Capitalism*, London: SCM Press.

Preston, Ronald H. (1983), *Church and Society in the Late Twentieth Century: The Economic and Political Task*, London: SCM Press.

Pribram, Karl (1983), *A History of Economic Reasoning*, Baltimore, MD and London: The Johns Hopkins University Press.

Priestley, J.B. ([1934] 1977), *English Journey: Being a Rambling but Truthful Account of What One Man Saw and Heard and Felt and Thought During a Journey Through England During the Autumn of the Year 1933*, London: Penguin.

Pufendorf, Samuel von ([1673] 2003), *The Whole Duty of Man According to the Law of Nature*, reprinted in Ian Hunter and David Saunders (eds), *The Whole Duty of Man According to the Law of Nature*, Indianapolis, IN: Liberty Fund.

Pufendorf, Samuel von (1703), *Of the Law of Nature and Nations*, Basil Kennett (ed.), Oxford: Lichfield.

Pullen, John M. (1981), 'Malthus' theological ideas and their influence on his principles of population', *History of Political Economy*, **13** (1), 39–54.

Reeve, C.D.C. (2006), 'Aristotle on the virtues of thought', in Richard Kraut (ed.), *The Blackwell Guide to Aristotle's Nicomachean Ethics*, Oxford: Blackwell Publishing, pp. 198–217.

Richards, Jay W. (2007), *Environmental Stewardship in the Judeo-Christian Tradition*, Grand Rapids, MI: Acton Institute.

Richardson, J. David (1994), 'What should Christian economists do? . . . economics!', *Bulletin of the Association of Christian Economists USA*, **23** (Spring), 12–15.

Robbins, Lionel (1932), *An Essay on the Nature and Significance of Economic Science*, London: Macmillan.

Robbins, L. (1970), *Jacob Viner: A Tribute*, Princeton, NJ: Princeton University Press, p. 6.

Robertson, William ([1769] 1996), 'The history of the reign of the Emperor
    Charles V', in Jeffery Smitten (ed.), *The Collected Works of William
    Robertson*, vol. IV, London: Routledge/Thoemmes.
Robertson, William ([1794] 1996), 'An historical disquisition concerning
    the knowledge the ancients had of India', in Jeffery Smitten (ed.), *The
    Collected Works of William Robertson*, vol. X, London: Routledge/
    Thoemmes.
Rothbard, Murray N. (1995), *Economic Thought before Adam Smith: An
    Austrian Perspective on the History of Economic Thought*, vol. 1,
    Aldershot, UK and Brookfield, US: Edward Elgar.
Sanderson, Michael (1972), *The Universities and British Industry
    1850–1970*, London: Routledge and Kegan Paul.
Sanguineti, Juan José (1991), *Ciencia aristotélica y ciencia moderna*,
    Buenos Aires: Educa.
Schlossberg, Herbert, Vinay Samuel and Ronald Sider (eds) (1994),
    *Christianity and Economics in the Post-Cold War Era: The Oxford
    Declaration and Beyond*, Grand Rapids, MI: Wm. B. Eerdmans.
Schluter, Michael and John Ashcroft (eds) (2005), *Jubilee Manifesto: A
    Framework, Agenda and Strategy for Christian Social Reform*, Leicester:
    Intervarsity Press.
Schmitt, Charles B. (1973), 'Towards a reassessment of Renaissance
    Aristotelianism', *History of Science*, **11**, 159–93.
Schmitt, Charles B. (1983), *Aristotle and the Renaissance*, Cambridge:
    Harvard University Press.
Schumpeter, Joseph A. (1954), *History of Economic Analysis*, edited by
    Elizabeth Boody Schumpeter, New York: Oxford University Press.
Schwartz, Barry (2007), 'Stop the treadmill!', *London Review of Books*, 8
    March.
Scott, R.H. (1990), *The Economic Society of Australia: Its History
    1925–1985*, Canberra: Economic Society of Australia.
Selby, Peter (1997), *Grace and Mortgage: The Language of Faith and the
    Debt of the World*, London: Darton, Longman & Todd.
Sen, A. (1977), 'Rational fools: a critique of the behavioural foundations
    of economic theory', *Philosophy and Public Affairs*, **6** (4), 317–44.
Senior, Nassau W. (1836), *An Outline of the Science of Political Economy*,
    London: Longmans.
Shaftesbury, Lord ([1711] 1999), *Characteristics of Men, Manners,
    Opinions, Times*, reprinted in Lawrence E. Klein (ed.), *Characteristics of
    Men, Manners, Opinions, Times*, Cambridge: Cambridge University
    Press.
Shannon, Thomas A. (2005), 'Commentary on *Rerum Novarum* [The
    Condition of Labor]', in Kenneth R. Himes (ed.), *Modern Catholic*

Social Teaching: Commentaries and Interpretations, Washington, DC: Georgetown University Press.

Sher, R.B. (1985), *Church and University in the Scottish Enlightenment: The Moderate Literati of Edinburgh*, Princeton, NJ: Princeton University Press.

Sherlock, Charles H. (1996), *The Doctrine of Humanity*, Downers Grove, IL: Intervarsity Press.

Siebert, W. Stanley (2005), 'Labour market regulations: some comparative lessons', *Economic Affairs*, **25** (3), 3–10.

Silverstein, Michael J. and Neil Fiske (2003), *Trading Up: The New American Luxury*, New York: Portfolio.

Sirico, Robert A. (1997), *Toward a Free and Virtuous Society*, Grand Rapids, MI: Acton Institute.

Sirico, Robert A. (1998), 'The economics of the late Scholastics', *Journal of Markets & Morality*, **1** (2), 122–9.

Sirico, Robert A. (2001), *The Entrepreneurial Vocation*, Grand Rapids, MI: Acton Institute.

Skinner, Quentin (1969), 'Meaning and understanding in the history of ideas', *History and Theory*, **8** (1), 3–53.

Smith, Adam ([1759] 1982), *The Theory of Moral Sentiments*, published 1977 in D.D. Raphael and A.L. Macfie (eds), *The Glasgow Edition of the Works and Correspondence of Adam Smith*, vol. 1, Indianapolis, IN: Liberty Fund.

Smith, Adam ([1776] 1904), *The Wealth of Nations*, vol. 1, Edwin Cannan (ed.), New Rochelle, NY: Arlington House.

Smitten, J. (1992), 'The shaping of moderation: William Robertson and Arminianism', *Studies in Eighteenth-century Culture*, **22**, 281–300.

Snow, C.P. (1951), *The Masters*, London: Macmillan.

Solnik, S. and D. Hemenway (1996), 'The deadweight loss of Christmas: comment', *American Economic Review*, **86** (5), 1299–305.

Southey, Robert (1803), 'Malthus's essay on population', *Annual Review*, 292–301.

Stackhouse, Max L. and Dennis P. McCann (1991), 'Post-communist manifesto: public theology after the collapse of socialism', reprinted in Max L. Stackhouse, D. McCann, S. Roels and P. Williams (eds) (1995), *On Moral Business: Classical and Contemporary Resources for Ethics in Economic Life*, Grand Rapids, MI: Wm. B. Eerdmans, pp. 949–54.

Stackhouse, Max L., D. McCann, S. Roels and P. Williams (eds) (1995), *On Moral Business: Classical and Contemporary Resources for Ethics in Economic Life*, Grand Rapids, MI: Wm. B. Eerdmans.

Stark, Rodney (2005), *The Victory of Reason: How Christianity Led to Freedom, Capitalism, and Western Success*, New York: Random House.

Steedman, Ian (1994), 'Wicksteed: economist and prophet', in H. Geoffrey
    Brennan and Anthony M.C. Waterman (eds), *Economics and Religion:
    Are They Distinct?*, Boston, MA and Dordrecht, Netherlands: Kluwer
    Academic, pp. 77–101.
Sternberg, Elaine (2004), 'Corporate governance: accountability in the
    marketplace', Institute of Economic Affairs Hobart Paper 147, London.
Stone, R. and J.D. Corbit (1997), 'The accounts of society', *American
    Economic Review*, **87** (6), 17–29.
Storkey, Alan (1993), *Foundational Epistemologies in Consumption Theory*,
    Amsterdam: Free University Press.
Tawney, R.H. (1937), *Religion and the Rise of Capitalism: A Historical
    Study*, London: Penguin.
Temple, William (1942), *Christianity and Social Order*, London: Penguin.
The Holy Bible: New International Version (1984), Grand Rapids, MI:
    Zondervan Bible Publishers.
The New American Bible, accessed at www.nccbuscc.org/nab/bible.
The Pew Global Attitudes Project (2003), *Views of a Changing World*,
    Washington, DC: The Pew Research Center for the People and the Press.
Tiemstra, John P. (ed.) (1990), *Reforming Economics. Calvinist Studies in
    Method and Institutions*, Lewiston, NY: Mellen.
Tiemstra, John P. (1994), 'What should Christian economists do? Doing
    economics, but differently', *Bulletin of the Association of Christian
    Economists USA*, **23** (Spring), 3–8.
Tiemstra, John P., W. Graham, G. Monsma, C. Sinke and A. Storkey
    (1990), *Reforming Economics: A Christian Perspective on Economic
    Theory and Practice*, New York: Mellen.
Tollison, R. (1990), in B. Goff and R. Tollison, *Sportometrics*, College
    Station, TX: Texas A&M University Press.
Trueman, Carl R. and R.S. Clark (eds) (1999), *Protestant Scholasticism:
    Essays in Reassessment*, Carlisle: Paternoster Press.
van Asselt, Willem J. and Eef Dekker (eds) (2001), *Reformation and
    Scholasticism: An Ecumenical Enterprise*, Grand Rapids, MI: Baker
    Book House.
van Steenberghen, Fernand (1955), *Aristotle in the West: The Origins of
    Latin Aristotelianism*, translated by Leonard Johnston, Louvain,
    Belgium: E. Nauwelaerts.
van Til, K. (2007), 'Morality and economics: yes, the twain meet – a review
    essay', *Christian Scholars Review*, **39** (4) (summer).
van Wensveen Siker, Louke (1989), 'Christ and business: a typology for
    Christian business ethics', *Journal of Business Ethics*, **8** (11), 883–8.
Veblen, Thorstein ([1899] 1994), *The Theory of the Leisure Class*, Mineola,
    NY: Dover.

Veblen, Thorstein (1918), *The Theory of the Leisure Class: An Economic Study of Institutions*, New York: The Modern Library.

Vickers, Douglas (1975), *Man in the Maelstrom of Modern Thought: An Essay in Theological Perspectives*, Nutley, NJ: Presbyterian and Reformed Publishing Company.

Vickers, Douglas (1976), *Economics and Man: A Prelude to a Christian Critique*, Nutley, NJ: Craig Press.

Viner, Jacob (1927), 'Adam Smith and laissez faire', *Journal of Political Economy*, **35** (2), 198–232.

Viner, Jacob (1972), *The Role of Providence in the Social Order*, Philadelphia, PA: American Philosophical Society.

Viner, Jacob (1978), *Religious Thought and Economic Society: Four Chapters of an Unfinished Work by Jacob Viner*, edited by Jacques Melitz and Donald Winch, Durham, NC: Duke University Press.

Volf, Miroslav (1996), *Exclusion and Embrace*, Nashville, TN: Abingdon Press.

Waldfogel, J. (1993), 'The deadweight loss of Christmas', *American Economic Review*, **83** (5), 1328–66.

Walsh, Vivian C. (1961), *Scarcity and Evil*, Englewood Cliffs, NJ: Prentice Hall.

Waterman, Anthony M.C. (1991a), 'The intellectual context of *Rerum Novarum*', *Review of Social Economy*, **49** (4), 465–82.

Waterman, Anthony M.C. (1991b), *Revolution, Economics and Religion: Christian Political Economy 1798–1833*, Cambridge: Cambridge University Press.

Waterman, Anthony M.C. (1996), 'Why William Paley was "the first of the Cambridge economists"', *Cambridge Journal of Economics*, **20** (6), 673–86.

Waterman, Anthony M.C. (2003), 'Romantic political economy: Donald Winch and David Levy on Victorian literature and economics', *European Journal of the History of Economic Thought*, **25** (1), 91–102.

Waterman, Anthony M.C. (2004), 'The sudden separation of political economy', in Anthony M.C. Waterman (ed.), *Political Economy and Christian Theology Since the Enlightenment: Essays in Intellectual History*, London: Palgrave Macmillan.

Weber, Max (1905), *The Protestant Ethic and the Spirit of Capitalism*, republished in 1976, London: Allen and Unwin.

Wells, H.G. (1932), *The Work, Wealth and Happiness of Mankind*, London: Heinemann.

Werpehowski, William (2003), *American Protestant Ethics and the Legacy of H. Richard Niebuhr*, Washington, DC: Georgetown University Press.

Wesley, John (1760), 'On the use of money', sermon no. 50 text from the 1872 edition, Thomas Jackson (ed.), accessed at http://new.gbgm-umc.org/umhistory/wesley/sermons/50/.

West, Andrew (2006), *NOW Australia: Inside the Lifestyles of the Rich and Tasteful*, Melbourne, VIC: Pluto Press.

Whately, Richard (1832), *Introductory Lectures on Political Economy*, London: J.W. Parker.

White, Andrew Dickson (1896), *A History of the Warfare of Science with Theology in Christendom*, 2 vols, New York and London: D. Appleton and Company.

White, L. (1967), 'The historical roots of our ecological crisis', *Science*, **155** (3767), 1195–319.

Widow, Juan Antonio (1997), 'The economic teachings of the Spanish scholastics', in Kevin White (ed.), *Hispanic Philosophy in the Age of Discovery*, Washington, DC: Catholic University of America Press.

Wieland, Wolfgang (1996), 'El individuo y su identificación en el mundo de la contingencia', in W. Wieland, *La razón y su praxis*, translated by A. Vigo, Buenos Aires: Biblos, pp. 117–46.

Wieland, Wolfgang (1999), 'Norma y situación en la ética aristotélica', *Anuario Filosófico*, **63**, 107–27, translated by A. Vigo from 'Norm und Situation in der aristotelischen Ethik', in R. Brague and J.-Γ. Courtine (eds) (1990), *Herméneutique et ontologie. Mélanges en Hommage à Pierre Aubenque*, Paris: Presses Universitaires de France, pp. 127–45.

Wiener, Martin J. (1981), *English Culture and the Decline of the Industrial Spirit 1850–1980*, Cambridge: Cambridge University Press.

Williams, Oliver F. and John W Houck (eds) (1982), *The Judeo-Christian Vision and the Modern Corporation*, Notre Dame, IN: University of Notre Dame Press.

Winch, Donald N. (1996), *Riches and Poverty: An Intellectual History of Political Economy in Britain 1750–1834*, Cambridge: Cambridge University Press.

Wojytla, Karol (1994), *Person and Community: Selected Essays*, in Andrew N. Woznicki (ed.), *Catholic Thought from Lublin*, translated by Theresa Sandok, New York: Peter Lang.

Wolf, Martin (2004), *Why Globalization Works*, New Haven, CT: Yale University Press.

Woods Jr, Thomas E. (2005), *The Church and the Market: A Catholic Defense of the Free Economy*, Lanham, MD: Lexington Books.

Yezer, A., R.S. Goldfarb and P.J. Poppen (1996), 'Does studying economics discourage cooperation? Watch what we do, not what we say or how we play', *Journal of Economic Perspectives*, **10** (1), 177–86.

Yoder, John Howard (1996), 'How H. Richard Niebuhr reasoned: a critique of *Christ and Culture*', in Glen H. Stassen, D.M. Yeager and John Howard Yoder (eds), *Authentic Transformation: A New Vision of Christ and Culture*, Nashville, TN: Abingdon, pp. 31–89.

Young, Jeffrey T. (1997), *Economics as a Moral Science: The Political Economy of Adam Smith*, Cheltenham, UK and Lyme, US: Edward Elgar.

Young, Jeffrey T. and Barry Gordon (1992), 'Economic justice in the natural law tradition: Thomas Aquinas to Francis Hutcheson', *Journal of the History of Economic Thought*, **14** (1), 1–17.

Young, Robert M. (1985), *Darwin's Metaphor: Nature's Place in Victorian Culture*, Cambridge: Cambridge University Press.

Yuengert, Andrew M. (1999), 'The uses of economics in papal encyclicals', in James M. Dean and Anthony M.C. Waterman (eds), *Religion and Economics: Normative Social Theory*, Boston, MA: Kluwer.

Yuengert, Andrew M. (2004), *The Boundaries of Technique: Ordering Positive and Normative Concerns in Economic Research*, Lanham, MD and New York: Lexington Books.

Index